European Political History, 1815–1870

Aspects of Liberalism

The CONTEMPORARY ESSAYS Series

GENERAL EDITOR: LEONARD LEVY

European Political History
1815–1870

Aspects of Liberalism

Edited by
EUGENE C. BLACK

HARPER TORCHBOOKS
Harper & Row, Publishers
New York, Evanston, and London

EUROPEAN POLITICAL HISTORY, 1815–1870

Introduction, notes, and compilation copyright © 1967 by Eugene C. Black.

First edition: HARPER TORCHBOOKS 1967, Harper & Row, Publishers, Incorporated, 49 East 33rd Street, New York, N.Y. 10016.

Library of Congress Catalog Card Number: 67–21564.

Designed by Darlene Starr Carbone

Contents

Introduction

Eugene C. Black

❖❖

Europe has yet to exhaust the legacy of the French Revolution. H. M. S. *Bellerophon* could remove Napoleon in 1815, but the Congress of Vienna could neither undo twenty-five years of change nor redirect the dynamics of the age. Nor could the Nottingham Luddite or the Westphalian handloom weaver hold back the tidal surge of industrialism and the factory system. Nourished by new ideas, values, and the hard facts of the industrial age, a revolutionary generation grew up under the restraints of Metternich's Europe. Events, forces, and thought tended to merge into or in response to that state of mind or attitude that we call liberalism.

The most important fact about post-Napoleonic Europe was that there were more people—over ten per cent more each decade. Population increased everywhere, save in Ireland after the famine of 1846. Not only did numbers grow at this staggering rate; population concentrated in towns and cities. Rural economic, social, and cultural values slowly lost their primacy. Political substance and forms might or might not change; statesmen might opt for war or peace; ideology might or might not be addressed to the reality of the situation; apprenticeship laws might stand or be swept aside in laissez-faire fervor; private or state capital might promote or retard factories and machine technology—but there were still more people.

Demographic revolution brought economic revolution and massive social change, regardless of national or political organization. Fear and distress, often engendered by factors over which no contemporary had any control, exploded in riot and revolution. This turbulence compounded in varying proportions with the social and political ambition of individuals and groups. Both unrest and ambition—the circumstances and those ready to exploit them —were essential to political success as the contrast between 1819– 1820 and 1830, or 1848, would clearly show. Turmoil reverberated in men's minds and upset their lives. No regime was immune, no way of life exempt. Britain and Russia were sufficiently detached from Europe to be able to adapt to or reject many of the principal continental forces. After the Crimean War (1854– 1856), Russia was effectively isolated from Europe for twenty years, which proved to be the crucial decades in the remaking of the continent.

Many of the ideas and forces of the post-Napoleonic era continued by little more than force of habit to radiate politically from France. Germany had become the new center of thought; Britain of economic development. The restored French Bourbons had learned nothing and forgotten nothing, even after being chased once more from their throne with ridiculous ease during Napoleon's Hundred Days. Nor was it sufficient, as Louis-Philippe found to his cost, when lacking *la gloire* to build railroads. Political revolution came to assume a jaded, imitative quality, like eighteenth-century court life. Revolutions usually emanated from Paris, spreading to other regions and countries following a prescribed ritual. The most successful political revolutions, however, were significant exceptions to this pattern. The movement in Britain which culminated in the Reform Act of 1832 emanated from the provinces. The Belgian Revolution of 1830 started in Liège, not Brussels. But the ritual of revolution achieved its widest political currency in 1848. Almost every large or petty German principality enjoyed that formality of revolution, the erection of barricades. The paving blocks went up whether there was a revolution or not. Many barricades were empty symbolic gestures, but they were characteristic and revealing aspects of the age.

European political considerations came, during the years from the fall of Napoleon to the revolutions of 1848, to revolve around liberalism and nationalism. First the continent and then the world was to be remade on these two principles. Many first-generation liberals pledged themselves to the achievement of both, little realizing that they would prove incompatible—an easy error since the French revolutionaries had held that liberty and equality were in no way mutually exclusive (a far less self-evident truth). The generation of 1848 had yet to learn that they were. The electro-plated empire of Napoleon III saw France's greatest push towards economic liberalism in spite of fraudulent representative institu-tions. Then Bismarck seemed to demonstrate that ideas must ulti-mately give way to the weight of power, a pragmatic if cynical philosophy that is still in vogue.

The first generation of modern Europe suffered from shellshock after twenty-five years of the French Revolution and war. It in-vented new words for self-definition. Almost every "ism" in our vocabulary derives from these years, although the substance has, in many cases, significantly changed. Political and economic lib-eralism became an intellectual guideline for the period. Together with nationalism and socialism, liberalism would eventually de-stroy the remains and reconstructions of dynastic states and tra-ditional power. Yet the persistence of dynasties and aristocracies proved more surprising than their fall, for the logic of social and economic development worked strongly against them. Russian autocracy survived into the twentieth century, and the inevita-bility of its violent overthrow is still a matter of debate. The Junker social order of Prussia retained power in spite of Ger-many's becoming the leading industrial power of the continent. The French upper classes, as redefined by the revolution, main-tained social control throughout the century. The English aris-tocracy lost power rapidly in the last third of the century, but it took the agricultural catastrophe of the 1870's to turn a dignified retreat into a precipitous rout. Cultural forms showed the per-sistence of social forces. Romanticism, the cultural hallmark of the age, was, as Alfred North Whitehead remarked, "a revolu-tion in metaphysics," but it was never an unchallenged ideological or cultural victor.

Some "isms" derived from the ideas and forces released by the French and industrial revolutions; others in response to them. Each "ism" developed its philosophic rationale and utilitarian value, although these varied from country to country and even within nations. Moreover, every "ism" changed in content and meaning through the years from 1815 to 1870, conservatism and monarchism no less than socialism and Communism. That the times demanded such words after 1815 suggests the depth of the need.

Whatever the play of ideas, facts remained facts. French hegemony of Europe had ended; the German century had not yet begun. In the interval from 1815 to 1870, the construction of liberal Europe proceeded. The Crimean War, the only major European conflict between the defeat of Napoleon and the Prussian conquest of Germany (1866–1871) was fought to eliminate Russia from Europe and to enable the process of liberalization and nation-building to continue without her hindrance. Russian liberalism, at its best something of a bad joke, had aspects which either set it off from western and central Europe, or else set Russian liberals off from Russia. The Decembrist Rising of 1825 which would loom so large in liberal mythology was a somewhat overblown snowball fight to climax a Gilbert-and-Sullivan conspiracy. Many of the troops shouting for Constantine and Constitution seem to have thought that Constitution was Constantine's wife. On the other hand, British success in economic, social, and institutional adjustment enhanced England's position as Europe's liberal model, but the British case never appeared to be, nor was it, completely relevant: the virtues of free trade, for example, always appeal to a country in command of the economic situation.

That complex of facts we call the industrial and demographic revolutions inexorably refined a new context in which ideas and institutions had to establish their meaning. There had been earlier population explosions in European history and earlier periods of sharp economic advance, but a Malthusian check always appears to have functioned. Lacking technology, increase in productivity can be achieved only by increasing population. (Conversely, a declining population results in a fall in productivity.) The technology of the industrial and agricultural revolutions enabled the nineteenth century to leap ahead of the constraints of population. In many ways the new technology also overleaped the imagination of man, but in spite of the problems the industrial revolution brought in its train, it made the nineteenth century bearable.

Economic and demographic pressures demanded social change. Dr. Thomas Arnold, the reforming headmaster of England's Rugby School, remarked on the coming of the railroad, "Feudality is gone forever." His relation of cause to effect may have been simplistic, but his conclusion was correct. Fundamental social reconstruction, not mere amendment, lay ahead. Existing social forms seemed irrelevant to many, but there was little harmony of interests in the new elements of industrial society. Initially, particularly on the continent, liberal agitation sprang from middle-class professional men: lawyers, teachers, doctors, bureaucrats, and those in the liberal arts. There was no necessary relationship between these groups and industrialism. But the augmented mercantile and newly-growing industrial classes included leaders (middle-class and otherwise) who sought social and political expression for their enhanced economic position. For the first time an organized industrial proletariat, taking advantage of the discipline and organization of the factory system, began to articulate its grievances and hesitantly attempt to redress them.

Social tension characterized the two generations after Waterloo. The spread of fundamental technological and economic changes meant an increasing attack upon vested interests and the exacerbation of social distress. A series of myths have developed about the social problems of the industrial revolution which display a striking resistance to refutation by facts. Take the instance of the legendary nobility and skill of the handloom weaver. Their sources and rationale need not concern us here. This characteristic productive technique in textiles was actually easy to learn, and the rudimentary machinery was cheap. Apprenticeship regulations and other trade restrictions had gone by the board in western and central Europe long before the competition of machine-produced textiles became severe. But the most pathological industrial conditions developed in those areas where handworkers fought a grim, losing battle against machine production. But they were still not the most depressed or exploited workers. The most brutally exploited workers were not involved in productive occupations of any sort. Nor did they have any hope of redress—at least not until the emancipation of women and the development of new occupations provided alternatives. These workers were domestic servants, a class which grew rapidly through the liberal years. Their employers, moreover, tended increasingly to be *arrivistes* to whom a carriage and servants were essential badges of status. These new masters all too often lacked social self-confidence or a capacity for tactful management. They were alternately lax and brutal; perhaps always a little frightened.

The machine, that characteristic feature of the modern scene, demanded discipline, which implied organization. Organization and association refined new social groupings, developed economic opportunities, and exploited potential political advantage. Industrial organization and discipline enabled parts of the working classes to demand economic regulation and social concession. The strength and influence of some older forms of organization were clearly waning. Religion had difficulty adjusting to the inroads of science and secularism, and began to crumble as a successful form of social cement. The traditional unity of church and state weakened rather than strengthened the position of each. The problem ran deeper than the obvious identification of ruling elites, established churches, and political as well as social privilege. Dissenting religious creeds which gained varying degrees of legal toleration often discovered that adversity and persecution had been a principal source of their strength. Liberal political philosophy implied a toleration of the opinions of others difficult to square with the more traditional demands of Christian belief. Since the religious sense of denominational superiority could be developed through national and class lines, the emotional current of religion could and did flow increasingly through secular wires. Religious loyalties, when translated into political terms, tended to follow regional or national divisions rather than liberal or social lines.

Liberalism was an ideology or state of mind that dealt in terms of "almost," "the best we can," "acknowledge the possibility of error," and "seek constitutional, pragmatic answers." This doctrine was well suited to an age of incomplete, uneven progress and disrupted or uprooted societies attempting to discover themselves. Even modern industrialism, a traditional guideline, while well developed in parts of Europe, proceeded unevenly through the 1870's, and not until then was there social stability (itself a relative term) comparable to the previous century. England and Wales, the most highly industrialized part of the world, only achieved an urban-rural balance of population by the 1850's. With the exception of Belgium, other countries trailed considerably behind. Within industries, much continued to be done in old ways. Lacking even the Bessemer process, steel remained a precious metal through the first half of the century. Machine tools, the foundation of sophisticated industry, were also a product of the last half of the century. The textile industry is often called the bellwether of the industrial revolution, but textiles as a whole was one of the last industries to be fully mechanized.

Uneven and inconsistent development characterized everything in these liberal years. Edwin Chadwick, the great British civil servant and leading champion of public health reform, believed that the germ theory of disease was nonsense. Illness came from smells and faulty drains. His error set back the cause he sought to promote during the cholera epidemics of the 1840's. Medicine generally remained at best sophisticated, but all too often crude, butchery. By mid-century, anesthesia had numbed the pain, but the continuing lack of antiseptics claimed many lives. The surgeon washed after, not before, an operation. The mid-Victorian was entitled to derive what consolation he could from the fact that his death pains would be eased, but die he would.

These essays are addressed to a series of important problems any student should consider in his appraisal of post-Napoleonic Europe. Some relevant questions are not discussed, and eastern Europe is much neglected. I have omitted many vital areas of culture and ideas—religion, for example—and there remain unanswered many fundamental questions in historical sociology, the elaborate analysis of society that is only now receiving proper attention. There is also less discussion of liberal institutions and their operation than I should like; but no set of selections will answer all purposes or satisfy everyone.

The first essays touch on precise questions about the general context of the liberal era—one on the social impact of the industrial revolution, the other on the social significance of cholera. Essays on Metternich and Guizot, both offering reassessments of these highly controversial leaders, focus on specific and general problems of statesmanship and politics in the first post-Napoleonic generation. Two essays deal more generally with the problem of liberalism in nineteenth-century Europe, particularly during the critical years of the middle third of the century. Articles on the Crimean War, the Risorgimento, Napoleon III, and Bismarck offer a series of new views of political life and aspects of liberalism during the middle of the century. The last essay provides a new, controversial view of liberal imperialism, which suggests some of the range, media, and limitations of western European liberalism.

Brandeis University
December 1966

1.

The Rising Standard of Living
in England, 1800–1850[1]

R. Max Hartwell

❖❖

EDITORIAL NOTE: *This essay is another installment in the heated academic debate on the industrial revolution; in this instance it is between Max Hartwell and Eric Hobsbawm. Hartwell deals directly with one aspect of the social impact of the industrial revolution—the crucial question of the standard of living of the working classes in England. No one disputes the necessity of industrialization. Only a revolution in nineteenth-century productivity could have fed, clothed, and housed the exploding population of Europe, so that industrialism was a necessity for survival. However, it engendered many problems and much anguish. Perhaps the cardinal question is, did the industrial revolution mean progress or retrogression for the workers who came to be involved in the factory process?*

This debate also highlights a salutary new trend in the study of history. For the past century historians have tended to regard the newer social sciences as interlopers—unwanted stepchildren. Now, however, as this essay suggests, historians are beginning to realize that any meaningful examination of industrialism and the society it produced requires the use of the techniques of other social sciences. Even an investigation of the industrial revolution in social terms demands economic analysis. To comprehend the range of problems produced by industrial society, historians must think to some extent as anthropologists, sociologists, and psychologists. Perhaps there may be reciprocal understanding. The social sciences, in their turn, may come to see the poverty of an ahistorical approach to their disciplines.

Hartwell makes a strong case for maintaining a historical perspective. We react emotionally as well as intellectually to the prob-

[1] This article has benefited from the criticisms of T. S. Ashton, A. J. Taylor, E. Russell, C. P. Kindleberger.

lems of early industrial society. There were and still are industrial abuses. Child labor was exploited. And nothing can remove the ugly factory suburb with its "salubrious dwellings for industrious artisans." But the situation of the people had not necessarily worsened. More than a century earlier, Daniel Defoe had written of part of the West Country, "Not a child of six but can make his way in the world." The much-vaunted insecurity of factory employment was by no means new. Eighteenth-century stewards' handbooks speak approvingly of estate cottages with floors made of sand, dung, and ash.

Hartwell also asks that we set aside ideological prejudices and preconceptions. If you are determined to find economic and social retrogression, you will. No evidence will convince you of the contrary; and of course the facts point both ways. There are many pitfalls awaiting the historian. The most obvious are unquestioned assumptions: that rural life is better than town life; that self-employment is more secure than being employed; that the putting-out system of cottage industry was preferable to the factory system; that the exploitation of man by man is an evil produced by industrialism; or even that the good old days were better because they were old.

Other problems are not discussed here. Some investigators, for example, sought only the worst conditions; others were more balanced. An investigator who wanted to talk about a bad factory town used Manchester; if he wanted a good one, he took Birmingham; similarly with Lyons and Lille. Careful distinctions should be made between rural and industrial labor, between factory and handicraft cottage industry producers. Regional economic variations persisted until the railroad system was widespread, and even in England it still had far to go by 1850. There were restrictions, physical and legal, on the migration of labor. An immature and inadequate banking and credit system produced unnecessary social hardship.

Every question Hartwell raises about England is relevant to other European countries. While the specifics vary, the general questions are germane. A knowledge of Hartwell's exhaustive enquiry is essential to any thoughtful political analysis.

I

The most interesting and most inconclusive debate on the industrial revolution in England has been concerned with the standard of living of the workers, particularly the industrial and urban poor, during the first half of the nineteenth century. In the past, those who have argued for deterioration have outnumbered those who believed that conditions of life improved, and the intransigency of both has resulted inevitably in extreme points of view.[2] To a large extent the argument has been, not an objective debate on the interpretation of the facts as known, but a controversy about values, about the desirability of social and economic change.[3] Disagreement has stemmed also from the conflicting character of the evidence, which has allowed plausible allegiance to opposed theories; from the facts that there was, for much of the period, no *marked* trend in living standards, and that the increase in per capita real income still left the majority of workers at a low standard of living, aware more of their unfulfilled wants than of their increasing prosperity. And so historians have argued—often exaggerating trends and over-dramatizing events—without feeling that they have done violence to the facts. The *exact* measurement of the standard of living in the years 1800 to 1850 may be impossible, but, eschewing prejudice and preconceived theories, a firm statement about the trend of living standards can be derived from the mass of evidence that has survived, and from an analysis of the likely changes in income distribution during a long period of economic growth. This article argues for an upward trend in living standards during the industrial revolution; in section II, from an examination of national income and other aggregate statistics that have survived (or can be calculated or guessed with some certainty), from wage-price data, and from analogy; in section III, from an analysis of consumption figures; and in section IV, from the evidence of vital

[2] Thus, for example, J. Kuczinski (*A Short History of Labour Conditions in Great Britain from 1750 to the Present Day*. London: F. Muller, 1947 ed., p. 16) declared that the period "brought about a rapid deterioration of the condition of the working class," whereas J. H. Clapham (*An Economic History of Modern Britain. The Early Railway Age 1820–1850*. Cambridge University Press, 1925, p. 561) argued, for the same period, that "for every class of urban or industrial labour about which information is available . . . wages had risen markedly." Herbert Heaton, however, claims that Clapham can be excused for his "extremism," for he entered "a field occupied largely by neoliberal or socialist intellectuals. . . . It took courage, skepticism, caution, and patient industry to breast that tide, to put popular and often legendary generalizations to the test of measurement and proportion" (*Journal of Economic History* [September 1957], 489).

[3] See R. M. HARTWELL, Interpretations of the Industrial Revolution in England: A Methodological Inquiry. *Journal of Economic History* (June 1959).

statistics, from a comparison with eighteenth century living standards, and from details of the expansion after 1800 of social and
economic opportunities. Briefly the argument is that, since average
per capital income increased, since there was no trend in distribution against the workers, since (after 1815) prices fell while money
wages remained constant, since per capita consumption of food and
other consumer goods increased, and since government increasingly
intervened in economic life to protect or raise living standards, then
the real wages of the majority of English workers were rising in
the years 1800 to 1850.[4]

II

Economic growth implies an increase in per capita national income,
and, if distribution leaves labor with at least the same relative
share of the increasing product, an increase in the average standard
of living. Generally, as the historical analyses of economic development have shown, an increase in per capita income has been accompanied by a more equal income distribution.[5] In Britain, contemporary estimates of the national income between 1800 and 1850
indicate that average real income doubled in this period, and,
although the upward trend was uneven, with stagnation during
the war and a possible small decline in the thirties, average per
capita income had already increased fifty per cent by 1830.[6] No

[4] See E. J. HOBSBAWM, The British Standard of Living, 1790–1850. *The
Economic History Review* (August 1957), for a vigorous plea for deterioration. This article is marred, however, by carelessness in the use of
evidence, argument and language: for example, the statement that the
controversy is only thirty years old, and that "the consensus of informed
and intelligent contemporaries . . . took the dark view," ignoring Tooke,
Porter, Macaulay, etc.; or the unqualified claim that "there is no a priori
reason why the standard of living should rise markedly under early
industrialism," prejudicing the argument by inserting "markedly," and
ignoring a priori reasons (and historical evidence) why the standard of
living might well rise under early industrialism; or the consistent use of
trough years of the cycle to indicate "normal" vagrancy figures; or the
insertion of adjectives to make otherwise reasonable statements unreasonable—"there is no evidence of any major rise in the per capita consumption"; or the assumption, without any proof, of deterioration—"Eggs seem
to have been of small importance. Per capita consumption can hardly
have risen."

[5] See S. KUZNETS, Economic Growth and Income Inequality. *American
Economic Review* (March 1955). Theoretically there may be an increase
in inequality in the early stages of growth to allow for larger savings and
more investment. This possibility is discussed below.

[6] P. DEANE, Contemporary Estimates of National Income in the First Half of

juggling of the figures could suggest deterioration, but the estimates are inadequate both in their methods of compilation and in their statistical bases, so that they can be used only as an indication of trend, and not as a measure of change. This probable increase, of uncertain size, in per capita income becomes more plausible, however, when three other phenomena are taken into account: the increase in the output of manufacturing industry relative to the increase in population; the increasing and substantial proportion of manufacturing income in the national income; and the increasing and substantial proportion of the total working population employed in manufacturing industry. According to W. Hoffmann, the rate of growth of industrial output between 1782 and 1855 was 3 to 4 per cent per annum (except during the war years when the rate was about 2 per cent);[7] over the same period the annual rate of growth of population varied from 1.2 to 1.5 per cent, with the highest rate between 1811 and 1831, and a declining rate thereafter. This, however, would have been of little significance if industrial output was so small a part of national income that changes in it could not have affected the average standard of life. But the contribution of manufacturing industry to the national income increased from about one fifth in 1770, to one quarter in 1812, to one third in 1831. Census figures for 1841 and 1851 show that about one third of the occupied population of England and Wales was engaged in manufacturing industry and that the 1851 proportion "was not exceeded until 1951."[8] In 1850, M. Mulhall estimated, manufacturing industry provided £269 mil-

---

the Nineteenth Century. *Economic History Review* (April 1956) ; and The Industrial Revolution and Economic Growth: The Evidence of Early British National Income Estimates. *Economic Development and Cultural Change* (January 1957). Miss Deane uses the contemporary estimates of H. Beeke (1800), B. Bell (1802), P. Colquhoun (1806 and 1815), J. Lowe (1822), P. Pebrer (1833), W. F. Spackman (1843 and 1847), W. R. Smee (1846) and G. R. Porter (1847), supporting them with the later estimates of M. Mulhall, R. D. Baxter, L. Levi and R. Giffen. Her consequent index of "average real incomes" is as follows: 1800–100, 1812–94, 1822–114, 1831–174, 1836–168, 1841–145, 1846–160, 1851–193. See also the figures (*not* the conflicting text) of C. CLARK, The Trend of Real Income in Great Britain. *Review of Economic Progress* (July 1952) ; and PAUL STUDENSKI, *The Income of Nations*. New York University Press, 1958, ch. 7.

[7] W. HOFFMANN, *British Industry, 1700–1950.* Oxford: Blackwell, 1955, and C. SNYDER, Measures of the Growth of British Industry. *Economica* (November 1934).

[8] E. A. G. ROBINSON, The Changing Structure of the British Economy. *Economic Journal* (September 1954), 447, 459.

lions (about 40 per cent) of a British national income of £690 millions.[9] It is probable, therefore, that by 1830 manufacturing had a similar role as income producer as it has had since 1850, and that the growth of manufacturing output substantially affected living standards.

Of the factors that raised per capita output the most important were capital formation, technical progress, and improved labor and managerial skills. It is necessary, from a combination of those, to explain the shift between 1760 and 1840 from a situation where population and incomes were rising very slowly to one where population was increasing at the annual rate of c. 1.5 per cent, and incomes at c. 3 per cent. This could be explained by assuming that the capital income ratio increased from 1 or 2 to 1, to 3 to 1 (something like the modern ratio), and the savings ratio from 3 to 5 per cent to over 12 per cent, from 1 or 2 per cent to 4.5 per cent to keep capital stock intact in a growing population, and a further 9 per cent to increase incomes 3 per cent annually. Contemporary and subsequent analyses of the industrial revolution have assumed such ratios, without quantifying them. The rate of capital formation certainly increased over the period, but to determine accurately its effect on real income it would be necessary to know both the savings ratio and the capital output ratio, neither of which can be determined. Of the various possibilities (a high savings ratio, S/Y, and a high capital output ratio, C/O; high S/Y and low C/O; low S/Y and high C/O; low C/O and low S/Y), however, the most likely up to about 1840, when railway investment was becoming important, was a modest rate of savings and a low capital output ratio. Modern analyses of underdeveloped economies in process of growth often assume low savings and low capital income ratios. In the England of the industrial revolution, likewise, the rate of saving was necessarily relatively low in a society where average incomes were still not much above subsistence, and where the capital market was imperfect; and the replacement of men by machines, of wind and water by steam power, and of the home by the factory, marked an increase in productivity that was often spectacular. But whereas the productivity of much new industrial equipment was high, its cost was often low. Thus the comparatively low capital output ratio was

[9] P. DEANE, Contemporary Estimates of National Income in the Second Half of the Nineteenth Century. *Economic History Review* (April 1957), 458.

not incompatible with rising real incomes. By 1800 improvements in techniques and management were already making capital more fruitful, and it is certain that over the whole period the rate of growth of output depended as much on the rate of technical progress as on the rate of capital accumulation, on the quality as much as on the quantity of investment. The productivity effect of better machinery during the industrial revolution was both large and rapid in impact, and the growth of output, because the output-increment per unit of investment was large, was rapid. As Robert Owen declared in 1816: "in my establishment at New Lanark . . . , mechanical powers and operations superintended by about two thousand young persons and adults . . . now completed as much work as sixty years before would have required the entire working population of Scotland." [10]

The employment effect, however, was also potentially large. Many of the new machines required less labor per unit of output, so that, theoretically, the consequent labor displacement could have been large enough to have prevented real wages from rising. On the other hand, because the new machines generally reduced costs, including the cost of goods consumed by the workers, there was at the same time a tendency for real wages to rise. It is because of this tendency, J. R. Hicks has suggested, that capital accumulation in the nineteenth century was so favorable to the standard of living. [11] Moreover, money wages were stable between 1820 and 1850, a period of falling prices, indicating that there was insufficient competition from underemployed and unemployed labor to pull down wages. In spite of pockets of technological underemployment, [12] the displacement of labor by machinery did not result in

[10] R. OWEN, *The Life of Robert Owen. Written by Himself*. London, 1857, vol. I, p. 125.

[11] J. R. HICKS, *Value and Capital*. Oxford University Press, 1939, p. 292. "The fact that the things whose production has been facilitated have been particularly articles of mass consumption has worked in the same direction. If there are any goods in terms of which wages have fallen as a result of the accumulation of capital, they are not goods of much importance to the wage-earner."

[12] *Report of the Commissioners for Inquiry into the Conditions of Unemployed Hand-Loom Weavers in the United Kingdom* (*Parliamentary Papers,* 1841 [296] X), showed that handloom weaving was not only a dying trade, but that, because it was an easy trade to learn and had early relaxed apprenticeship rules, it had become "the refuge of the surplus numbers from nearly all other trades" and from Ireland, and that "wages had begun to decline before any machinery was introduced."

a decline in average real wages. And the existence of groups of
wage-earners whose real wages were stable or declining—industrial
groups like the handloom weavers, or national groups like the
Irish—bias the averages downwards and disguise the gains in the
growing sectors of the economy. Indeed, to some extent, the displacement of labor was theoretical: the new machines required less
labor per unit of output than did old plant making the same
products; but much new plant was an addition to total plant, not
a displacement of existing plant, and when this was so, the net
effect on the total demand for labor was an absolute increase. Thus,
for example, railways did gradually displace canals, but the displacement effect on canal labor was insignificant compared with
the massive labor requirements for railway construction and maintenance.[13] There was in this period a continually increasing demand
for industrial labor, a demand that caused a differential between
agricultural and industrial wages, and a consequent continuous
migration towards the industrial areas.[14] As a spokesman of the
agricultural laborers declared bitterly, "it is well known that in
the great trading towns, such as Manchester, Sheffield, Birmingham, etc., four days work in a week amply supply the dissolute
and the drunken." [15]

Wages were higher and employment more constant in England than in
Ireland, but Irish social habits often remained unchanged by emigration.
(Reports from Commissioners [15] Poor Laws (Ireland), Parliamentary
Papers, 1836 [XXXIV], Appendix G, pp. ix–xii.) The Irish, therefore,
although they improved their lot by emigration to Lancashire, often
provided contemporary critics of industrialism with their best examples.
Thus Place declared that Kay-Shuttleworth's horrifying picture of squalor
and disease in Manchester in 1832 was based almost exclusively on Irish
immigrants. (M. D. GEORGE, London Life in the Eighteenth Century. London, 1951 ed., p. 323; New York: Harper Torchbooks, 1964.)
[13] T. Tooke and W. Newmarch (A History of Prices, and of the State of
Circulation, during the Nine Years 1848–1856. London, 1857, p. 368)
estimated that "the population supported by the Railway Works [in
1847–8] was nearly . . . as large . . . as the total population employed
in the whole of the Factories of the United Kingdom." T. Brassey (On
Work and Wages. London, 1873, p. 39) tells how, in the period of the
railway boom, when admittedly the demand for labor was "excessive,"
"look-outs [were] placed on the roads to intercept men tramping, and
take them to the nearest beershop to be treated and induced to start work."
[14] See E. W. GILBOY, Wages in Eighteenth Century England. Harvard University Press, 1934, and A. REDFORD, Labour Migration in England, 1800–
50. Manchester University Press, 1926.
[15] D. DAVIES, The Case of Labourers in Husbandry. Bath, 1795, p. 163.
Compare C. D. Brereton (A Practical Inquiry into the Number, Means

But factories have to be administered, and machines have to be tended, and even the best equipment is of little value without able entrepreneurs and skilled laborers. The industrial revolution was as much a revolution in industrial organization as in technology. Entrepreneurs increasingly centralized production into factories, worked out the problems of factory management, accounting, financing, merchanting and labor-relations. Not the least problem was to change craft and agricultural laborers into factory workers, with their different skills, different rhythm of work, different incentives, different social attitudes, and different way of life. This necessary transformation was certainly painful, but it was gradually achieved without political revolution, and with labor simultaneously increasing its opportunities, its industrial skill and its bargaining strength. The quantitative effect of such changes on output cannot be measured accurately, but they certainly tended to increase productivity.

Ricardo, who regarded economics as "an inquiry into the laws which determine the division of industry amongst the classes who concur in its formation," argued that the combination of the laws of population and of diminishing returns to land determined wages at subsistence according to the price of corn, and thus limited economic progress because of the tendency of profits to decline as rents increased.[16] Thus was established the theory that wages inevitably stabilize at subsistence, which so influenced the early socialists and Marx, and all since then who have cherished the theory of exploitation. "By the present constitution of society, the millions are a doomed class," wrote J. F. Bray in 1839, "from the position in which they stand with regard to capital and the capitalist, their condition is unimprovable and their wrongs irremediable."[17] After 1830, however, it became increasingly difficult for the classical economists to reconcile theory with facts, and, in

---

of Employment, and Wages, of Agricultural Labourers. Norwich, 1826, p. 1) who contrasted the "improving . . . knowledge, comfort, and conduct" of town workers with the depression of "the peasantry."

[16] Ricardo to Malthus, October 9, 1820. P. SRAFFA, ed., *The Works and Correspondence of David Ricardo.* Cambridge University Press, 1952, vol. VIII, p. 278. Even so, Ricardo was conscious of progress, remarking in *The Principles* that "Many of the conveniences enjoyed in an English cottage, would have been thought luxuries at an earlier period of our history." *Ibid.* vol. I, *On the Principles of Political Economy and Taxations,* p. 97.

[17] J. F. BRAY, *Labour's Wrongs and Labour's Remedy.* Leeds, 1839, p. 67.

particular, with the facts that corn production was more than keeping pace with population, and that real wages were rising.[18] Theoretically it is possible that economic growth could result in reduced real incomes in the short run, but it is quite unreasonable to assume, over a long period of a half century, during which per capita national income was rising, that the rich were getting richer and the poor poorer.

There is some evidence that the distribution of income in England in 1850 was less unequal than it had been in 1800. C. Clark, for example, by estimating Pareto coefficients, reckons that income distribution was more unequal in 1812 than in 1848;[19] income tax assessments of 1812 and 1848 show, also, that the number of assessments between £150 and £500 increased more than those over £500; a comparison of fundholders of 1831 and 1848 reveals that the largest increase was in those receiving dividends of under £5.[20] These figures, however, are no conclusive proof of a significant change in distribution. In any case, as E. H. Phelps Brown points out, "the changes in real wages due to distributive shifts have been very small compared with those associated with the movements of productivity." [21] There has been generally the simultaneous rise, at not dissimilar rates of growth, of capital stock, output, and real incomes.[22] Study of the long-term trends in the wage-share of the national income show that since about 1860 that

---

[18] This difficulty has been extremely well surveyed by M. BLAUG, The Empirical Content of Ricardian Economics. *The Journal of Political Economy* (February 1956).

[19] C. CLARK, *The Conditions of Economic Progress.* 2nd ed., London: Macmillan, 1951, pp. 534, 538.

[20] W. R. GREG, *Essays on Political and Social Science.* London, 1853, vol. I, pp. 318–19.

[21] E. H. PHELPS BROWN, The Long-Term Movement of Real Wages, in J. T. DUNLOP, ed., *The Theory of Wage Determination.* London, 1957, p. 53.

[22] See P. H. DOUGLAS, *The Theory of Wages.* New York: Macmillan, 1934, ch. VII, showing the close correlation between productivity and wages; also his An Estimate of the Growth of Capital in the United Kingdom, 1865–1909. *Journal of Economic and Business History* (August 1930), p. 683. See also E. H. PHELPS BROWN, *op. cit.,* showing how real wages per worker have usually moved in step with both capital accumulation and productivity; for example, the doubling of real capital per head and real income per head in the United Kingdom between 1870 and 1938. A. K. CAIRNCROSS (The Place of Capital in Economic Progress, in L. H. DUPRIEZ, ed., *Economic Progress.* Louvain, 1955) argues also that "capital and income do tend to increase at about the same rate" (p. 238), and notes the stability over a long period of the ratio between the two.

share has remained almost constant.[23] If this stability has a longer history, the wage bill would have been increasing proportionately with the national income from some earlier date, possibly from the beginning of the industrial revolution. It is not unlikely, however, that the share of wages was less in 1780–1800 than in 1860, and thus, that wages were rising between those dates more quickly than national income. That this was probable is indicated by the continuous increase over the period of those employed in manufacturing industry. Agricultural wages lagged behind industrial wages, and as more workers transferred to higher productivity occupations, average real wages increased. Census figures show that the percentage proportions of agricultural to all families in 1811 and 1831 were 35.2 and 28.2, and that the percentage proportions of adult males employed in agriculture to all male workers in 1831, 1841 and 1851 were 31.7, 25.7 and 21.1.[24] Further confirmation is provided by the increasing proportion over these years of total population engaged in commerce, finance and the professions, "a fairly precise measurement of the degree of economic advancement." [25] Occupational statistics before 1841, except in broad categories, are not very helpful, but other evidence shows that there were large increases in the numbers employed in services— in transport, commerce and finance, in government, and in the professions—between 1780 and 1850.[26] Between 1841 and 1851 the census figures show an increase in services, excluding domestic service, of from 9.1 to 12.2 per cent of the population, or, as corrected by C. Booth, of from 14.0 to 16.5 per cent.[27] At the

[23] The literature on this subject is large, "partly because of the general interest in the fortunes of labor in a class-conscious society; . . . partly because of an attempt to use the wage share as a measure of the degree of monopoly" (s. KUZNETS, Distribution of National Income by Factor Shares. *Economic Development and Cultural Change* (April 1959), 55, but no adequate explanation of the phenomenon exists. See A. L. BOWLEY, *Wages and Income in the United Kingdom since 1860.* Cambridge University Press, 1937, for basic statistics, and the following for comment on the phenomenon: J. M. KEYNES, Relative Movements of Real Wages and Output. *Economic Journal* (March 1939); J. H. RICHARDSON, Real Wage Movements. *Economic Journal* (September 1939); and E. H. PHELPS BROWN and P. E. HART, The Share of Wages in National Income. *Economic Journal* (June 1952).

[24] G. R. PORTER, *The Progress of the Nation.* London, 1847, pp. 53, 64.

[25] C. CLARK, *op. cit.,* pp. 397, 401.

[26] See, for example, A. M. CARR-SAUNDERS and P. A. WILSON, *The Professions.* Oxford: At the Clarendon Press, 1933, pp. 294–97.

[27] C. CLARK, *op. cit.,* p. 408; E. A. G. ROBINSON, *op. cit.,* p. 459. The Booth

same time the proportion of gainfully occupied in the population increased, as the underemployed labor of the predominantly agricultural economy of pre-industrial Britain was gradually absorbed into fuller employment in industry and services. Thus, for example, the much publicized and criticized employment of women and children, though common in the farms and domestic industries of pre-industrial revolution England, was certainly more productive and generally more humane during the industrial revolution.

The workers' standard of living is affected by the redistribution of income by government, especially through taxation and expenditure on social welfare. The tax structure between 1800 and 1850 was certainly regressive, although there was income tax during the war (the heaviest of the century) and again after 1842 when it yielded £5 millions annually. Government revenue came mainly from indirect taxation, of which customs revenue provided an increasing proportion until 1840, and thereafter a stable one. The reduction of tariffs after 1824, and especially after 1840, gave general benefit by lowering the price of many goods of common consumption and by encouraging the demand for goods which hitherto had been considered luxuries. Other taxation, also mainly indirect, was reduced after the war, and remained relatively stable at £3-4 millions between 1825 and 1856. Total government revenue also declined after 1815 both absolutely (until 1843) and as a proportion of national income, and in terms of average per capita contributions. On the expenditure side, the national debt service was the largest and most regressive item, but its incidence remained stable in money terms, varying from £33.9 to £28.1 millions between 1815 and 1845, so that it was a decreasing proportion of national income even though in real terms its incidence increased in the period of falling prices. The civil and pensions list, to which *The Black Book* gave so much publicity, was a small item and it decreased absolutely. "Social services" cost from £2 to £5 millions, increasing after 1830, but the benefit to the worker must have been very small. Much more important was the expenditure for the relief and maintenance of the poor through the poor and county rates, which increased to £7.9 millions in 1818, varied from £5.7 to £7.0 millions from 1818 to 1832, fell to

estimates also come from Clark quoting Booth's estimates in *The Journal of the Royal Statistical Society* (1886).

£4.0 millions in 1834, and increased to £6.2 millions in 1848.[28] All that can be said in summary about these collections and disbursements of government is that there was no marked trend, although there was a reduction in the average contributions, and an increase in the average receipts, of the laboring poor. In another way, however, government action was important. Government legislation which involved private expenditure in improving the condition of the working classes was considerable. Such legislation included protective acts like the factory and truck acts, enabling acts such as the legislation for savings banks and friendly societies, and acts of general benefit such as those improving municipal government. Under such legislation, for example, hours of work were reduced in factories and limits were set to the age at which children were allowed to work, women and children were excluded from mines, some educational facilities were enforced for factory children, and the provision of water and the disposal of sewage by municipal authorities were facilitated. Such legislation, J. M. Ludlow and L. Jones declared, secured "the primary elements of health, safety and well-being" for the people at large, and enabled them "to become a better fed, better clothed, better housed, more healthy, more orderly, more saving, more industrious, more self-reliant, better educated population." [29] There is no doubt that humanitarian and legislative pressure increased the social-overhead cost of industry, directly benefiting the workers, and driving out of business those employers at the margin whose inefficiency had previously been protected by the exploitation of labor.

III

Evidence of the condition of the working class during the industrial revolution can be found also in the statistics of savings, wages and consumption. After the establishment of savings banks in 1817 deposits increased to £14.3 millions by 1829, and to almost £30 millions by 1850, when the number of depositors totalled 1,112,-999. "The £30 millions of deposits in 1847 were predominantly the savings of wage-earners, among whom domestic servants and artisans occupied the most prominent places." [30] Friendly and

[28] G. R. PORTER, *op. cit.*, section IV.
[29] J. M. LUDLOW and L. JONES, *Progress of the Working Class 1832–1867*. London, 1867, pp. 69, 82.
[30] H. O. HORNE, *A History of Savings Banks*. Oxford University Press, 1947,

Benefit Societies, of which there were 20,000 in 1858 with a membership of about 2,000,000, had also accumulated £9 millions.[31] Other societies catering for working-class savings, such as Building and Land Societies (after 1816) and Co-operative Societies (after 1844), did not advance with such rapidity, although their foundation in this period is evidence of the increasing ability of the working class to save.[32]

A large and long economic expansion like the industrial revolution was possible only with a large extension of the market, with the creation or discovery of increasing and accessible markets with consumers willing and able to buy the expanding output of goods and services. For a shorter period, however, it is relevant, in an inquiry into living standards, to know how much of the increased production went into savings and investment rather than into consumption, and how much went abroad without immediate repayment in other goods. But, whatever the amount of savings and exports in the short run, in the long run capital accumulation would have increased productivity, and sales abroad would have resulted in increased imports.[33] In any case neither capital accumulation nor exports, nor the two together, could have completely absorbed the increase in production in this period: capital accumulation was not so large as to make exorbitant demands on current output; and exports, as a proportion of national income, increased

p. 116. The trend of savings was upwards except for the years 1828–29, 1830–32, and 1847–48. The range of depositors is best seen in examples: of the 14,937 depositors of the Manchester and Salford Savings Bank in 1842, 3,063 were domestic servants, 3,033 were children whose parents saved for them, 2,372 were tradesmen, clerks, warehousemen, porters, artists, and teachers, and the remainder were laborers and industrial workers. (W. R. GREG, *op. cit.*, p. 318.)

[31] C. HARDWICK, *The History, Present Position, and Social Importance of Friendly Societies*. Manchester: Heywood, 2nd ed., 1869, p. 22.

[32] J M.. LUDLOW and L. JONES, *op. cit.*, p. 125 *et seq.*; G. J. HOLYOAKE, *The History of Co-operation*. London: Unwin, 1906, vol. 1, p. 266 *et seq.* Thus for example, the deeds for houses registered by Building Societies in the West Riding [of Yorkshire] totalled 192 between 1843 and 1847, 1,372 between 1848 and 1852, and 3,044 between 1853 and 1857.

[33] Unless, of course, the terms of trade deteriorated so much that the increase in productivity was exported. The quantum (at 1694 prices) of imports increased from 4 (1811–18) to 15 (1847–53) and exports from 4 to 15; the terms of trade (export prices divided by import prices, 1913 = 100) fell from 123 to 90. Thus, although some of the increase in productivity went abroad, imports increased at much the same rate as exports. (W. A. LEWIS, *Economic Survey, 1919–1939*. London: Allen and Unwin, 1949, pp. 195, 202.)

from 12 per cent in 1820 to 15 per cent in 1850 (retained imports meantime increasing from 12 to 18 per cent), while the balance of merchandise trade became increasingly *unfavorable* (averaging £8.66 m. in 1816–20, about 3 per cent of national income, and £26.8 m. in 1846–50, about 5 per cent of national income).[34] There was, however, the period of the war, when much production went either into unproductive war effort at home, or into loans and subsidies for allies abroad. As G. W. Daniels has pointed out, "the increased power of production, instead of improving the material welfare of the community, had to be devoted to the prosecution of the war." [35] The failure of living standards to rise much before 1815 was due, therefore, not to industrialization, but to war.

The extension of the market was made possible more by reduced prices than by increased money wages.[36] While money wages after the war remained relatively constant, the prices of manufactured and agricultural goods declined. The goods of the industrial and agricultural revolutions tended to be cheap and plentiful, for the new entrepreneurs were fully aware that great expansion of production was possible only by supplying goods suitable for mass markets. Thus, Robert Bakewell's object in breeding new sheep was "not to produce meat for the tables of the rich, but to supply substantial nourishment for the working classes." "I do not breed mutton for gentlemen," he said, "but for the public." [37] Similarly

[34] Percentages reckoned from the figures of E. A. G. ROBINSON, *op. cit.*; P. DEANE, *op. cit.*; and L. LEVI, *History of British Commerce*. London, 1872.

[35] G. W. DANIELS, *The Early English Cotton Industry*. Manchester University Press, 1920, pp. 147–48. The memory of war hardships persisted throughout the nineteenth century resulting, for example, in such statements as that of J. E. Thorold Rogers: "Thousands of homes were starved in order to find the means for the great war . . . the resources on which the struggle was based, and without which it would have speedily collapsed, were the stint and starvation of labor, the overtaxed and underfed toils of childhood, the underpaid and uncertain employment of men" (*Six Centuries of Work and Wages*. London, 1884, p. 505). See also SIR GEORGE NICHOLLS, *A History of the English Poor Law*. 1st ed., 1860. (New ed. by H. G. Willink, London, 1904), vol. II, 165–66; and W. CUNNINGHAM, *The Growth of English Industry and Commerce in Modern Times*. 1st ed., 1882. (Cambridge University Press, 1925 ed.), vol. III, section III.

[36] For example, G. R. PORTER, *op. cit.*, p. 459: "The diminution in the weekly earnings . . . has been but small in any case, and certainly not commensurate with the diminished cost of most of the necessaries of life, comprehending in this list most articles of food, and every article of clothing."

[37] A. REES, *The Cyclopaedia*. London, 1819, vol. 32, article on "Sheep";

A. Redgrave of Yorkshire reported that "the efforts of the majority of West Riding manufacturers have been chiefly directed to the production of cheap cloth; they can unquestionably sell a moderately well got up cloth at a low price; . . . they can also produce in enormous quantity."[38] If only manufactured goods had fallen in price, however, the gain in real wages to a working class that spent a high proportion of its income on food and fuel would not have been large. But food prices also declined after 1815, along with the prices of most other consumer goods. R. S. Tucker's index of consumer goods prices—for food, fuel and light, and clothing, the most important items in working class budgets—shows a downward trend from 1813–15 to 1845, as also does Miss E. B. Schumpeter's index for 22 articles of food and drink, and 9 articles of fuel, light and clothing.[39] Money wages, in contrast, rose slightly less than prices during the war, and remained stable, or fell less than prices after the war, as the wages indices that have been compiled for this period show.[40] The facts that aggregate money national income increased substantially, money wages remained stable, and prices of key foodstuffs remained stable or fell, suggest clearly that food supplies at least kept pace with population. When

---

R. WALLACE, *Farm Live Stock of Great Britain*. Edinburgh, 1907, 4th ed., p. 575.

[38] A. URE, *Philosophy of Manufactures*. Rev. ed. by P. L. Simmonds, London, 1861, p. 710.

[39] R. S. TUCKER, Real Wages of Artisans in London, 1729–1935. *Journal of the American Statistical Society* (1936). E. B. SCHUMPETER, English Prices and Public Finance, 1660–1822. *Review of Economic Statistics* (1938).

[40] For example, see the articles of A. L. BOWLEY in *The Journal of the Statistical Society* (1895, 1898, 1899, 1902) and *The Economic Journal* (1895, 1896) and his book *Wages in the United Kingdom in the Nineteenth Century*. Cambridge University Press, 1900; G. H. WOOD, The Course of Average Wages between 1790 and 1860. *The Economic Journal* (1899); N. D. KONDRATIEFF, Die Preisdynamic der Industriellen und Landwirtschaftlichen Waren. *Archiv für Sozialwissenschaft und Sozialpolitik* (1930); E. H. PHELPS BROWN and S. V. HOPKINS, Seven Centuries of Building Wages. *Economica* (1955); R. S. TUCKER, *op. cit.* Moreover, those who have argued for deterioration have too often depended, not on indices, but on individual statements of hardship that were exaggerated; thus W. Felkin (*Remarks upon the Importance of an Inquiry into the Amount and Appropriation of Wages by the Working Classes*. London, 1837, p. 7), comparing workers' statements about wages received with wages actually received as recorded in employers' account books, wrote, "The results are, No. 1 says 16s, he received 18s; No. 2 says 15s, he received 18s; No. 3 says 16s, he received 20s; No. 4 says 18s, he received 26s; No. 5 says 15s, he received 25s."

other commodities are taken into consideration, the implication is clear: an increase in real wages, at least after 1815, which it would be irresponsible to deny, and which, indeed, has been confirmed by the industrial histories of the period.[41]

Although consumption statistics before 1850 are inadequate and unreliable, they do indicate modest though fluctuating increases in the consumption of most foodstuffs and other consumption goods.[42] M. G. Mulhall, for example, has reckoned that between 1811 and 1850 the per capita consumption of meat, sugar, tea, beer and eggs increased, while that of wheat decreased somewhat between 1830 and 1850, increasing thereafter.[43] Import statistics are the most accurate of the measures of consumption in this period, and these show important long-term gains in a wide range of commodities; for example, in tea, "from about 1815 there is a secular rise, notably accelerated in the last decade of the period"; in tobacco, also a "persistent upward trend"; and in sugar, "the trend move-

[41] For example, S. J. CHAPMAN, *The Lancashire Cotton Industry*. Manchester University Press, 1904, p. 75; T. S. ASHTON, *Iron and Steel in the Industrial Revolution*. Manchester University Press, 1924, p. 75; T. S. ASHTON and J. SYKES, *The Coal Industry of the Eighteenth Century*. Manchester University Press, 1929, p. 141; F. A. WELLS, *The British Hosiery Trade*. London, 1935, pp. 128–29. See also A. D. GAYER, W. W. ROSTOW, and A. J. SCHWARTZ, *The Growth and Fluctuation of the British Economy 1790–1850*. Oxford: At the Clarendon Press, 1953, vol. II, ch. XI, Cyclical Patterns Relating to the Condition of Labour. See also the contemporary general books: for example, G. R. PORTER, *op. cit.*, p. 459; P. GASKELL, *The Manufacturing Population of England*. London, 1833; J. WARD, *Workmen and Wages at Home and Abroad*. London, 1868; S. SMILES, *Workmen's Earnings, Strikes and Savings*. London, 1861; J. R. MC CULLOCH, *The Principles of Political Economy*. 4th ed., London, 1849.

[42] E. J. Hobsbawm argues that the case for deterioration, if it can be established, "will be done on the basis of consumption data" and declares that "there is no evidence of any major rise in the per capita consumption of several foodstuffs, and in some instances evidence of a temporary fall" (*op. cit.*, p. 57). The use of "major" makes this statement difficult to refute, but Dr Hobsbawm's evidence about the consumption of meat, wheat, milk, cheese, butter, eggs, tea, sugar and tobacco (the commodities he considers) is ambiguous: he admits increases in the last three items; bases his figures of meat and wheat consumption on very dubious statistics (see below); argues that consumption of dairy produce must have declined because "cow-keeping must have declined with urbanization (no statistics provided), and that they were, in any case, inferior substitutes for meat; states that consumption of eggs "can hardly have risen" (no evidence).

[43] M. G. MULHALL, *The Dictionary of Statistics*. London, 1892, pp. 286, 542, 354, 281, 158, 120. Mulhall also gives statistics for increasing per capita consumption of soap, leather, linen, cotton and coal.

ment is upward." [44] By 1840, to take one source of imports, steamships were pouring into England an almost daily stream of Irish livestock, poultry, meat and eggs. During "the hungry forties" there were increases in the average per capita consumption of a number of imported foodstuffs: butter, cocoa, cheese, coffee, rice, sugar, tea, tobacco, currants.[45] For this reason Peel, in his election letter to the electors of Tamworth in July 1847, noting the large increase in the import of nonessential foodstuffs between 1841 and 1846, declared: "Can there be a doubt that if the consumption of articles of a second necessity has been thus advancing, the consumption of articles of first necessity, of meat and of bread for instance, has been making at least an equally rapid progress?" [46] Certainly, when P. L. Simmonds considered national eating habits in the 1850's he concluded "how much better an Englishman is fed than anyone else in the world." [47]

There are, unfortunately, no adequate statistics for bread and meat consumption. The main statistical uncertainties in the case of bread are the acreage and the yield of cereal crops, especially wheat. There is no convincing evidence for Dr. Hobsbawm's statement that, "The fundamental fact is that, as contemporaries already knew, wheat production and imports did not keep pace with the growth of population so that the amount of wheat available per capita fell steadily from the late eighteenth century until the 1850's, the amount of potatoes available rising at about the same rate." [48] On the contrary, as T. Tooke, G. R. Porter, J. R. Mc-

---

[44] GAYER, ROSTOW and SCHWARTZ, op. cit., vol. II, pp. 957–65.

[45] L. LEVI, op. cit., p. 497. It could be argued that food imports increased to compensate for inadequate home supplies, without any per capita increase in total food supply. More plausibly, however, it can be argued that Britain increasingly specialized to benefit from her comparative advantages in industrial production. That such specialization increased living standards, even in this period, is indicated by the "luxury" character of many of the food imports. An absolute increase in demand occurred both when tariffs, and hence prices, were reduced (for example, tea prices were reduced from 2s. 9d. per lb. in 1831 to 1s. in 1853), and also when prices remained relatively stable (for example, with sugar and coffee).

[46] Memoirs by the Right Honourable Sir Robert Peel. London, 1857, vol. II, p. 104.

[47] P. L. SIMMONDS, The Curiosities of Food. London, 1859, p. 2.

[48] E. J. HOBSBAWM, op. cit., p. 59. Dr. Hobsbawm's wheat statistics come from R. N. Salaman (The History and Social Influence of the Potato. Cambridge University Press, 1949, appendix IV) who took them from Lord Ernle (English Farming Past and Present. 1st ed., London: Longmans, Green, 1912).

Culloch and even J. S. Mill pointed out, agricultural output increased faster than population.[49] When F. M. Eden wrote in 1797, barley, oat and rye breads were common, especially in the north; when McCulloch discussed bread in his commercial dictionary in 1859 he commented on the disappearance of barley and oat breads, the inconsiderable use of rye bread, and the universal consumption in towns and villages, and almost everywhere in the country, of wheat bread.[50] Such a substitution in a rapidly growing population—and one usually associated with increasing living standards—would not have been possible without a large increase in the home production of wheat, for it cannot be accounted for by the increase in imports. In the century of the agricultural revolution, however, this is not surprising: between 1760 and 1864 the common fields and wastes of England were enclosed, increasing both the area of, and yield from, arable. Even without other improvements, enclosure generally increased yields substantially. The largest increase in cultivation was during the war, and exactly how much increase there was after 1815 is not known.[51] Drescher estimated, however, that wheat cultivation in England and Wales increased from 3 to 3.8 million acres between 1798 and 1846, and

[49] Thus, for example, J. S. Mill, who probably believed that living standards had been lowered by industrialization, argued that, "In England and Scotland agricultural skill has of late increased considerably faster than population, insomuch that food and other agricultural produce, notwithstanding the increase of people, can be grown at less cost than they were thirty years ago" (written in 1848). (*Principles of Political Economy*, W. J. Ashley, ed., London: Longmans, Green, 1915, p. 704.)

[50] F. M. EDEN, *The State of the Poor*. A. G. L. Rogers, ed., London: Routledge, 1928, pp. 103–04; J. R. MC CULLOCH, *A Dictionary, Practical, Theoretical and Historical of Commerce and Commercial Navigation.* H. G. Reid, ed., London, 1869, p. 197. Even as early as 1795 Count Rumford (*An Essay on Food and particularly on Feeding the Poor*, new ed., Dublin, 1847, p. 48) commented on the "strange dislike" of rye bread in England.

[51] Agricultural historians of this period do agree, however, that the area of cultivation expanded after 1815; for example, W. H. R. CURTLER, *The Enclosure and Redistribution of our Land.* Oxford: At the Clarendon Press, 1920, pp. 231–32; A. H. JOHNSON, *The Disappearance of the Small Landowner.* Oxford: At the Clarendon Press, 1909, p. 99; J. A. VENN, *Foundations of Agricultural Economics.* Cambridge University Press, 1923, p. 314; G. E. FUSSELL and M. COMPTON, Agricultural Adjustments after the Napoleonic Wars. *Economic History* (February 1939), 202; L. DRESCHER, The Development of Agricultural Production in Great Britain and Ireland from the Early Nineteenth Century. *The Manchester School* (May 1955), 167.

that yields increased from 20–24 bushels per acre to 32–34 bushels. In a study of wheat yields over seven centuries, M. K. Bennett showed that "the most rapid rate of increase in British wheat yield was probably in the century between 1750 and 1850," that whereas 15 bushels was "broadly representative of British wheat yield per acre in the middle of the eighteenth century," the representative yield in 1850 was 26–28 bushels.[52] On Drescher's estimates, wheat production just failed to keep pace with population. On other and reasonably plausible assumptions—for example, that yields were under 20 bushels per acre in 1800, and nearly 30 bushels in 1850 —domestic wheat production (without wheat imports) was keeping pace with population.[53] Wheat and bread prices certainly support the view that there was no long-term shortage of wheat and flour. Wheat prices fell sharply after 1815 and were relatively stable, though with a discernible downward trend, after 1822, the yearly average reaching 70s. only on one occasion, 1839, before 1850, and the price in 1835, 39s.4d., being the lowest for half a century.[54] The price of bread was also relatively stable in these years; for example, the London 4 lb. loaf fluctuated from 6.8d to 11.5d between 1820 and 1850, but with a range of 6.8d to 10.5d in all but seven years, and with decade averages of 9.7d, 9.1d and 9.3d.[55]

Far less is known about potato consumption than wheat consumption, although R. N. Salaman reckoned that per capita daily consumption in England and Wales increased from 0.4 to 0.6 lbs. between 1795 and 1838.[56] The theory that this increase was not a net addition to total diet, associated after 1815 with the increasing

[52] M. K. BENNETT, British Wheat Yield per Acre for Seven Centuries. *Economic History* (February 1935), 28.

[53] T. Tooke and W. Newmarch (*op. cit.*, vol. V, p. 132) wrote in 1857 that "during the last thirty years, the increase in England on the Average Acreable Produce of Wheat is very much greater than it is the habit to suppose," with supporting evidence. Compare J. R. McCulloch's statement (1869) that "the produce of the wheat crops has been, at the very least *quadrupled* since 1760" (op. cit., p. 197).

[54] W. PAGE, ed., *Commerce and Industry*. London: Constable, 1919, vol. II, p. 216; T. H. BAKER, *Records of the Seasons, Prices of Agricultural Produce, and Phenomena observed in the British Isles*. London, 1883, p. 249 *et seq.*

[55] *Wheat*, Return to House of Commons, August 7, 1912.

[56] R. N. SALAMAN, *op. cit.*, p. 613. It is interesting that consumption of potatoes today is almost exactly the same as in 1838, between 3 and 4 lbs. per person per week. (*Economic Trends*, no. 59 [September 1958], xvii; and *The Times* [London], April 21, 1959.)

use of allotments by the working class, but a necessary substitution of an inferior vegetable for wheat bread, is based on the doubtful assumptions that bread consumption was declining, and that the potato was an inferior food. Prejudice against the potato stemmed partly from dislike of the Irish, and certainly the half million Irish in England in 1850 help to explain the increasing popularity of the root. But increasing consumption was due also to the simple facts that people liked potatoes and that they were good food, as Adam Smith demonstrated.[57] Moreover the potato was but one of many vegetables and fruits whose consumption was increasing.[58] Vegetables, that in 1800 had only been grown casually, like watercress, were by 1850 commercialized; fruits that were not imported at all, or in very small quantities in 1800, were regularly imported by the 1830's—for example, cherries and apples—and in large quantities by 1850.[59] In London, Covent Garden was rebuilt in 1827, and by 1850 there were in addition five other important markets supplying the metropolis with fruit and vegetables. By 1850 every large town had its market gardens and orchards, and for London, the largest and richest market, the movement was well under way which by 1870 had almost filled the Thames Valley with fruit trees and vegetable crops.[60]

"Next to the *Habeas Corpus* and the Freedom of the Press," Charles Dickens wrote, "there are few things that the English people have a greater respect for and livelier faith in than beef."

[57] ADAM SMITH, *The Wealth of Nations*. Cannan edition, New York: The Modern Library, 1937, p. 161: "The Chairmen, porters, and coal-heavers in London, and those unfortunate women who live by prostitution, the strongest men and the most beautiful women perhaps in the British dominions, are said to be, the greater part of them, from the lowest rank of people in Ireland, who are generally fed with this root. No food can afford a more decisive proof of its nourishing quality, or of its being peculiarly suitable to the health of the human constitution."

[58] See G. DODD, *The Food of London*. London, 1856; H. MAYHEW, *London Labour and the London Poor*. London, 1851; B. POOLE, *Statistics of British Commerce*. London, 1852; and *The Commissariat of London*. *The Quarterly Review* (September 1854), for the fruit and vegetable markets of London.

[59] DODD, *op. cit.*, pp. 377–78.

[60] See, for example, J. CUTHILL, *Market Gardening round London*. London, 1851, and C. W. SHAW, *The London Market Gardens*. London, 1879, for a description of the Thames Valley gardens and orchards. Shaw commented that "the price paid now for fruits deviates but slightly from that paid half a century ago; although the quantity which we receive is fifty times greater, yet the demand has increased accordingly, and thus the price has been kept up" (pp. 82–83).

In the first fifty years of the nineteenth century, the English working class came to expect meat as a part of the normal diet.[61]
Above all other foods, wheat bread and meat were to them the
criteria of increasing living standards and superiority over foreigners. "Until the 'Roast beef of old England' shall cease to be one
of the institutions of the country—one of the characteristics
whereby foreigners believe, at any rate, that they may judge us as
a nation—butchers' meat will continue to be (with the exception
of bread) the chief article in our commissariat," G. Dodd declared
in 1856.[62] The fifty years before had been a period of widespread
livestock improvement. For example, the story of the English sheep
in this period was one of substituting mutton for wool as the main
criterion of breeding, a substitution firmly based on economic incentives; the flock owners were turning away from the ancient
breeds to larger, stronger and quickly-maturing breeds like the
New Leicester and the Southdown.[63] As with sheep, so with cattle
and pigs.

The only detailed statistics of meat consumption, however, are
for London, based on killings at Smithfield, where, between 1800
and 1850, the slaughter of cattle increased 91 per cent and sheep
92 per cent while London population meantime increased 173 per
cent.[64] But these figures ignore any increase in carcass weight, and,
also, the supply from other markets. Smithfield killings cannot be
accepted as a reliable index for London meat consumption—as
E. J. Hobsbawm does[65]—for there were other fast growing markets
—Newgate, Leadenhall, Farringdon and Whitechapel—in addition
to a number of smaller markets, all of which were largely dependent on country-killed meat and on imported "preserved" meats,

---

[61] *Reports from Commissioners* (13), *Poor Laws* (*Ireland*), *Parliamentary
Papers,* 1836 (XXXIV), p. xii, comments that the English working class
have meat most days, in contrast to the Irish. See also C. S. PEEL, Homes
and Habits, in *Early Victorian England 1830–1865.* Oxford, 1934, vol. I,
pp. 126–43) showing working-class budgets 1824–59, all with meat.
[62] DODD, *op. cit.,* p. 211.
[63] LORD ERNLE, *op. cit.,* p. 371; R. TROW-SMITH, *A History of British Live-
stock Husbandry 1700–1900.* London: Routledge and Kegan Paul, 1959,
pp. 156–58; J. BISCHOFF, *A Comprehensive History of the Woollen and
Worsted Manufactures.* London, 1842, vol. II, p. 255. Bischoff reckoned
that by 1850 eight million sheep were slaughtered annually to give the
Englishman his mutton.
[64] Averaging 1798–1802 and 1848–52.
[65] HOBSBAWM, *op. cit.,* p. 65.

like bacon and salt pork.[66] Even in the mid-eighteenth century, when London was smaller and Smithfield relatively more important, perhaps only two-thirds of the fresh meat for London went through Smithfield, "because the London butchers bought at the country markets and at fairs in Cambridge, Northampton and Norfolk as well as bringing carcases in." [67] In the nineteenth century the limitations of Smithfield [68] and the growth of London led inevitably to the development of other sources of supply, other markets that increased in size more rapidly than Smithfield. Newgate had 13 principal salesmen in 1810, and by 1850, 200, who were handling half as many sheep, three-quarters as many cattle, and more calves and pigs than Smithfield; in 1850, 800 tons of country-killed meat arrived there weekly, mainly by railway. In the same year Poole estimated that the yearly sales at Newgate and Leadenhall amounted to 76,500 tons.[69] Certainly the railways much increased the supply of country-killed meat to London, but well before their time increasing quantities had been transported in wagons and carts. At the same time the import of bacon, ham and salt pork increased. Little wonder, therefore, that McCulloch concluded that "the . . . extraordinary increase in the supply of butchers' meat" was evidence of "a very signal improvement . . . in the condition of the population, in respect of food." [70] Nor, of course, was the increased supply confined to London. As a farmer noted significantly in 1836, the fat stock of Gloucestershire and Cumberland were then going, not to London as before, but increasingly to Birmingham, Liverpool and the other industrial towns.[71]

[66] DODD, *op. cit.*, p. 267 *et seq.*, p. 276 *et seq.; Report of the Commissioners Appointed to make Inquiries relating to Smithfield Market and the Markets in the City of London for the sale of Meat* (*Reports of Commissioners* (12), *Parliamentary Papers*, 1850, XXXI), pp. 16–18; *The Commissariat of London, op. cit.*, pp. 280–87.

[67] G. E. FUSSELL and C. GOODMAN, Eighteenth-Century Traffic in Live-Stock. *Economic History* (February 1936), 231.

[68] In 1854 Smithfield market occupied under seven acres (*The Commissariat of London, op. cit.*, p. 280).

[69] DODD, *op. cit.*, p. 273; B. POOLE, *op. cit.*, p. 225; MC CULLOCH, *Dictionary, op. cit.*, pp. 281–83; LEVI, *op. cit.*, p. 497; *Report of Commissioners . . . for the Sale of Meat, op. cit.*, p. 16; *The Commissariat of London, op. cit.*, p. 287. See also, A. B. ROBERTSON, The Suburban Food Markets of Eighteenth-Century London. (*East London Papers*, II, 1, p. 21 *et seq.*), for an account of the expansion of market facilities in London up to 1801.

[70] MC CULLOCH, *Dictionary, op. cit.*, p. 197.

[71] *Parliamentary Papers* 1836 (465), VIII, part 2, pp. 181, 210; also, 1833

Increased supply was reflected in prices, with steady prices generally from 1819 to 1841, and fluctuating prices in the forties.[72]

Another important food whose consumption was increasing at this time was fish.[73] Before 1815, except during gluts, fish was expensive, and appeared regularly only on the tables of the well-to-do. Early in the nineteenth century, consumption was small, partly because of religious prejudice,[74] partly because of the difficulty of transporting such a perishable commodity, partly because of a preference for meat. After 1815 increasing supply and decreasing prices (the average price for all fish at Billingsgate in 1833 was 2½d. per lb.)[75] led to a large increase in consumption; but even in 1833 the clerk of Billingsgate declared that "the lower class of people entertain the notion that fish is not substantial food enough for them, and they prefer meat." [76] Nevertheless the poor by this time were becoming large purchasers of fish, taking particular advantage of price fluctuations (which were much greater than for meat) to increase consumption. When, for example, mackerel and herring were cheap, the poor ate "a great deal of them" and at any time the news of cheap fish spread throughout London "with wonderful celerity." [77] Official statistics, unfortunately, are confined mainly to the Scottish herring export industry. We know, however, that "a large proportion of the Fish caught upon the English coast [was] supplied by hand carriage to the London and Inland Markets," and, also, that the supply of fish increased after the abolition of the salt tax in 1825, and, after 1830, with technical innovations in fishing that increased yields, particularly the development of deep-sea trawling and of drift fishing; with improvements

---

(612) V, p. 59, saying that meat "sells well in the large towns," "the mechanics having more money to lay out."

[72] TOOKE and NEWMARCH, op. cit., vol. II, pp. 85, 135, 257; vol. VI, pp. 454–60.

[73] Commissariat of London, op. cit., pp. 273–80; C. L. CUTTING, Fish Saving. London, 1955, pp. 207–30.

[74] "The Reformation seems almost to have abolished the use of fish among this class of the community; they have contracted, I know not how, some obstinate prejudice against a kind of food at once wholesome and delicate, and everywhere to be obtained cheaply and in abundance, were the demand for it as general as it ought to be." R. SOUTHEY, Sir Thomas More, or Colloquies on the Progress and Prospects of Society. London, 1829, vol. I, p. 175.

[75] Parliamentary Papers 1833 (676), XIV, p. 95.

[76] Ibid., p. 94.

[77] Ibid., pp. 94, 100.

in the handling of fish, for example, the use of fast cutters, walled steamers and the railways, and the increasing use of ice; and with the discovery of new fishing waters, for example, the Great Silver Pitt, south of the Dogger, in 1837.[78] By 1840 ice and fast transport were enabling trawlers to fish farther north, and were opening up new markets in the inland towns.[79] The kipper was invented in 1843.[80] By 1850 steamship and railway combined to transport catches quickly to the centers of consumption all over England: steamships linked the Channel, North and German Seas to the English ports; railways linked the ports to the internal towns and London. In season, herrings alone were arriving in London from Yarmouth at the rate of 160 tons an evening, and even the humble periwinkle, Simmonds estimated, was consumed at the rate of 76,000 baskets (or 1,900 tons) annually.[81]

The conclusion from consumption figures is unquestionably that the amount and variety of food consumed increased between 1800 and 1850. Even an uncritical reading of those entertaining and informative volumes of G. R. Dodd (*The Food of London*) and H. Mayhew (*London Labour and the London Poor*), and of the article "The Commissariat of London" in *The Quarterly Review* (1854), will reveal the size, range and quality of London's food supplies. By 1850, using the admittedly rough calculations of Dodd, McCulloch, Mayhew, Poole, Mulhall and Levi, the Londoner was consuming each week 5 oz. of butter, 30 oz. of meat, 56 oz. of potatoes, and 16 oz. of fruit, compared with an English consumption today of 5 oz. of butter, 35 oz. of meat, 51 oz. of potatoes, and 32 oz. of fruit.[82] Even allowing for contemporary ex-

[78] *Parliamentary Papers* 1833 (676), XIV, p. 12; J. T. JENKINS, *The Sea Fisheries*. London, 1920, p. 145, and chs. II and V; *The Commissariat of London, op. cit.,* pp. 278–79.
[79] CUTTING, *op. cit.,* p. 220.
[80] *Ibid.,* p. 277.
[81] SIMMONDS, *op. cit.,* p. 345; DODD, *op. cit.,* p. 341 *et seq.* London streets in the forties were crowded with barrows. When Jorrocks and the Yorkshireman went from Covent Garden to Surrey they met, among others, "an early breakfast and periwinkle stall," "three water-cress women," "one pies-all-ot! -all-ot man," "a whole covey of Welsh milk-maids" (*Jorrocks's Jaunts and Jollities* [1843]). By 1854 there were probably 30,000 costermongers, hawkers and stallkeepers in London (*The Commissariat of London, op. cit.,* p. 307).
[82] The 1850 calculations are made by simple division of yearly totals, when given, by London population; the modern figures come from *The Times*, April 21, 1959.

aggeration and enthusiasm, the consumption of *basic* foods in 1850 London was not wildly inferior to that of modern England.[83]

IV

What conclusion follows from the evidence so far presented? Surely, since the indices point in the same direction, even though the change cannot be measured with accuracy, that the standard of living of the mass of the people of England was improving in the first half of the nineteenth century, slowly during the war, more quickly after 1815, and rapidly after 1840. And, if expectation of life depends partly on living standards, the increase in average life over these years is further proof of increasing well-being. As Macaulay argued, "that the lives of men should become longer while their bodily condition during life is becoming worse, is utterly incredible." The expectation of life at birth in 1840–50 was higher than in 1770–80; by the 1840's infantile mortality rates had been reduced from "the terrifying levels of the eighteenth century," and "the death rate for ages 0–4 . . . was very low, at least for a highly urbanized country at that time." [84] McKeown and Brown have shown that medical improvements could have had little effect on life expectation before 1850, and suggest that it was an improvement in the economic and social environment that lengthened life.[85] People lived longer because they were better

[83] Of other foodstuffs mentioned by Dr. Hobsbawm, milk and eggs deserve some attention. Of milk, he wrote, "it is difficult to see anything but a decline . . . because cow-keeping must have declined with urbanization" (p. 59). But this was a period of "a new race of enlightened cowkeepers" when the railway enabled "the evening's milk from the country to be on the London doorstep the next morning." As Trow Smith points out: by 1853 on some farms in Surrey "100 to 150 cows are kept and the milk sent to the Waterloo terminus of the South Western Railway" (*op. cit.*, pp. 305, 309). There were, in any case, about 20,000 cows in metropolitan and suburban dairies in 1854 (*The Commissariat of London, op. cit.*, p. 287). Of eggs, Simmonds wrote of "the sixty wholesale egg merchants and salesmen in the metropolis, whose itinerant carts are kept constantly occupied in distributing their brittle ware" and the "railways and steamers bring up large crates, and carefully packed boxes of eggs, for the ravenous maws of young and old" (*op. cit.*, p. 138). Mayhew also refers to the change in the egg trade due to the "immense quantities from France and Belgium" (*op. cit.*, vol. 1, p. 129).

[84] H. J. HABAKKUK, The Economic History of Modern Britain. *Journal of Economic History* (December 1958), 496; J. T. KRAUSE, Changes in English Fertility and Mortality. *Economic History Review* (August 1958), 66–67.

[85] T. MC KEOWN and R. G. BROWN, Medical Evidence Related to English Population Changes in the Eighteenth Century. *Population Studies* (No-

nourished and sheltered, and cleaner, and thus were less vulnerable to infectious and other diseases (like consumption) that were peculiarly susceptible to improved living standards.[86] Factory conditions also improved. R. Baker, one of the early factory inspectors, in a paper to the Social Science Association at Bradford in 1859, declared of the years 1822 to 1856 that "all the diseases which were specific to factory labor in 1822 have as nearly as possible disappeared," and, quoting a Dr. Smith of Leeds, referred particularly to "the wonderful change in the condition of the female part of the population . . . So striking a difference in twenty-five years I could not have believed, had I not marked and seen it with my own eyes."

But increasing life expectation and increasing consumption are no measures of ultimate wellbeing, and to say that the standard of living for most workers was rising, is *not* to say that it was high, *nor* is it to affirm that it was rising fast, *nor* that there was no dire poverty, and cyclical fluctuations and technological unemployment of a most distressing character. It is as foolish to ignore the sufferings of this period as to deny the wealth and opportunities created by the new industry. Moreover little understanding comes from trying to attribute blame for the suffering that did exist. The discomfort of the period was due in large part to an inability to handle new problems or old problems enormously magnified; prob-

---

vember 1955). In so far as the population increase was due to an increased birth rate, whether from a lower marriage age, or from increasing fertility without a change in the age of marriage, economic factors again were probably important. Improved conditions, also, would help to explain "the failure of births to fall as soon as one would have expected under the pressure of population" (HABAKKUK, *op. cit.*, p. 495), a phenomenon puzzling to those who take for granted a Malthusian situation in England at this period.

[86] Dr. Hobsbawm argues that a greater regularity of supply in per capita consumption does not imply a rise in living standards, even though it causes a reduction in mortality. "It is quite possible for the industrial citizen to be worse fed in a normal year than his predecessor, so long as he is more regularly fed" (p. 46). This is double talk; the final criterion is surely death? Some people may prefer a combination of feasts and famine, with an uncertain expectation of life, but surely most people would prefer regular consumption, the certainty of longer life, and the hope of improved conditions. And, in any case, there were no feasts in pre-industrial, or modern non-industrial societies: the alternatives were (and are) subsistence, and, when crops fail, less than subsistence. In the classic definition of welfare, a person is better off if his income is larger, or more evenly distributed over time.

lems of increasing population, of urbanization, of factory conditions, of fluctuating trade and employment. And the tensions of
the period arose naturally from the rapidly changing social and
economic relationships. As the Hammonds point out: "When . . .
society is passing through changes that destroy the life of custom,
the statesman who seeks . . . to command man's will and not
merely his deeds and services has a specially difficult task, for these
changes bring into men's minds the dreaded questions that have
been sleeping beneath the surface of habit." [87] On the easier practical problems, to take an example, municipal authorities did not
have the knowledge, and usually not the adequate authority, to
deal with the various problems of sanitation in rapidly growing
cities. Such problems required study, experiment and experience,
as well as a change of attitudes, before they could be solved, so
that it was ignorance rather than avarice that was often the cause
of misery. In any case, much of the ill that has been attributed
solely to the industrial revolution existed also in the pre-industrial
age. "Appalling as was the state of things revealed by the nineteenth-century reports (1840–45) on the sanitary state of towns
it can hardly be doubted that the state of London was far worse
in the eighteenth century." [88] And by 1854 London was "the
healthiest metropolis in Europe." [89]

Thus much misunderstanding has arisen because of assumptions
—mainly misconceptions—about England before the industrial
revolution; assumptions, for example, that rural life was naturally
better than town life, that working for oneself was better and
more secure than working for an employer, that child and female
labor was something new, that the domestic system (even though
it often involved a house crammed with industrial equipment) was
preferable to the factory system, that slums and food adulteration
were peculiar products of industrialization, and so on; in other
words, the perennial myth of the golden age, the belief that since
conditions were bad, and since one did not approve of them, they
could not have been worse, and, indeed, must once have been
better! But, as Alfred Marshall pointed out: "Popular history

[87] J. L. and B. HAMMOND, *The Bleak Age.* Pelican ed., 1947, p. 30.
[88] M. D. GEORGE, *London Life in the Eighteenth Century, op. cit.,* p. 103. See
also, T. S. ASHTON, Changes in the Standard of Comfort in Eighteenth-Century England. *Proceedings of the British Academy* (1955).
[89] D. ROBERTS, *Victorian Origins of the British Welfare State.* Yale University Press, 1960, p. 325.

underrates the hardships of the people before the age of factories." [90]

Rural life was just as appalling as urban life: on the estates of the Marquis of Ailesbury much later cottage conditions exhibited "a violation of all decency," "altogether filthy and disgusting," with, in extreme cases, twelve persons in one room and "depravity which the towns could scarcely have rivalled." [91] Insecurity, as T. S. Ashton has demonstrated, was as much a characteristic of the eighteenth as of the nineteenth century, with regular cycles of trade complicated by harvest failures for which there was no adequate redress.[92] In any case, already before the industrial revolution, large numbers of employees worked as wage-laborers for clothiers, ironmongers, hosiers, and the government. "In the textile trades, in particular, there must have been thousands of workers who never set eyes on their employer. The notion that the coming of factories meant a 'depersonalization' of relations to industry is the reverse of the truth." [93] Again, in the eighteenth century the domestic system and agriculture (the largest employer before the coming of the factories) depended heavily on the labor of women and children.

Similarly, food adulteration, which Dr. Hobsbawm seems to think was suddenly discovered in the 1850's, was well known to Smollett in 1771, when he complained that: "The bread I eat in London, is a deleterious paste, mixed up with chalk, alum, and bone-ashes; insipid to the taste and destructive to the constitution." "I need not dwell upon the pallid contaminated mash, which they call strawberries; soiled and tossed by greasy paws through twenty baskets crusted with dirt; and then presented with the worst milk, thickened with the worst flour, into a bad likeness of cream." "The milk . . . the produce of faded cabbage-leaves and sour draff, lowered with hot water, frothed with bruised snails; carried through the streets in open pails." [94] Likewise with morals. It cannot be assumed that the moral standards of the working class

[90] A. MARSHALL, *Industry and Trade*. 3rd ed., London, 1920, p. 73 n.
[91] F. M. L. THOMPSON, English Landownership: The Ailesbury Trust, 1832–56. *Economic History Review* (August 1958), 128.
[92] T. S. ASHTON, *Economic Fluctuations in England 1700–1800*. Oxford: At the Clarendon Press, 1959.
[93] T. S. ASHTON, *An Economic History of England: The 18th Century*. London: Methuen, 1955, pp. 102–03.
[94] T. SMOLLETT, *The Expedition of Humphry Clinker*. (1771); World Classics Edition, Oxford, 1938, pp. 144, 146.

had deteriorated, or, indeed, that they were worse than those of
their betters. The Webbs were certainly shocked by the morals of
the eighteenth century where they discovered "a horrifying mass
of sensual and sordid delinquency" and "private licentiousness." [95]
Moreover, the evidence about morals is, to say the least, ambiguous; and, in any case, immorality in the slums was no worse, in
quantity or kind, than immorality in high society.

But if misery was not a new phenomenon, the range and possibility of opportunities for workmen were new. As A. Toynbee
admitted: "The artisan's horizon became indistinct; there was no
visible limit to subsistence." [96] Economy and society were in process
of rapid change, and the opportunities for wealth and social advancement were greater than they had ever been before. The result
was the increasing self-respect of the poor that so pleased Francis
Place and the young Edwin Chadwick.[97] One might well ask,
however, as did the Hammonds: "Why did this age with all its
improvements create such violent discontent?" [98] But discontent
is not merely a simple product of living standards. The vision of an
age of plenty, stimulated by the obvious productivity of new machines that seemed to compete with labor, roused both anger and

[95] Webb Local Government Collection, London School of Economics and
Political Science, report (unpublished) by Ruth Atkins.
[96] A. TOYNBEE, Lectures on the Industrial Revolution of the Eighteenth Century in England. London, 1913 ed., Malthus and the Law of Population,
p. 91.
[97] See M. D. GEORGE, London Life in the Eighteenth Century, op. cit., pp.
103, 105; quoting Chadwick commenting in 1828 of "considerable improvements . . . in the domestic habits of artisans; they are more cleanly
and regular, their houses are better constructed, they have acquired some
notions that fresh air is conducive to health, and the streets where they
reside are less filthy and pestilential than formerly." Professor Schultes of
Baden, visiting London in 1824, also noted a habit that showed the increasing refinement of the poor: "the poor Londoner who cannot afford
to buy what is beautiful, will still obtain . . . something green to decorate
the window of his dark little attic, and give his last farthing for a bit
of verdure . . . the poor artisan of the French capital, he only thinks of
vegetable productions as they are fit for culinary uses." (SIR W. J. HOOKER,
Botannical Miscellany. London, 1831–33, vol. I, pp. 72–73.)
[98] J. L. HAMMOND, The Industrial Revolution and Discontent. Economic
History Review (January 1930), 215. A. V. Dicey (Law and Public Opinion in England during the Nineteenth Century. 2nd ed., London, 1914, pp.
lxviii–lxix) argued that discontent "is often due far less to the absolute
amount of the suffering endured among men . . . than to the increased
vividness of the contrast between given institutions and the desires of
persons who suffer, or think they suffer, from the existing state of things."

ambition. The breaking-up of the old social relationships was a liberating and stimulating experience that made possible, for the first time, an effective working-class movement. And although the standard of living was rising, it was not rising quickly, and the individual was aware only that his wages were meager and not sufficient to satisfy his wants and needs. As A. L. Bowley has pointed out: "The idea of progress is largely psychological and certainly relative; people are apt to measure their progress not from a forgotten position in the past, but towards an ideal, which, like an horizon, continually recedes. The present generation is not interested in the earlier needs and successes of its progenitors, but in its own distresses and frustration considered in the light of the presumed possibility of universal comfort or riches." [99] Discontent, even disorder, were indeed understandable, and both, like suffering, it must be remembered, were also characteristic of the previous age. But the disorder of the forties was far less violent and destructive than the Gordon Riots, and this restraint was due, not only to better police, but "to the fact that the English industrial working class was on the whole better housed, better fed, better educated, and far less degraded than in preceding years." [100] And the important thing about suffering during the industrial revolution was that it brought with it its own solution: increasing productivity in industry and agriculture, and, in society, faith that social conditions should and could be improved, and that economic progress was inevitable.

Amidst the varied reflections which the nineteenth century is in the habit of making on its condition and its prospects [wrote J. A. Froude later in the century] there is one common opinion in which all parties coincide—that we live in an era of progress . . . in every department of life—in its business and in its pleasures, in its beliefs and in its theories, in its material developments and in its spiritual convictions—we thank God that we are not like our fathers. And while we admit their merits, making allowance for their disadvantages, we do not blind ourselves in mistaken modesty to our own immeasurable superiority. [101]

[99] A. L. BOWLEY, *Wages and Income in the United Kingdom since 1860.* Cambridge University Press, 1937, p. x.
[100] F. C. MATHER, *Public Order in the Age of the Chartists.* Manchester University Press, 1959, pp. 12–13.
[101] J. A. FROUDE, *Short Studies on Great Subjects.* London, 1907 ed., vol. III, "On Progress," pp. 149–50.

The new attitude to social problems that emerged with the industrial revolution was that ills should be identified, examined, analyzed, publicized and remedied, either by voluntary or legislative
action. Thus evils that had long existed—child labor, for example
—and had long been accepted as inevitable were regarded as new ills
to be remedied rather than as old ills to be endured. It was during
the industrial revolution, moreover, and largely because of the economic opportunities it afforded to working-class women, that there
was the beginning of that most important and most beneficial of
all the social revolutions of the last two centuries, the emancipation
of women.

2.

Cholera and Society in the Nineteenth Century

Asa Briggs

✣✣

EDITORIAL NOTE: *The historian sometimes misses a point merely because it is obvious; seeking the finer shades of truth, his sophistication may sometimes conceal rather than illuminate. Take, for example, the problem of unspoken assumptions. The late G. M. Young, dean of the modern school of Victorian historical study, claimed that he studied social history by so immersing himself in the literature of an age that he could hear the people talking. Then he discovered that the things people really talked about or meant often did not get into the books. The immediacy of death, for instance, must have been the cardinal consideration of the fifteenth century, haunted as it was by plague, murrain, famine, and war. By the same token, there is a relationship just now being studied between the evolution of political liberalism and cholera.*

Louis Chevalier in his Classes laborieuses et classes dangereuses (*1958*) *was one of the first to call attention to "the social significance of cholera," and Asa Briggs extends the discussion and raises cognate questions in a review essay of that volume and Chevalier's* Le Choléra (*1958*). *Almost no general histories discuss the severe epidemics, although the coming of cholera to Britain and France in 1831 sharpened social tension, spurred the development of new governmental institutions and attitudes, and, as Briggs suggests, "inspired not only sermons but novels and works of art."*

Many hitherto neglected social factors might serve to illuminate the context of evolving liberal society, but cholera is one of the most useful. It is directly related to problems in demographic history; cholera epidemics posed new questions requiring novel answers, were instrumental in the development of such new institutions as public health boards, and even led to reassessments of social roles. Cholera helped to create the new image of the doctor, the nurse, the civil servant; the epidemics contributed to the respect the nineteenth-century public learned to pay to experts; and the fear of cholera helped to prepare the public for extensive state intervention in private life while refining new attitudes toward sickness and health.

Disease was an ancient problem. It seemed to be part of the revenge nature took, but in the nineteenth century man determined to master nature. The difference in the reaction to and handling of the first cholera epidemic of the 1830's (discussed by Chevalier) and those of the mid-century (analyzed by Briggs) are testimony to the growing capacity of liberal society and government to fulfill their responsibilities. The article is also historiographically important; it develops the range and subtle inter-relationships of social and political history.

There were several world outbreaks of "Asiatic Cholera" during the nineteenth century. The Asian center of the disease was India. There it exercised "habitual dominion." From the "alluvial swamps and malarious jungles" of Asia it passed through Russia and the Middle East to the teeming cities of Europe and from Europe across the Atlantic.[1] Nor was Africa immune.[2] The disease "mastered every variety of climate, surmounted every natural obstacle, conquered every people." [3] In Europe it was thought of preeminently as "a disease of society." [4] "It attacks towns, multitudes of men rather than sporadic dwellers in the wilderness." In Asia and Africa it was thought of as a disease of the great thoroughfares of trade and commerce: it appeared to have the "predilection of an alderman for easy traveling or the empressement of a courier for rapid movement" since it seemed almost invariably to select the best roads for its "dreadful invasion." "Like man, it travels along the high roads from town to town, gradually, and attacks the most populous and commercial first. In its visits to an uninfected country, it selects the principal port or frontier town, and from there it takes the most frequented thoroughfare to reach

[1] See Sir John Simon's 1853 *Report* as Medical Officer of the City of London. For a brief account of American experience see W. S. SMILLIE, The Period of Great Epidemics in the United States, in F. H. TOP, ed., *The History of American Epidemiology.* St. Louis, 1952.
[2] See, for example, J. CHRISTIE, *Cholera Epidemics in East Africa.* London, 1876.
[3] *Quarterly Review*, XVI (1832), 170.
[4] *Economist,* January 20, 1849.

the largest cities." [5] It was a disease of society in a more profound sense also. It hit the poor particularly ruthlessly, thriving on the kind of conditions in which they lived.[6] Whenever it threatened European countries, it quickened social apprehensions. Wherever it appeared, it tested the efficiency and resilience of local administrative structures. It exposed relentlessly political, social and moral shortcomings. It prompted rumors, suspicions and at times violent social conflicts. It inspired not only sermons but novels and works of art. For all these reasons a study of the history of cholera in the nineteenth century is something far more than an exercise in medical epidemiology, fascinating in themselves though such exercises are; it is an important and neglected chapter in social history.[7]

Professor Louis Chevalier has recently directed attention to certain aspects of the social significance of cholera in his book *Classes laborieuses et classes dangereuses* and in a volume of essays which he has edited called *Le choléra, La première épidémie du XIXe siècle*.[8] He has done well to open discussion of this difficult and long-neglected topic. The reasons for studying it carefully are self-evident. Yet it is scarcely mentioned in standard national histories,[9] and no attempt has hitherto been made to ex-

---

[5] *Quarterly Review, loc. cit.* Dr. Anthony Low, to whom I owe the reference to Christie's book on East Africa, has used data relating to the movement of cholera as a guide to the movements of African trade.

[6] Cholera is propagated by a micro-organism, *vibrio cholerae,* propagating only in the human intestinal tract. Infection is always oral, and the disease is disseminated by ingestion of excreta. The organism is easily killed either by carbolic disinfectants or the chlorination of filtered water. In bad living conditions, as C. V. Chapin, an American authority, bluntly puts it, "it requires only a little observation to demonstrate that the path from intestines to mouth is not always a circuitous one." See *The Sources and Modes of Infection.* New York, 1910.

[7] By far the best account of British cholera outbreaks in the nineteenth century is that of c. CREIGHTON, *A History of Epidemics in Great Britain.* 2 vols., Cambridge, 1891–94. Vol. II, ch. 9 is concerned with "Asiatic Cholera." Creighton clearly recognized that epidemiology comes into "close contact with social and economic history" (vol. II, p. vi).

[8] L. CHEVALIER, *Classes laborieuses et classes dangereuses.* Plon, 1958; ed., *Le choléra, La première épidémie du XIXe siècle.* Imprimerie Centrale de l'Ouest, 1958.

[9] As Mr. Eversley points out (p. 158, note 4) it is not referred to by Halévy in his account of events in England between 1830 and 1832. Trevelyan, even in his *English Social History,* London, 1944, refers to it only

amine the response to the cholera comparatively, against an international background. Detailed comparative history will allow us to understand its chief features, and the material for such history is readily available.[10] The purpose of this article is to show that, valuable though Professor Chevalier's initiative has been, it is far from having exhausted the possibilities of comparative studies. The following reflections, stimulated by his work, are therefore in the nature of a call for further research.

Both Professor Chevalier's books are byproducts of his search for a new synthesis, for social history with demography not at the margin but at the base. *Le choléra* contains essays on the first great epidemic of the nineteenth century not only in Paris, but in Lille, Normandy, Bordeaux, Marseilles, Russia and England. Like most collective works, the volume is extremely uneven, though, given Professor Chevalier's purpose, it is perhaps surprisingly so. In a few of the essays demography plays little part even at the margin of the narrative. In others little attention is paid to those contemporary social reactions to cholera on which the editor himself lays much stress. The book as a whole has three other major general weaknesses. First, all comparisons in it are implicit. No

---

in passing and not to the epidemics as such. Sir Llewellyn Woodward, however, describes the main events in *The Age of Reform*. Oxford, 1938. An old work like Lavisse and Rambaud's *Histoire Générale* briefly mentions cholera in Paris in 1832 but associates its outbreaks not with social tension in the capital but with "une sorte de trêve" in parliament "la plupart des députés ayant fui" (1898, vol. X, p. 382). The fact that Casimir Périer, the French prime minister, died of cholera makes it difficult to avoid mention of the epidemic altogether. The drama of the situation has been brought out in a lively popular book by J. LUCAS-DUBRETON, *La grande peur de 1832, Le choléra et l'émeute*. Gallimard, 1932. It is impossible either from the *Peuples et Civilisations* series, edited by Halphen and Sagnac, or from the American series *The Rise of Modern Europe,* edited by Langer, New York: Harper & Row to gain any knowledge of the chronology or social consequences of cholera in nineteenth-century Europe.

[10] The amount of writing by doctors alone is considerable. For example, the Sunderland outbreak of 1831 is covered in a large number of contemporary pamphlets. Two particularly interesting ones, cited by Mr. Eversley, are W. HASLEWOOD and W. MORLEY, *History and Medical Treatment of Cholera at Sunderland*. London, 1832, and W. F. AINSWORTH, *Observations on the Pestilential Cholera at Sunderland*. London, 1832. A French study by a doctor from Rouen, not mentioned in the essay on Normandy in *Le choléra,* was E. DUBUC, *Rapport sur le choléra morbus à Sunderland*. Rouen, 1832. The Indian literature alone is very considerable.

attempt is made to pull together the scattered evidence from different places, to draw conclusions from it, least of all to test Professor Chevalier's own hypotheses. A fuller and less general introduction or a tidy and systematic epilogue might have remedied this weakness. Second, it has a curiously narrow range of reference. The first cholera outbreak, which began in India in 1817 and reached Britain and France in 1831 and 1832, is not related to other cholera outbreaks later in the century. I shall suggest below some possible results of such a comparison.

The third weakness affects the whole study. Reference is frequently made to the role of doctors—both to the careful and suggestive surveys they often prepared of local manifestations of cholera and to the divided opinions they held about the nature of the disease and the mode by which it was transmitted. Nothing is said, however, concerning the light that is thrown by later medical conclusions about cholera on the experiences of 1831 and 1832. There is no reference, for example, to John Snow whose famous writings on the transmission of cholera remain invaluable sources for the social as well as the medical historian,[11] or to the works of Max von Pettenkofer, who continued to argue in "environmental" terms against Snow in the last decade of the nineteenth century.[12] Several years after Robert Koch had identified *vibrio cholerae* in 1883, Pettenkofer and a group of his pupils swallowed virulent cultures of the bacillus to try to prove that it could not cause cholera without other factors being present. The debate about "other factors" seems as distant as the debates about "miasma" and "contagion" in the early nineteenth century, and modern writers prefer to argue about epidemiology in sophisticated terms of "patterns of causes" or "multiple causation."[13] The conclusions of later doctors are relevant, however, in that they do not reveal as simple a connection between misery and cholera as Professor Chevalier and some of the other writers of essays in his volume suggest. Cholera was in a real sense "the disease of the poor," but it was not the disease of all the poor. Many places with bad

---

[11] There is a convenient American reprint (New York, 1936) of his main works, *On The Mode of Communication of Cholera*. 2nd ed., London, 1849, 1855, and *On Continuous Molecular Changes, more particularly in their relation to Epidemic Diseases*. London, 1853.

[12] For Pettenkofer's work, see C. E. A. WINSLOW, *The Conquest of Epidemic Disease*. Princeton, 1943.

[13] See *inter alia*, J. N. MORRIS, *Uses of Epidemiology*. Edinburgh, 1951.

sanitary conditions escaped it, and in many places the rich (partly because of the mode of communication of the disease by water supplies) were not immune. "It has attacked the palaces of princes," wrote an English commentator in 1832, "and an English camp which may vie with these in cleanliness, equally with the filthiest habitations of the Tartar or the Polish Jew." [14] When Mr. Eversley, in a useful and informative essay on cholera in England, writes that "la misère était une des principales causes de la maladie," [15] his use of the word "causes" needs a gloss.

Surprisingly the gloss brings out points which are not uninteresting to social historians. Mr. Eversley does not mention, for example, that many of the cotton towns in Lancashire with very high "normal" mortality rates were virtually untouched by cholera not only in 1831–32 but in 1849–50. They included Preston, Blackburn, Bury, Rochdale, Oldham, Bolton and Halifax. Wigan was left unscathed in 1831–32 although there were over 500 cases in 1849–50. Contemporaries noted that few factory hands caught the disease. Some percipient workmen argued that the "insects" which caused it could not survive factory temperature:[16] Snow gave other explanations.[17] Whatever the cause, the social consequences are interesting. In the most advanced industrial region of the world, the center of the sharpest class conflicts, cholera was absent as a disturbing factor. Orator Hunt in the House of Commons talked not of the misery of Preston, his own constituency, but of Spitalfields. Furthermore there was virtually no cholera in Birmingham. It is very surprising that Mr. Eversley, writing from Birmingham about a period when Birmingham was in a position of almost undisputed leadership in the political reform agitation, does not mention Birmingham in his chapter at all and he does not give the reason. Although the Black Country was particularly hard hit by cholera—Bilston alone had at least 693 deaths[18]—

---

[14] *Quarterly Review, loc. cit.,* p. 202.

[15] *Le choléra,* p. 170.

[16] CREIGHTON, *op. cit.,* vol. II, pp. 823 ff.

[17] Preston and Oldham, for example, were supplied with water from surface drainage on the neighboring hills: SNOW, *op. cit.,* p. 102.

[18] There is a good account of the cholera in Bilston by W. LEIGH, *An Authentic Narrative of the Melancholy Occurrences at Bilston . . . during the Awful Visitation of that Town by Cholera.* Wolverhampton, 1833. Leigh was incumbent of St. Leonard's, Bilston and a county magistrate. He took the chair at several reform meetings in 1832 when Staffordshire was not only hard hit by cholera but in the thick of the fight for reform.

Birmingham was almost untouched not only in the cholera outbreak of 1832 (when there were 21 deaths)[19]—but in the more
serious outbreak of 1849, when there were only 29.[20] The comparative figures for Manchester were 706 and 878.[21] For Liverpool, the hardest hit of English cities, they were 1,523 and 5,308.
More people died of cholera in Portsea Island in 1866 than in all
the nineteenth-century epidemics in Birmingham. In talking of
"l'incidence inégale de l'épidémie," [22] Mr. Eversley should surely
have mentioned this kind of locational differentiation. The equation
of dirt, disease and political disturbance is one that always needs
careful and critical treatment.

France provides just as interesting a case as England. Among
the cities which do *not* figure in the collection of essays on local
cholera outbreaks in France is Lyons, like Birmingham (and for
reasons which deserve comparative study)[23] a key center in the
development of nineteenth-century social and political modes of
action. The reason for this—also not given—is that there was
virtually no cholera in Lyons either. Pettenkofer, indeed, made a
special pilgrimage to Lyons to examine the basis of its immunity.
He rightly pointed out that for social reasons it should have had

---

"It is impossible to describe the enthusiasm which prevails in [these]
districts," a local writer noted. (*Reports of the Principal Staffordshire
Reform Meetings,* May 14, 1832, Birmingham Reference Library.)

[19] CREIGHTON, *op. cit.,* vol. II, p. 821, gives a number of basic statistics.
These and all nineteenth-century cholera statistics should be used to the
full, but treated with caution. This was emphasized by contemporaries.
Thus the General Board of Health in its *Report on the Epidemic Cholera
of 1848 and 1849* warned that "there were in 1832 no means of obtaining
an accurate return of the number of attacks and deaths; nor has there
been any return that can be relied on of the number of attacks in the late
epidemic. We adopted all available means to obtain such a return, but
we know that the disease was prevalent in several places from which no
returns at all have been made, and that in others, the attacks and deaths
have been much understated."

[20] CREIGHTON, *op. cit.,* pp. 841 ff. There were 1,365 deaths in the Wolverhampton area, including Bilston, in 1849. On the immunity of Birmingham
there are some interesting comments by Isaac Aaron, medical officer of
the Local Board of Health in 1831 and 1832, and later medical officer of
Sydney in Australia. See *Sydney Magazine of Science and Art,* II (1859),
193 ff.

[21] *Ibid.* There is a full and able account of cholera in Manchester in 1832
by H. GAULTER, *The Origins and Progress of the Malignant Cholera in
Manchester.* Manchester, 1833.

[22] *Le choléra,* pp. 170–74.

[23] See my article, Social Structure and Politics in Birmingham and Lyons,
1815–48. *British Journal of Sociology,* I (1954).

a cholera outbreak. It had highly insanitary districts, at least its fair share of "classes dangereuses," and regular commercial intercourse with infected regions. Lyons puzzled Pettenkofer. "I cannot believe," he once remarked, "that the inhabitants of Lyons or Würzburg have intestines or privies any different from those of Marseilles, Paris and Rothenfels." [24]

Cholera thus not only created panic: it posed puzzles. It was characterized by what M. Guiral, the author of an excellent essay on Marseilles, calls a certain "bizarrerie." [25] Nineteenth-century writers spoke of its "eccentricity." It struck hard but it struck strangely. Some of the strangeness was the strangeness of coincidence. But not every coincidence was accidental. In Leith the first case in 1848 was in the same house as in 1832: in Bermondsey it was near the same ditch. In Pollokshaws the first victim died in the same room and even in the same bed as sixteen years before.[26] As early as 1832 a doctor argued that "generally speaking the disease fixed its residence in such places as medical men could have pointed out a priori." [27] Out of the coincidences and the "bizarrerie"—the fact that some houses were spared while neighboring houses were devastated, one side of a street left untouched, another plague-ridden—Snow drew a skillful and commanding analysis. But he did not explain everything. "The history of cholera," a recent writer has noted, "teaches the epidemiologist to be humble." [28]

This article is concerned with the scope of the subject rather than with detailed conclusions. It takes the material of Professor Chevalier and his colleagues as given and seeks to consider more fully the three points discussed above—comparison, perspective and the use of medical evidence. All three are related and cannot be completely separated. Perspective must be considered first, however, since it influences the whole approach to the study.

Professor Chevalier starts with Paris in the early nineteenth century. His background is "cette longue crise qui va des dernières

[24] M. VON PETTENKOFER, Boden und Grundwasser in ihren Beziehungen zu Cholera und Typhus. *Zeitschrift für Biologie*, V (1869).

[25] *Le choléra*, p. 128.

[26] General Board of Health, *Report on the Epidemic Cholera of 1848 and 1849*, p. 18.

[27] W. R. CLANNY, *Hyperanthraxis; or the Cholera of Sunderland*. London, 1832, p. 42.

[28] H. PAUL, *The Control of Communicable Disease*. London, 1952, p. 383.

années de la Restauration aux premières années de la Monarchie de Juillet." [29] He sees the cholera outbreak of 1832 not so much as a catastrophe as a culmination—"la conséquence de l'évolution antérieure et la révélation d'un état biologique, économique et social." [30] He refers on several occasions to "cet état pathologique de la ville dont la mortalité normale et la mortalité cholérique ne sont qu'un aspect." [31] The choice of this particular point of entry to the subject—Paris in a period of demographic expansion and "inadaptation du cadre urbain à la population"—determines the treatment. Paris was a city of social conflicts. Cholera, if only because of its mode of communication (not touched on by Professor Chevalier), was predominantly a disease of the poor. In metropolitan Paris not only did inequality of life and inequality of death move together, but reactions to the epidemic were closely associated with social conflict. "Le choléra précise les fondements biologiques des antagonismes de classes." [32] Contemporaries recognized this: cholera thereby exacerbated class hatred.

The vivid demonstration of the social pathology of Paris which cholera provided is admirably discussed by Professor Chevalier, but in other places and at other times cholera can provide different social demonstrations. Class hatred is a social not a biological phenomenon. In colonial India, to take a different setting, cholera does not appear to have sharpened social conflicts, although there was an obvious contrast between the condition and vulnerability to the disease of the European and the Indian. A commentator in 1818 noted local Indian reactions rather in the same fashion as Camus noted social reactions to plague in *La peste*.[33]

> Those who enjoy the happiness to have escaped personal knowledge of the calamity of a residence in "the city of the plague" can with difficulty form an idea of the state of mind of its inhabitants; the first feeling of dismay, the reflux of levity, the agitation and bustle at the commencement, and the immediately following unconcern to all that is going on; the mild workings of charity—the cautious guarded intercourse with

[29] *Classes laborieuses*, p. xvi.
[30] *Le choléra*, p. 8.
[31] *Ibid.*, p. 6.
[32] *Ibid.*, p. 13. See also the interesting article by R. BAEHREL, La Haine de Classes en temps d'Épidémie. *Annales*, VII (1952), 351-60.
[33] *La peste* (1947) is interesting in that it says little about social conflicts. The main influence of the plague, indeed, was to draw the town together as a collective unit, with a sense of a "collective destiny."

others, maintained by selfishness—the active energies, in short, of the good, and the heartless indifference of the bad, are all presented in their several extremes.[34]

The light that cholera throws on the operation of charity—other light was being thrown on the same subject in Britain by writers on the poor law—is merely one aspect of its social significance. Charity, however, is a facet of religion, and the relative appeal to the "plague-stricken" of religion and politics (both interpreted in the broadest sense), obviously depended on local social conditions.

That conditions in Paris provide only one point of entry in relation even to early nineteenth-century France is well brought out in M. Guiral's study of Marseilles. The inhabitants of that city were reminded each year by religious ceremonies of the plague of 1720. The events of 1834–35 (cholera arrived late in Marseilles) recalled the past and had the effect of stimulating a return to Catholic religion. The *Gazette du Midi* commented that the cholera epidemic had quickened the religious zeal of the inhabitants of Marseilles, a conclusion well amplified by M. Guiral.[35] In many other parts of the world cholera was not so much associated with "inadaptation du cadre urbain à la population" as with the latest visitation in new form of an old scourge, with "terrible and affecting circumstances which have arisen out of the dispensation of the Almighty." [36] It is notable that in their brief study of Russia in *Le choléra,* Mme. Netchkina, K. V. Sivkov and A. L. Sidorov dwell on the role of charity and of religion in the Russian situation of 1831 and 1832. It would have been interesting to have had a fuller account of differences between Moscow and St. Petersburg, for in the former city there were no "cholera disturbances" at all.[37]

Religion plays an interesting part in the story of cholera in all parts of the world, not least in India where outbreaks were (and are) often associated with massing of crowds at religious festivals. In Paris and London in 1831 and 1832 there might be signs of anti-clericalism sharpening class hostility during the epidemic, but in Dieppe and Le Havre, where there were heavy cholera casualties, fishermen began by attributing the cholera to divine displeas-

[34] *Quarterly Review, loc. cit.,* p. 171.
[35] *Le choléra,* pp. 136 ff.
[36] *Quarterly Review, loc. cit.,* p. 170.
[37] *Le choléra,* pp. 143–55.

ure threatening the end of the world and went on to declare that
the divine displeasure was caused by the legitimate sovereign of
France having been expelled from the throne.[38] In Ireland, where
cholera seems to have played no part in social disturbance, lumps
of smoldering peat were offered in lieu of medical assistance with
the words: "The plague has broken out; take this and while it
burns up offer seven paters, three aves and a credo in the name of
God and the holy St. John that the plague be stopped." [39] Even
in Britain, the House of Lords on the initiative of Bishop Blomfield of London added the phrase "whereas it has pleased Almighty
God to visit these kingdoms . . ." to the Cholera Morbus Prevention Bill of 1832. Bishop Blomfield's speech on this occasion is
particularly interesting since he was a close friend and consistent
supporter of Edwin Chadwick in the battle for public health. On
this occasion he chose to look back rather than forward, recalling
the plague of the seventeenth century when "there was a devout
acknowledgment that that calamity had been caused by the Providence of God." [40]

The absence of such a reference to God in the draft Bill offered
by the government to the Commons in 1832 had provoked strong
opposition from a group of members of parliament, and they were
not appeased when the Cholera Prevention Bill (Scotland) included such a clause. The odd situation thereby arose that "the
Scotch seemed to be monopolizing Providence to the exclusion of
the English." [41] The debates on this subject, briefly referred to by
Mr. Eversley, are as interesting for the light they throw on religion as on politics. Philosophical radicals, notably Joseph Hume,
joined with popular radicals—notably the group associated with
the *Poor Man's Guardian*—in describing religious measures to
combat cholera as "cant, humbug and hypocrisy." [42] Other members, the great majority, claimed that in referring to God they
were simply "recognizing the Divine power." One member said
that he trusted it was not yet necessary for any gentleman to
apologize for proposing such recognition.[43] Briscoe, the leader of

[38] *Ibid.,* p. 106.
[39] CREIGHTON, *op. cit.,* vol. II, pp. 186 ff. He quotes the *Gentlemen's Magazine* (June 1832).
[40] *Hansard,* 3rd ser., X, cols. 443–44.
[41] *Ibid.,* col. 439. The phrase was Hume's.
[42] *Ibid.,* col. 438.
[43] *Hansard, loc. cit.,* col. 392.

this group, added in a later debate that "whenever ministers of the crown ceased to lend the influence of their high station to support religion, from that hour the sun of the country's prosperity was set for ever." [44] These debates should be set in the context not only of the struggle for the Reform Bill but the debates on tithes and religious privilege.

There is room for a fuller study of the impact of cholera on religious opinion. Yet cholera touched other concerns as well. When neither class hatred nor religion entered the debate, there were other social irritants. The most powerful of them was the fear of bureaucracy. In Russia, for example, as in Camus' novel *La Peste,* great irritation was caused, as the Russian historians who have contributed to *Le choléra* show, by the enforcement of *cordons sanitaires.* Differences of opinion about the value of *cordons sanitaires* tended to divide "conservatives" (particularly conservatives with military experience) and "reformers." Yet the reformers themselves were often divided too. In England Hume tended to dismiss all cholera precautions as alarmist—he does not emerge well from the debates despite his professed concern for "civil liberties"—while Henry Warburton, philosophical radical and pioneer of medical reform, made it clear that enlightened laissez–faire was not the same as "Turkish indolence." When George Robinson pressed as hard as he could for "gentle" control of cholera in the interests of commerce, Warburton retaliated that while "the mercantile interest was no doubt of great moment . . . the public safety was a matter of permanent importance." In his view it was because of "mercantile activity and mercantile avarice and jealousy" that cholera had spread around the world.[45]

Since cholera tended to break out in "great commercial marts," [46] merchant reactions to cholera are as interesting in this period of business expansion as the reactions of the poor. They can be traced fairly fully in many of the places described in this article. In Sunderland itself, for example, they exacerbated the situation during the early days of the epidemic. Lord Londonderry and the local shipping interest did their best to prove that it was "a wicked and

[44] *Ibid.,* col. 440.
[45] *Ibid.,* cols. 267–68. Both Blomfield and Warburton are historical characters who deserve further attention from historians of nineteenth-century Britain.
[46] *Quarterly Review, loc. cit.*

malignant falsehood" that there was Asiatic cholera in the town.[47]
In Marseilles there were complaints of "centralization" from Paris
as well as of bureaucratic interference.[48] It is impossible to tell
from *Le choléra* what reactions were in Bordeaux, for Dr. Fréour
in his brief note scarcely mentions them.[49] The local reaction to the
various nineteenth-century attacks in Hamburg would make a fascinating study in itself.

"Great commercial marts" and capital cities provide different
insights into the significance of cholera. So too do small communities, particularly those which were very badly hit like Bilston in
the Black Country. In Paris cholera might in a real sense be a
"culmination"—as Professor Chevalier clearly shows, for instance,
in his details of quinquennial mortality rates.[50] In Bilston it was
an unanticipated calamity. Leigh described public health in Bilston
as being "in general good" before the outbreak. So too was political
morale. Bilston was in the vanguard of the reform agitation. Despite a local "depression in trade" (a more potent influence on
positive radicalism in England than cholera) the Bilston wake on
July 29, 1832 was well attended and there were the "usual orgies."
Cholera was brought into the community from Manchester by a
canal boatman. It ravaged the community mercilessly. No fewer
than four hundred fifty Bilston children under the age of twelve
were left orphans by the cholera, and a special Cholera Orphan
School was established by public subscription. It is scarcely surprising that religion (and not radicalism) was the main gainer
from this terrible experience. "A reformation of morals and revival
of religion is said to have followed the scourge." [51]

The story of later cholera outbreaks in the nineteenth century
reflects not only changes in social structure but basic changes in
social attitudes, particularly concerning the possibility of exercising
"social control." Many comments were made, particularly in

---

[47] See HAZLEWOOD and MORBEY, *op. cit.*
[48] P. GUIRAL, Marseille, in *Le choléra,* pp. 121–40.
[49] Dr. Fréour (no initial given) in *ibid.,* pp. 109–20.
[50] *Ibid.,* p. 8.
[51] LEIGH, *op. cit., passim;* CREIGHTON, *op. cit.,* vol. II, p. 823. It is interesting
to compare a religious work cited both by Creighton and Eversley—
G. GIRDLESTONE, *Seven Sermons Preached during the Prevalence of Cholera
in the Parish of Sedgley.* London, 1833—with the two contrasting sermons
preached by Father Paneloux in Camus' *La peste.*

Britain, which qualify the view that cholera above all diseases was associated with "class hatred." "The epidemic was no respecter of classes," wrote Dr. Sutherland, one of the medical inspectors of the General Board of Health in 1849. "Rich and poor suffered alike or escaped alike, according as they lived in the observance or violation of the laws of their physical wellbeing." [52] There was more emphasis on the need for sanctions to secure the observance of these laws in 1849 than there had been in 1832. The Public Health Act of 1848, which set up the General Board of Health, had been carried within the shadow of cholera in Europe. Chadwick watched the progress of the disease and the progress of the legislation with equal attention. When cholera reached Moscow, he warned Lord Morpeth that "if preparations be not soon made only the Sanitary Commissioners who have recommended them will be held blameless if it should reach us. You will remember the difficulty there was [in 1831] in forming a Board of Health at the Privy Council office. I fear that we might not now under existing circumstances get the voluntary service we might have done then. Will not the service fall to the new Board and be a means of introducing it to the country?" [53]

It is the purpose of this article not to examine the administrative response of the Central Board of Health to the second cholera outbreak, but to set the outbreak and the reactions it inspired into perspective. The second great outbreak, like the first, had its origin in Lower Bengal. Indeed between 1817, when cholera first burst out of Bengal to start its international career, it had never been absent from some part or other of the Indian Peninsula. [54] In 1847 it entered European Russia again, as it had done in 1829, and reached Britain, again by way of the Baltic, in 1848. The second outbreak was far more serious, at least as far as Britain was concerned, than that of 1831–32 and, as Sutherland wrote, it affected all sections of the population, "cutting off many beyond the limits of the destitute and reckless class who were its most usual victims on the first occasion. Many of the respectable class of workmen and shopkeepers

[52] *Report of the General Board of Health on the Quarantine* (1849), p. 73.
[53] Chadwick to Lord Morpeth, May 24, 1848 (Chadwick Papers, University College, London).
[54] *The Report of the General Board of Health on the Epidemic Cholera of 1848 and 1849* claimed that according to Parliamentary Returns from 1825 to 1845 cholera caused the deaths of nearly one in eight of British soldiers and one in five of Indian soldiers who died in India.

were among the victims." [55] There was consequently far less talk
in 1848 than there had been in 1832 of cholera selecting its victims
"generally among the lower classes . . . and chiefly from those
who were most intemperate and dissolute in their habits." [56] The
barriers of class and character had been battered down.

The same point was made in countries where even less attempt
had been made than in England to improve "sanitary institutions."
In Moscow, for instance, the disease extended itself "over the
whole city" and attacked "all classes": in Constantinople it attacked "the upper as well as the lower classes." [57] There were
popular complaints in St. Petersburg, reminiscent of 1831 and
1832, that the water had been poisoned by the upper classes, but
in most places the epidemic was regarded as a universal lesson in
the need for public health. Where endemic disease and statistics relating to it—including the terrible differential mortality statistics
—could not convince people of the gravity of the problem of public
health, cholera could. As a writer in the *Edinburgh Review* put it
in 1850, "Cholera is in truth a Health Inspector who speaks
through his interpreter, the Registrar General, in a language which
reaches all ears." [58] A modern historian has made the point somewhat differently. "Cholera, like plague, was a sensational disease,
and it aroused the petty parochialism of the mid-nineteenth century
as effectively as plague had aroused the corrupt bureaucracy of the
eighteenth century." [59] It is interesting to note that in a region
where there was no outbreak of cholera—Australia—sanitary reformers sometimes expressed a wish that there had been an outbreak to rouse public opinion. "Epidemics," wrote a Melbourne
doctor in 1861,

are of signal service by procuring indirectly those sanitary reforms which offer a comparative immunity from their recurrence.
It might savor of inhumanity to wish that this colony, hitherto
in a measure free from the devastating scourges which have
periodically swept over Europe and Asia, shall become the scene
of an unsparing pestilence; and yet, judging by the capacity of
those who should be the first to move in bringing about the

[55] CREIGHTON, *op. cit.,* vol. II, p. 841.
[56] *Hansard, loc. cit.,* col. 345.
[57] *Report of the General Board of Health on the Epidemic Cholera of 1848 and 1849.*
[58] *Edinburgh Review,* CLXXXIV (1850), 389.
[59] M. C. BUER, *Health, Wealth and Population.* London, 1926, p. 230.

preventive conditions, it would seem that this terrible stimulus is required, in order that we may obtain them.[60]

For all the lessons of cholera in Europe there were only limited improvements in urban health and housing conditions during the middle years of the century—the full story of improvements and resistances to them remains to be told—and the "sanitary idea" was the crusade not of the majority but of an enlightened minority. The minority was not only enlightened but dedicated. It believed that the conquest of disease was the conquest of Fate, that where Asia acquiesced Europe should act. "Man could by first principles . . . get behind Fate itself, and suppress the forces which led up to it at their prime source." [61] Cholera appears in this setting as a catalyst of public opinion, an ally in the service of the "sanitary reformers." It was not until the late nineteenth century that public health became an "expert service," and it is only in the twentieth century that social control has become genuinely international.

The last two big British outbreaks of cholera in 1853–54 and 1866 were far less serious than the earlier epidemics. The 1853–54 outbreak followed further attacks of disease in the Baltic parts. These may have been caused either by "a new approach from Asia" or, what seems more likely, a "rekindling of smoldering fires" in Europe itself. Among the most interesting reactions to the outbreak was that of Lord Palmerston, then home secretary in Aberdeen's government. When the presbyters of Edinburgh asked him to proclaim a day of fasting and humiliation to check the progress of the cholera he replied that only when Edinburgh freed itself of the "gaseous exhalations" arising from overcrowded dwellings and undisposed filth, would it be time to ask the Maker of the Universe to interpose.[62] This mood of practical concern may usefully be compared with the mood of 1831–32. So too can the reports published on the two occasions. One of the most interesting local reports about the 1853–54 outbreak was drawn up by H. W. Acland in Oxford. Acland emphasized the existence of "sanitary laws which our Creator has imposed upon us." "The consequence of the violation of these laws is punishment to the *community* for its *common* crime; as it is in the case of the individual for his in-

[60] The Public Health. *Australian Medical Journal* (October 1861).
[61] B. W. RICHARDSON, Introduction to *The Health of Nations: A Review of the Work of Edwin Chadwick*. London, 1887.
[62] See H. C. F. BELL, *Lord Palmerston*. London, 1936, vol. II, p. 76.

dividual crime." Acland compared the Oxford attacks of 1832, 1849 and 1854 and drew general social deductions from them. The deductions ranged widely over social questions: the need for improved housing and sewage disposal; and moral questions—the need for better and wiser "living." He recognized that "to enumerate the arrangements which a wise Community would adopt beforehand to mitigate the terrible scourge of coming Epidemics . . . would lead the reader into questions of the most extensive nature —social, so called, political and religious." [63]

Yet while the 1854 outbreak in Oxford inspired these relatively sophisticated reflections, parallel and later outbreaks in other parts of the world often duplicated earlier patterns of experience and response. The 1866 British outbreak entered Britain not from Russia and the Baltic but from Egypt. It was kept carefully under control. In Egypt there was the same grim story of panic, flight of the rich (including the Viceroy), suspension of commerce, and mass-murder mortality among the poor, which had characterized the earlier outbreaks.[64] The contrast of experience between Britain and Egypt was a foretaste of some of the international contrasts of experience in the twentieth century. In the Indian epidemic of 1937, for example, over 10,000 out of 442,000 Indian villages were infected with cholera, and there were 236,143 deaths, well over twice as many as in all the nineteenth-century British epidemics put together. Yet not one British or Indian soldier in the Indian Army died of cholera in this terrible year.[65] In a post-war Egyptian outbreak in 1947 international action was immediately taken to deal with Egyptian problems. The action was medical as well as administrative. The World Health Organization transported enough anti-cholera vaccine to inoculate one out of six persons in Egypt.

It did not need anti-cholera vaccine to dispel cholera from most of Europe in the late nineteenth century. In the three late nineteenth-century outbreaks of 1873, 1884 and 1892 Britain, for instance, was left virtually untouched. The 1884 outbreak in the Mediterranean was the result of maritime contact with the East: the 1892 outbreak in Hamburg was almost a laboratory proof of the conclusions of Snow's theories on the role of water in the trans-

[63] H. W. ACLAND, *Memoir on the Cholera at Oxford.* 1856, p. 105.
[64] A brief account is given in D. S. LANDES, *Bankers and Pashas.* London, 1958, pp. 241–42.
[65] J. S. SIMMONS, T. F. WHYAYNE, G. W. ANDERSON and H. M. HORACK, *Global Epidemiology.* vol. I, London, 1944, p. 119.

mission of the disease. The death rate in Hamburg was 13.4 per
thousand: in the suburb of Altona it was 2.1 per thousand. Both
the city and the suburb received their water from the Elbe, but
in Altona there was an efficient filtration plant.[66] It was this last
great outbreak in Germany which stirred American authorities on
the other side of the Atlantic to look to their public health ap-
paratus. In New York the Hamburg outbreak was used to force
the case for the establishment of a Division of Pathology, Bac-
teriology and Disinfection, "perhaps the most important step in
modernizing public health practice in the United States." [67]

The vast store of material about cholera tempts the social historian to seek for comparisons. There certainly have been parallel
phenomena in different parts of the world. The *Cholera Gazette*
in England had its counterpart, for example, in the *Cholera Bulle-
tin* in New York. Yet there have always been contrasts as well as
parallels. The desire to publicize facts, which lay behind the issue
of these publications, and the desire to conceal facts have often
conflicted. One English member of parliament told the Commons
that while serving in India "his plan had been to keep the ways of
the disease as much a secret as possible, and he had consequently
prohibited every soldier from mentioning the very name of cholera,
though they were much inclined to make it a topic of conversation." [68] He recognized that such a plan "would not be practicable
here." In every country where articulate opinions could be formed
and expressed, the question always arose of the extent to which
cholera would attack all sections of the community. In America, as
in Europe, cholera was specifically associated in 1832 with "the
most miserable and degraded of our population—white, black and
colored"—and it was said to "arise entirely from their habits of
life." [69] Yet in America and in Europe this familiar association did
not check the flight of the rich when cholera threatened. Marseilles
and Albany were alike in this respect. The rich were sometimes

[66] PAUL, *op. cit.,* p. 385.
[67] WINSLOW, *op. cit.,* p. 340. For appalling conditions in New York in the
1850's, see S. SMITH, *Report on the Sanitary Conditions of New York.* New
York, 1865.
[68] *Hansard, loc. cit.,* col. 387. The speaker was Sir James Malcolm.
[69] There is a fascinating account of the cholera outbreak in New York
State in the *New Yorker,* October 18, 1947 by S. H. ADAMS, That was Up-
State New York: My Grandfather and the Plague.

accompanied by the representatives of authority—the Prefect was conveniently away from Marseilles in 1835, for example, with an attack of gout.[70] Bishop Phillpotts, the target of the reformers of Exeter, was away in Torquay, during the terrible Exeter outbreak.[71] The Viceroy of Alexandria was absent on his boat for "a few days of rest" during the 1865 Egyptian outbreak.[72] It is scarcely surprising that given fear, verging on panic, cholera was associated with every kind of rumor, particularly with the two contradictory rumors leading to the same conclusion—the first that cholera was a fiction designed to suppress the rights of the poor and the second that the authorities had deliberately introduced cholera by poisoning as a means of attacking the poor.[73] In Paris, as Professor Chevalier shows, cholera had two distinct "images"— one *bourgeois,* and one associated with the *menu peuple.* In all parts of the world the disease had its folklore and its songs and ballads. "The cholera cometh," sang the Americans of the Mohawk Valley, "take care—take care!"

> Look well to thy dwelling—beware—beware!
> He breatheth corruption, and loveth the spot
> Where offal is suffered to lie and to rot;
> Then look to thy cellar, thy closet and yard—
> For all kinds of filth he hath special regard.[74]

This was a moral song. It pointed to the connection between dirt and disease, which was the first preoccupation of the sanitary reformers of the nineteenth century. Not the least interesting comparison that can be drawn between cholera epidemics in different parts of the world concerns the language of the lists of precautions

---

[70] *Le choléra,* p. 131.

[71] Details are given in R. S. LAMBERT's useful study, *The Cobbett of the West.* London, 1939, pp. 53–56.

[72] LANDES, *op. cit.,* p. 242.

[73] The rumors were widespread in Paris (*Le choléra,* p. 19), in St. Petersburg (*ibid.,* p. 148) and in England, where there was also the characteristic variant that it was a "job" (*ibid.,* p. 175). It was always easy in England to apply the term "job" to projects of sanitary reform. Colonel Sibthorp, the eccentric Tory critic of the Public Health Act of 1848 and all the other useful social legislation, had much in common with Cobbett. "I hate the commission, I hate all jobs, I suspect all governments," he declared. See A. BRIGGS, *Public Opinion and Public Health in the Age of Chadwick.* Chadwick Trust, 1946.

[74] ADAMS, *loc. cit.* Cf. the poem cited by M. Guiral—A. SAPET, *Le choléra morbus à Marseille.*

recommended by medical and administrative authorities. For many years more whitewash figured prominently near the head of the list. And what looked to be clean was often taken to be clean, particularly water. The General Board of Health in 1849 tried to deal with the evil smells of the sewers which its members thought contributed to the disease by flushing the sewers regularly into the Thames. Yet, as one of Chadwick's biographers has written, "the low districts of the capital might have been constructed by design to serve as a culture medium for the breeding and nourishment of the germs of the epidemic." [75]

Comparison of different national responses to cholera is revealing in illuminating general problems in comparative national history. There is an enormous amount of available literature since doctors and administrators were at pains to travel widely to see how other countries tackled questions which they knew or feared would soon confront them. Dr. Berry and Dr. Russell were sent from Britain, for example, to examine the first great cholera epidemic in Russia. In Germany Dr. Lichtenstädt translated the official Russian reports on cholera.[76] Sunderland, as has been shown, was a "Mecca" of doctors during the first British epidemic, and Indian experience was drawn on very freely in most parts of the world, particularly (at an expert level) by Pettenkofer. Comments made by foreigners usually concerned not only medical arrangements but such social factors as the willingness of the local population to go into hospital, the efficiency of local charity, the creation of ad hoc administrative machinery, and the policy (or lack of policy) of central government.

A systematic comparison of the role of cholera in modern social history at different times and in different places is thus already possible on the basis of available evidence. It would have to take account of at least five sets of facts—first, the facts of demography, including antecedent and later mortality rates and the incidence of cholera in terms of area, occupation, age and so on; second, the facts of economic and social structure, and economic and social reactions, including facts relating to the type and size of community and relations not only between rich and poor but between "authorities" and "subjects"; third, political circumstances, the immediate context of the cholera outbreaks; fourth, the structure

[75] LEWIS, op. cit., p. 202.
[76] J. R. LICHTENSTÄDT, Die Asiatische Cholera in Russland. Berlin, 1831.

of government, administration and finance, and the relationship of government effort to voluntary effort, including charity, and help from outside; and fifth, the extent of medical knowledge and popular attitudes towards that knowledge. Such a comparison would be of general interest to historians. It would go further than the limited task Professor Chevalier set himself and his colleagues—that of relating demography to history in the same way that demography is related to the study of contemporary societies, of giving a quantitative foundation to the analysis of social life.

The chief merit of Professor Chevalier's analysis is that it relates what contemporaries often thought of as an exceptional visitation of Providence to what many of them too readily accepted as the "normal" facts of life and death. He draws heavily on the work of the French pioneers of medico-social surveys. Cholera assisted them by providing them with sufficient material to make "une première expérience totale de ce fait de l'inégalité devant la mort qu'il n'avait jamais été possible de mesurer aussi complètement, dans ses caractères et dans ses causes." [77] The most important Parisian document from this point of view was one published in May 1834 by a commission of ten members: it reveals not only the demographic significance of cholera but the social geography of Paris and the composition of its population, including the large "floating population" which Professor Chevalier has studied so fully in other works.[78]

There is little doubt that in Britain also cholera stimulated what later in the century Dr. Haviland called "medical geography." [79] Snow's famous map of the distribution of the deaths from cholera in the Broad Street (Golden Square) area of London in 1854 was by no means the first. In 1833 Dr. Robert Baker illustrated his *Report of the Leeds Board of Health* with a "cholera plan," showing that the incidence of the disease was highest in the more densely populated area of the town. Dr. Shapter included a detailed map in his *History of the Cholera in Exeter* published in 1849, while three years later Augustus Petermann of Potsdam, a Fellow of the

[77] *Le choléra*, p. 26.
[78] *Ibid.* See also *Classes laborieuses et classes dangereuses* and *La formation de la population parisienne au XIXᵉ siècle.* Paris, 1950.
[79] A. HAVILAND, *Geographical Distribution of Disease in Great Britain.* London, 1892, p. 3.

Royal Geographical Society, brought out a *Cholera Map of the British Isles showing the districts affected in 1831–33*. Petermann vigorously upheld the claims of "geographical delineation" in the investigation of "the local causes" that might influence the progress of cholera and its "degree of fatality." [80]

Despite this close association between cholera and the development of medical geography, cholera probably played a somewhat smaller part in encouraging broader social investigation and demands for new social policies in Britain than Mr. Eversley suggests.[81] The study of occupational diseases in the industrial areas preceded the cholera outbreak,[82] and the extensive public enquiries into social conditions in the 1840's owed little to it.[83] The cholera outbreak of 1848–49 marked the culmination of a decade of enquiry, yet Viscount Morpeth himself emphasized that the purpose of the Public Health Act of 1848 was not to dispel a "transitory visitant" but to control "the abiding host of disease, the endemic and not the epidemic pestilence, the permanent overhanging mist of infection, the annual slaughter doubling in its ravages our bloodiest fields of conflict." [84] Contemporaries were as clear as Professor Chevalier that more commonplace and less dramatic diseases were at the heart of the problem of the improvement in social wellbeing. "It is possible," Snow himself wrote in 1855, "that seven times as many deaths have taken place from typhus as from cholera since the latter disease first visited England in 1831." [85] The significance

[80] An account of "Some Early English Maps of the Geography of Health and Disease" was given to the International Geographical Congress of 1952 by Professor E. W. Gilbert.

[81] *Le choléra*, pp. 170–71, where he says that the revelations of working-class conditions in Sunderland "pour la première fois" provided "une authentique désignation du rapport entre la saleté, la misère et la maladie."

[82] For example, C. T. THACKRAH, *The Effects of the Principal Arts . . . on Health and Longevity*. London, 1831. Chadwick's first published work of note was on the misleading picture of social conditions presented by the out-of-date life tables of insurance agencies. (*Westminster Review* [February 1828]). Chadwick quoted Villermé, who is in turn referred to by Professor Chevalier (*Le choléra*, p. 11). The *Westminster Review*, an invaluable utilitarian source, also included in its early numbers articles by DR. SOUTHWOOD SMITH on "Contagion and Sanitary Law" and plague, typhus fever and quarantine (*loc. cit.* [January and July, 1825]).

[83] For the significance of those reports, seen in proper perspective in relation to earlier ventures, see the important article by E. P. HENNOCK, Urban Sanitary Reform a generation before Chadwick? *Economic History Review*, 2nd ser., X (1957).

[84] *Hansard*, 3rd ser., XCVI, col. 392.

[85] SNOW, *On the Mode of Communication of Cholera*. 1855 ed., p. 137.

of differential urban mortality rates was understood if not always acted upon,[86] and it was the facts of typhus not cholera which induced the poor law commissioners in 1838 to summon Drs. Arnott, Kay and Southwood Smith to investigate the sanitary conditions of the towns. Some of the towns, like Preston, which were singled out in the famous 1842 *Report . . . on an Inquiry into the Sanitary Condition of the Labouring Population of Great Britain,* had almost completely escaped the cholera: yet it was Preston which provided Dr. Hall with some of the most effective statistics of differential mortality rates in "well-conditioned," "middling-conditioned," "ill-conditioned" and "worst conditioned streets." [87]

Too much emphasis on the social pathology of cities distorts the pattern of urban history in the nineteenth century. The forces of resistance to chaos and panic deserve as much attention as the chaos and panic themselves. A key theme in the history of the first cholera outbreak was the inability of doctors, despite their often heroic efforts in the sickroom, to reach agreement about the causes and the mode of communication of the disease. At best their approach was pragmatic: at worst their bitter disagreements promoted popular distrust and disapproval. In Russia public disapproval of the doctors was pushed so far that they were accused of trying to kill their patients.[88] In the United States a contemporary poetaster noted that

> Cholera kills and doctors slay
> And every foe will have its day[89]

In Britain, as elsewhere, the suspicion lingered late into the century. When in 1869 Snow urged the congress of the Social Science Association to press for an enlargement of machinery and the extension of governmental powers to achieve sanitary reform, *The Times* reported that the "stage of universal consent" still had not been reached. "What is needed is first information and then faith on the part of the public, and doctors must agree among themselves, if that be possible, before the outside world can be expected

[86] See MAJOR GREENWOOD, *Some British Pioneers of Social Medicine.* London, 1948.
[87] *Hansard, loc. cit.,* col. 395.
[88] *Le choléra,* p. 150.
[89] ADAMS, *loc. cit.*

to agree with them." [90] Snow himself was in frequent disagreement not only with some of his medical colleagues but with the more pragmatic supporters of sanitary reform—the foul smell and soap-and-water brigade. He urged that cleanliness should not be a cleanliness for mere appearance's sake; it should be "a rational cleanliness, like that by which the chemist keeps his tests pure and distinct and the farmer his land free from weeds." [91] The formulation of an articulate scientific approach was an important step forward in the history of the control of disease, but in Britain at least the practical effects of the application of scientific knowledge were not felt until the last quarter of the century. Cholera had already ceased to intrude when the Royal Sanitary Commission of 1868 was appointed, a commission which included four medical men, among them H. W. Acland, the investigator of cholera in Oxford. The setting up of the Local Government Board in 1871 and the Public Health Act of 1875 followed, but it was a medical journal, reporting a meeting called by Joseph Chamberlain in Birmingham, which warned Disraeli's government in 1875 that unless it aroused a national sense of "sanitary evils"—the motto *sanitas sanitatum* would have to be changed to *vanitas vanitatum*.[92]

The comparative side of this story still needs to be told—indeed, the English story itself has so far been neglected. Medical ideas might be shared or debated by doctors throughout the whole world, but sanitary institutions bore the stamp of their own national origin. There is room for new work on this subject. The improvement of the means of resistance to the "diseases of society," of which cholera was the most dramatic, provides just as interesting themes as the social pathology of Europe's very different cities in the early nineteenth century.

[90] *The Times* [London], October 5, 1869.
[91] SNOW, *On Continuous Molecular Changes*, p. 172.
[92] *British Medical Journal*, January 23, 1875.

3.

Metternich: A Reappraisal of His Impact on International Relations

Robert A. Kann

❋❋❋

EDITORIAL NOTE: *Clemens von Metternich (1773–1859) gave his name to the first post-Napoleonic generation in Europe. The age of Metternich, jolted by the revolutions of 1830, staggered on until 1848 when the statesman and his system collapsed together. Metternich's name became a byword for domestic and international reaction during his lifetime. Statesmen, like common stocks, rise and fall in popularity. Historians often execrate, then rehabilitate them. It would take a blindness to facts to defend Metternich's domestic policies. His ablest partisans, of whom Professor Kann is one, argue that in this respect he was a tool of historical forces beyond his control. This is really an evasion. Metternich's policy was the same at home and abroad. His self-appointed task was to thwart liberalism and nationalism. Within the traditional Hapsburg domains and in Europe at large, both threatened the Austrian Empire. Metternich used nationalism where he conceived that it suited his purposes, but he resisted the logical consequences of his own actions. Peasant nationalities could be invoked against their overlord aristocratic master nationalities, but the Hapsburg dynasty could never tolerate such a program of national conflict and class war. Sir Lewis Namier's essay (chapter 6) discusses the impossibility of any solution to these problems. Since Metternich's schemes for preventing revolution got no further than his office drawer, he was repeatedly thrown back on repression or inaction. The "coachman of Europe" quite properly despaired of order at home.*

A different view of Metternich has emerged since the second world war, but it is a reassessment strictly in terms of foreign affairs. Two generations ago, the victories of liberalism and nationalism were greeted as signs of "progress." Two world wars later and in a world still disrupted by the forces of nationalism,

Metternich, the old "internationalist," has come back into favor. Guglielmo Ferrero, Hans von Srbik, Henry Kissinger, and Robert Kann, among others, have portrayed a prescient and able diplomatist who understood world affairs better than any contemporary and most successors. After the first world war, everyone believed they could improve on Metternich's handiwork at the Congress of Vienna; their failure made Metternich look better by contrast. In more recent years Metternich has become doubly appealing. Substitute Communist for Jacobin, and he becomes a welcome defender of Cold War confrontation. In fact both Metternich's foreign and domestic policy were dictated by the facts. The survival of the Hapsburg Empire depended upon Metternich's capacity to make Austria a European necessity, a convincing answer for the unresolvable political and national dilemmas of eastern and central Europe. Austria could barely maintain domestic order, let alone run Italy and Germany (to which Metternich had committed her) without outside support. Metternich's principal task in foreign affairs was to convince the great powers of Europe that it was in their interest to sustain his employer's patchwork empire. The Hapsburg and Ottoman Empires, both nineteenth-century survivals on European tolerance, resembled two drunks staggering down the sidewalk, sustained only by each other and by the tolerance of their neighbors. If one collapsed, so did the other. The European powers reached decisions about both (as will be seen in the selection by A. J. P. Taylor, chapter 7) in the Crimean War.

Kann's able case for Metternich pleads for an assessment by results. He demonstrates Metternich's flexibility, his skill in dealing with liberal as well as reactionary powers, and points to forty years of peace after Waterloo as Metternich's contribution. But no power wanted to break the peace after twenty-five years of endemic war. Kann's argument rests partly, as he admits, on the assumption that the preservation of the Hapsburg Empire was a good thing, and about that—whatever the history of the successor states in the twentieth century—there may yet be some debate.

One of the supposed truisms of history is that the test of greatness in political action is its applicability to present-day conditions. When calling the roll of the eminent Western statesmen in the field of international relations in the last centuries—from Richelieu and Kaunitz to Cavour and Bismarck, to take only a few outstanding examples—one begins to wonder if this concept is not an oversimplification. Of the many who acknowledge the great contributions of these men to the policies of their countries, only a few would claim that their methods are in any way germane to the problems of our day. It appears that historical changes during the last generations make it necessary to differentiate between great action and action applicable in the modern world.

In the case of Prince Clemens Metternich, the "coachman of Europe," from the Congress of Vienna in 1814 to his enforced abdication from power at the beginning of the revolution of 1848, the situation seems to be rather the reverse. His character appears to many to have been as controversial as that of Richelieu, Talleyrand, or Bismarck; in his domestic policies he has found fewer defenders than any one of them. His greatness is still questioned today, though probably less so than half a century ago. Yet, as to the significance of his life's work for the present world, entirely irrespective of the issue of his personal greatness, he surpasses most of the outstanding statesmen that came before or after him.

Why is this true? So sweeping an assertion must of necessity be limited in its application. It is not to be applied to Metternich's role as the leading Austrian statesman for almost four decades, nor even to his suppression of nationalism and constitutionalism in central Europe. Metternich's active influence on the idea of the police state, censorship, and cultural isolationism, so frequently associated with Austrian internal administration in the restoration era, has been generally overrated. The same certainly cannot be said of the national and constitutional issues in the Germanies, the Hapsburg Empire, and Italy. Here, however, Metternich did not act very differently from many of his ministerial colleagues throughout the restoration period, both within and outside Austria. Like him, they conceived the chief task in domestic administration to be the preservation of ancient empire structures in a fast-changing world. Whatever Metternich did in these spheres has of course become part of the flow of cause and effect in the stream of history. Yet, whether he showed greater skill or perhaps less long-range insight than others, in these respects he appears more as the tool than the free agent of history.

The significance of Metternich for our times rests on a very different and almost unique contribution, a contribution which is perhaps comparable to that of only one Western statesman after him—Woodrow Wilson. The comparison seems strange. What does Metternich, the slightly frivolous, enlightened cavalier, never fully at home in the emotional, romantic era, have in common with the austere, puritan thinker Wilson? The answer is simple: the creation of a system of international politics according to supra-national and supra-party principles and based on supposedly self-evident reason. No attempt will be made here to stress this similarity further in personal terms. Wilson in many ways the liberal, Metternich the conservative; Wilson the deep thinker and luckless manager of international relations, Metternich the conventional though not shallow writer, the brilliant operator of foreign affairs and diplomatic agencies—there is no need to dwell on these great differences in character and the even greater ones in the political environment. What stands out, however, is the fact that both men forged a program not primarily tied to the national community, a program not conceived solely as a second step to an interrelationship between the great powers, as was the case with Bismarck or Cavour. Wilson, while by no means neglecting the interests of his country, perceived them first and last within the international community, just as Metternich in more modest terms simultaneously kept in view the Concert of Europe and, as a mere part of the whole, the Hapsburg Empire.

Among the formal international agreements in the three centuries from the Westphalian peace treaty to the present, these two systems share another—in this case negative—aspect that sets them apart from most other actively promoted systems of international relations of this period: the lack of a crusading or anti-crusading idea. True enough, the Wilsonian philosophy was permeated with the ideals of a supra-national democratic humanitarianism, but this had little to do with party ideology of any kind. In the same sense one might say that, appearances notwithstanding, Metternich's anti-revolutionary, anti-national, and anti-constitutional doctrine was in fact deeply rooted in an enlightened absolutism that placed equilibrium between the powers first and recognized ideological factors only insofar as they might disturb this equilibrium. One may well rate Wilson's political ideals far higher than Metternich's, and yet one cannot help being impressed by the latter's operation of a system of clear thought, reasonably free from the stresses of day-to-day political battles and the conflicts of specific personal interests. In this respect it is significant that the man whose name has been, and in all likelihood always will be, associated with this system of political thought clearly rejected the notion that international political doctrine and strategy should be linked to a specific individual and thus be weakened in their general validity.[1]

An admission that this "system"—the term used by Metternich's friends and foes alike—was clear, dispassionate, and rational within the limits of obvious human frailties implies but faint praise. Surely the chancellor did not produce an intellectual masterpiece of political strategy comparable to Machiavelli's *Prince*. Metternich was a voluminous and facile writer, but his lengthy ruminations on the nature of politics are not distinguished by any particular originality of thought. His correspondence on current events is far superior to his theoretical memoranda. In any event, the truly brilliant writings to which the system owed its fame derive primarily from Metternich's closest collaborator in the state chancellery, Friedrich von Gentz. This should in no way detract from the significance of Metternich's life work, which is based on a rare combination of thought and action, a sublime interplay between rigidity of doctrine and flexibility of application. This point was to some extent overlooked by Metternich's eminent biographer, Heinrich von Srbik, who represented Metternich's doctrines as a powerful work of political philosophy and his diplomacy as a kind of minor skill, not quite worthy of his hero. The observer of later days may well rate the rigidity and consistency of Metternich's political thought lower while he may appraise the flexibility of its execution considerably higher.

Basically, Metternich's theories consist in the combination and interpretation of a few simple and well-established concepts.[2] He believed in a principle of legitimacy in international relations which may not be quite as broad as has been claimed in a brilliant analysis by Henry Kissinger, who considers it an international order of

[1] See *Aus Metternichs nachgelassenen Papieren,* edited by his son Prince Richard Metternich-Winneburg. 8 vols., Vienna, 1880–84 (hereafter cited as *NP*), vol. VIII, pp. 186, 196–97, where Metternich deplores the tendency to link an idea to a specific individual and thereby weaken its impact. This applies in particular to the political phenomenon of Louis Napoleon in December 1848. See also (*ibid.,* pp. 462 ff.) Metternich's letter of January 17, 1849 to Prince Felix Schwarzenberg on the desirability of a depersonalized concept of government as he saw it practiced in England. See further the biography by H. V. SRBIK, *Metternich.* 3 vols.; Munich, 1925–54, vol. I, pp. 321–26, and the following passages from *NP* referred to in it: vol. VII, pp. 517, 612, 639; vol. VIII, pp. 200, 286, 239.

[2] See in particular SRBIK, *op. cit.,* vol. I, pp. 317–42.

limited conflicts always adjustable by negotiation between litigating powers.[3] It was something more than a restoration of divine right absolutism; it was a stable order determined by the consensus of the recognized great powers of the day. Here it is well to remember that after the French Revolution of 1789 and the Napoleonic Wars this order was not an established one but was merely restored or manufactured. As such it required this consensus, that is, the compromise between the great powers; and thus it could never be an exact replica of the old one. It was the good fortune of Metternich that the limited ideological differences between the great powers of this period made such a compromise possible. Compromise is indeed the salient feature in the second of Metternich's great principles: equilibrium among the great powers of the European pentarchy—at that time the world pentarchy—of Austria, France, Great Britain, Prussia, and Russia. Here again the notion of equilibrium, in the sense of a balance of power as attempted by the Westphalian peace treaty and actually achieved by the treaties of Utrecht, Rastadt, and Baden after the War of the Spanish Succession, was no more a new concept than legitimacy would have been in terms of divine right theory. What was new was the application of this concept: its extension from the sphere of power politics into that of ideological differences as represented by British constitutionalism and utilitarianism; a czarist mixture of metaphysically inspired enlightened absolutism and imperialism; a French drive for imperial restoration in very uncertain domestic political terms; a Prussian push for supremacy in the German orbit; and an Austrian effort to maintain a mediator's position within the framework of "the unified decentralized state." [4] A mediatorship of this sort in the service of the equilibrium could function only if it were assured of two further factors, related to but not similar to those previously mentioned. These were security and stability. To Metternich, security required not only military preparedness but also a compromise between the powers. He fully realized that the absolute security of one power is in purely military terms a threat to that of others. While it is true that in an age of

[3] HENRY A. KISSINGER, *A World Restored: Metternich, Castlereagh and the Problems of Peace, 1812–1822.* New York, 1957, pp. 1–3, 137, 204. See also R. A. KANN, *A Study in Austrian Intellectual History: from Late Baroque to Romanticism.* New York, 1960, pp. 259–302.
[4] SRBIK, *op. cit.,* vol. I, pp. 434–36; see also Metternich's memorandum of October 1817, *NP,* vol. III, pp. 66–75.

codified great-power dominance his concept cannot be described as collective security in the broad modern sense, it is entirely proper to refer to Metternich's security concept as based primarily on the consensus of the joint powers.

More controversial is the concept of stability, the interpretation and application of which has greatly contributed to Metternich's ill repute in the liberal camp. It is that part of his philosophy which is commonly associated more than any other with the notion of a blind restoration of the old regime and all that it involves in terms of direct and indirect restrictions of human liberties, of social emancipation and freedom of opportunity. Actually, Metternich never identified stability with the status quo, nor was he opposed to the idea of slow evolutionary reform in itself. Yet, such reforms were applied primarily to the realm of international politics, where he felt at home and was thus able and willing to make concessions, and not to the social-economic sphere, where change at home as well as abroad meant to him approaching the danger zone of revolution.[5]

What has particularly exasperated his critics is the kind of verbiage which seemingly intends to obscure the fact that he thought of consensus as deriving from government power not subject to control by public opinion, and freedom of thought as pertaining to an external forum and not merely to individual conscience.[6] It is perhaps noteworthy that these later, primarily nationalist critics took rationalizations of this kind for mere hypocrisy, whereas an extremely bitter contemporary liberal opponent like Heinrich Heine in his preface to *Französische Zustände* gives Metternich credit for the fact that he never "played the demagogue . . . that one always knew where one stood with him. . . . One knew that he did not act either out of love or petty hatred but grandly in the spirit of his system. . . ."[7] Apparently Heine knew the difference

[5] See the highly illuminating memorandum of June 1853 to his successor Count Buol in *NP,* vol. VIII, pp. 347–50 where he readily agrees to "manipulation" in the political sphere but categorically refuses what he terms "capitulation" in the social one.

[6] See for instance the strange concoction of the terms freedom, order and tyranny, all wrapped into one, in his so-called Political Testament of 1849–55, *NP,* vol. VII, pp. 633–42, and especially pp. 636–39, or his remarks addressed to Count Auersperg (Anastasius Grün) in 1838 on the identification of freedom of expression with freedom of thought. See SRBIK, *op. cit.,* vol. I, pp. 397–98.

[7] HEINRICH HEINE, *Sämmtliche Werke.* 12 vols.; Hamburg, 1851–65, vol. VIII, *Französische Zustände,* Preface of 1832, pp. 19, 20.

between hypocrisy and flexibility. For all Metternich's outstanding diplomatic skill and perspicacity, without this flexibility his entire political theory would have been fragile indeed.

It must be remembered, of course, that Metternich was spared the difficulty of the democratic and, to a degree, even of the totalitarian governments of today—namely, the necessity of obtaining at least a measure of public support for his policy. It was perhaps not so much the reactionary character but the seeming stability of the regime in Austria as well as his personal prestige that made him more impervious to the impact of public opinion than any contemporary leading statesman, Czar Alexander I not excluded.[8]

Lack of concern for the impact of public opinion, however, determines only one facet of diplomacy, and even that presumably only for a short period of time. Yet, by today's standards, Metternich's success was a long-range one and may well be measured in decades. This in spite of the fact that his disregard for mass support did not work entirely to his advantage. After all, there was a reverse side to this problem as well; namely, the lack of such strength as could have been drawn from such backing. It was precisely with the beginning of Metternich's tenure of office after the peace of Schönbrunn in 1809 that Austrian policy dismissed what Metternich considered the mere props of diplomacy. In its stead he introduced a foreign policy that was to be put into action after he was sure not only that Austria would not be isolated, but also that agreement existed as to the aims of the powers with which he wanted to cooperate. Hence, Austria's late but not belated joining of the anti-Napoleonic coalition in 1813 which, for all practical purposes, substituted a guarantee of success for the weight of popular support in the war of 1809.[9] This cautious policy was prompted largely by the strategic central position of Austria and the complexities of her ethnic-historic structure, threatened in the event of defeat by complete dismemberment, a danger to which the other key members of the great alliance, Great Britain and Russia, were not exposed.

But such a policy, slow and perhaps hesitant in execution, did not lack daring and imagination in planning. It should always be

[8] Though personally not oblivious to the effect of public opinion, Metternich conceived of it primarily as a gauge to measure the destructive forces of revolution. See, for instance, *NP,* vol. VIII, pp. 238–39, written in 1850.
[9] See Metternich's reflections in regard to Austria's policy at the beginning of the Crimean War, *ibid.,* pp. 364–71.

remembered that Metternich was the first to perceive the opportunity for the containment of France and was the last to agree to the destruction of Napoleon. He did so because he felt that a Napoleon, curbed in his foreign policy, would still be strong enough to check revolution, while his lesser successors would have to move into a power vacuum. Whether this belief, shattered by Napoleon himself during the Hundred Days in 1815, was correct is less important than his willingness to adjust the concept of legitimacy to stability rather than restoration.

Flexibility was demonstrated above all by the entire foreign policy of Metternich during that strange period of great-power conferences from 1815 to 1822. Somber features in this picture are not lacking. Yet, though criticism of the oppressive measures of the Concert of Europe against Naples and Spain may be justified in itself, the main point should not be overlooked that in a sense this policy was a price paid—perhaps all too willingly then—for the containment of Russia in close collaboration with Great Britain. Here again the chief evidence of flexible skill is the fact that Metternich cooperated sincerely and successfully with British statesmen whose philosophy of government was much more divergent from his own than that of Alexander I and his brother. Indeed, in 1821 it was no idle boast on Metternich's part when he wrote, "If I were not master of making [the Russian troops] retreat just as I made them advance, do you think I should ever have set them in motion?" [10]

It is quite true that after 1822 Metternich's grip on the European situation relaxed, slowly at first, then at an increasing speed. The ever more obvious deficiencies of the settlement of Vienna in regard to the rising issues of constitutionalism, liberalism, and nationalism (which are outside the province of this discussion) are not solely responsible for this fact. Even in the purely diplomatic sphere it became impossible to keep two alliance systems with different *raisons d'être* permanently in line. And surely the quadruple —later quintuple—alliance, primarily concerned with the preservation of the territorial status quo, and the Holy Alliance, emphasizing the necessity of domestic governmental patriarchies, proved to be wholly incompatible. Metternich's policy from the Congress of Verona in 1822 to his downfall at the very beginning of the March

[10] *Ibid.*, vol. III, p. 467; letter by Metternich to Count Stadion, quoted from KISSINGER, *op. cit.*, p. 280.

rising in 1848 is a continuous chain of rearguard actions to delay, to cover, and to argue away the breakdown of the Concert of Europe and all it stood for.

It cannot be denied that he achieved a limited success in his relations with the Orleans monarchy in France after the great July revolution of 1830, and a more modest but perhaps more difficult one, the Münchengraetz agreement with Russia of 1833, which for a time checked further Russian advances in the disintegrating Ottoman East. Undoubtedly, these policies helped also to give a limited renewal to Austria's lease on life in the German and Italian spheres. Metternich had, after all, succeeded in maintaining the great-power position of Austria, but the glorious period from 1812 to 1822 when the Hapsburg Empire, anticipating the late Victorian position of Great Britain, acted as European mediator and arbitrator in the service of peace had passed. Austria—very much against Metternich's original intention—had been forced to shift from an overall key position in the center of Europe to a kind of Austro-Russo-Prussian entente system. Her status, deprived of the flexibility desired by the state chancellor, was thus fatally weakened, even during Metternich's lifetime, by the deterioration of her relations with Russia resulting from the Crimean War crisis. This in turn presaged and to a point predetermined the loss of her position in Italy and Germany within less than a decade.

In a sense this steady undermining of Austria's position as a great power testifies to the eminence of Metternich the statesman, since what looked for a time like the operation of an infallible system turned out to be merely the temporary success of an eminent man. As the genuine Austrian that the Rhenish aristocrat had become, he was certainly pleased by his success, but never intoxicated by victory, always cognizant that he fought a delaying battle which he could not win in the end.[11]

What does it all add up to? An evaluation of Metternich's policies and of their relationship to the problems of our times might perhaps most conveniently move from the less controversial to the more controversial. Unfortunately for Metternich's reputation, this entails stronger and wider support for the negative criticism

[11] See, for instance, *NP,* vol. III, pp. 347-48 (1820), and p. 472 (1821); vol. V, pp. 193-96 (1831).

of his policies. There have been few who have maintained seriously that even within the standards of his own time the prince understood the impact of the social changes brought about by the industrial revolution and the gradual emancipation of the peasants, the Declarations of Independence and of Rights, the continental pattern of constitutional government, the rise of liberal nationalism. While he himself naturally enough believed in the correctness of "the system," he realized better than many of his more uncritical admirers that it had not stood the test of the times. Had he gone one step farther and realized that it was not merely the upheavals of the period but something less impersonal as well that had made things go wrong, he would not have been the man he was.

In the political field the verdict is somewhat less clear than in the social one. Unquestionably, the territorial settlement of 1814–15 was in a state of dissolution in the east by the end of Metternich's tenure of office. In western and central Europe the then established boundaries could still be held in a precarious kind of balance, but here the constitutional principles of the system were in rapid flux. Above all, the balance of power between east, west, and central Europe became increasingly disturbed. Here, however, it may well be argued that times like ours, subject to ever more rapid political change, might take a more tolerant view of the relative brevity of the preservation of established treaty provisions and principles.

Such comparisons of the relative similarity of historical situations should, of course, be based on complete confidence concerning the chain of historical causation itself. True enough, the bulk of evidence concerning the course of European political history from Metternich's time to ours is in. Yet before we can pass judgment on the character of the impact of his policies on our times, we would have to be very sure that he really exercised such an influence. To answer this question of causation in a fully satisfactory way is actually a far more difficult task than that of forming value judgments. Here we have to face the fact that we can assume but we cannot prove the degree to which Metternich influenced later events.

An assumption of this kind is usually based on three interrelated facts: the containment of Russia, the preservation of the Hapsburg Empire, and above all the establishment and maintenance of peace.

Hardly anybody will argue that Metternich's skillful containment of Russia was successful in the long run. Still, it is sometimes asserted that his policy at this particular time might well serve as a model for policies in our day. I do not believe this to be true. If historical analogies are meaningful, we must, of course, make a generous allowance for differences in historical situations. When we come to deal with personalities as different as Alexander I and his brother, and Messrs. Stalin and Khrushchev, the allowance must be very generous indeed. If we add to these differences the more important ones in ideology, we have reached a point where historical comparisons become unprofitable. Metternich's Eastern policy may have been wise or unwise; it teaches us no specific lessons.

Anyone who, like this writer, feels that the disintegration of the Hapsburg Empire at the end of World War I was a major tragedy in international relations cannot fail to be impressed by the argument that Metternich secured the preservation of Austria and therewith the European equilibrium, so tragically destroyed in 1918. While the effect of Austria's disintegration was demonstrably one major factor, though surely not the only one, responsible for the European crises that have continued since that time, the premise that Metternich's achievements helped to secure the great-power position of Austria up to that point is far more problematical. There can be no doubt that he made an outstanding contribution to the restoration of the Hapsburg Empire from the depths of defeat in the Napoleonic Wars to the key position she held for a decade after 1812 and to her continuation as a great power for some time subsequent to this. Yet restoration and preservation are by no means the same. Whether Metternich's part in establishing Austria's domestic policies and ideological alignments actually contributed to the preservation of the empire up to 1918 or, from a long-range viewpoint, possibly shortened her lease on life, is a question of extraordinary complexity. It merges with the more comprehensive question whether social and cultural change can be stopped at a certain point by governmental authority and, if so, for how long. Historians thus far have not found satisfactory answers.

The Russian and the Austrian problems are both linked to the supreme quest for the preservation of peace, the decisive test in any evaluation of Metternich. On the assumption (which, however, has not been proved) that Metternich's policies are largely responsible for the course of international relations from the Congress of Vienna to the outbreak of the war in 1914, the arguments present themselves as follows: Metternich's system secured for a full century the preservation, if not of peace, at least of an era without major war. Other schools of thought refuse to give Metternich credit at this point on the basis of the familiar and unanswerable argument that the extent of historical causation cannot be proved. More fruitful, however, is the examination of another line of thought which denies that peace was actually preserved during the century from 1815 to 1914. Here we may come close indeed to the core of the Metternich problem.

By and large, historiography prior to World War I took an unfriendly, even hostile attitude toward Metternich's foreign policy. This, of course, was due to several factors. Established Western liberalism, central European neoliberalism of the third quarter of the nineteenth century, and the German nationalism of the Second Empire, represented best perhaps by Treitschke's philosophy of history, rejected Metternich's doctrines and devices for obvious and specific reasons. Beyond this, however, one may well say that the people who reached manhood around 1848 and died before 1914 did not feel that they lived in an era of peace. To them the Crimean War, the Austro-Prussian War, and the Franco-Prussian War were big wars, and in view of the relative number of troops engaged and casualties suffered they had good reason to think so. Only the tragedy of two world wars has changed that picture. This, indeed, is the period when the reversal in the evaluation of Metternich, initiated by such eminent historians as Guglielmo Ferrero and Heinrich von Srbik, commences.[12]

It is psychologically quite understandable that the impact of the dark forces of our time should challenge the historian to portray Metternich in a favorable light. Undoubtedly such a shift in the frame of reference explains the motivation of those who contend that Metternich made a lasting contribution to peace. It neither proves nor disproves the contention itself. One thing only

---

[12] GUGLIELMO FERRERO (Eng. trans.), *The Principles of Power*. New York, 1942, and *The Reconstruction of Europe*. New York, 1941. The third volume of Srbik's biography deals with the historiographical evaluation of Metternich. See also A. WANDRUSZKA, Der Kutscher Europas. Fürst Metternich im Urteil der Historiker von Heute. *Wort und Wahrheit,* XIV (1959), 459 ff.

is certain. Metternich himself wanted peace, and peace not merely in terms of a Bismarckian saturation of power but on the basis of the status quo, adjusted by negotiations as he conceived them. Thus the living lesson of his work pertaining to international relations is not embedded in any particulars of political strategy but in principles which may be summarized as follows: moderation in success and perseverance in defeat, steadfastness of purpose as the intrinsic premise of compromise irrespective of conflicting ideologies, consensus based on reason and not on emotion. Surely not these principles in themselves but failure to apply them successfully is responsible for Metternich's equivocal position in history. Yet how could he have applied them successfully without linking them gradually to some kind of system of popular sovereignty? And how could he have done so without repudiating the tradition he stood for?

4.

A Reconsideration of Guizot

Douglas Johnson

❖❖

EDITORIAL NOTE: *Few Liberal statesmen have suffered more at the hands of historians than François Pierre Guillaume Guizot (1787–1874). A contemporary called him "the evil spirit of the French bourgeoisie." Revisionists avoided him for decades. Rightists rejected him as a liberal; but he was not liberal enough to share in the general approbation later accorded many inferior politicians and thinkers. Since he was a loser—one of the initial victims of the revolution of 1848—he has never received the plaudits of pragmatists. Professor Johnson argues that the devaluation of Guizot is misleading and unfortunate, for Guizot is important both in himself and for what he reveals about political development during the restoration (1815–1830) and July Monarchy (1830–1848).*

In a fundamental sense Guizot was detached from the France he helped to mold and govern. He was a Protestant—in fact, a puritanical Huguenot—and neither sympathized with nor attempted to understand the Roman Catholic church. There was a cultural rift between himself and the bulk of his countrymen. He had little sympathy for French institutions save when he felt they could be amended to imitate English forms. He sought the English parliament, not the French Chambre. He attempted to develop English self-help and social institutions in a relatively unreceptive France. As an historian (most nineteenth-century French political thinkers laid some claim upon history), Guizot was drawn, not to the French, but to the English Revolution of 1688. He believed it provided for a sound balance of social and political forces and interests while developing a framework for peaceful institutional change. In temperament, faith, and outlook Guizot was in many ways better suited to the seventeenth century than the nineteenth.

His contemporaries viewed him as a deep thinker, and he was certainly a popular teacher at the University of Paris. He edited Le Globe, *probably the periodical most widely read by the intellectuals. Guizot sought to involve cultivated and thoughtful men*

in politics and administration rather than bureaucratic or aristo-
cratic time-servers. He believed that it was the function of the
thinker and statesman to define general principles of government,
of foreign policy, of education, of belief. More important, he at-
tempted to put his principles into action. But Guizot had a sense of
human frailty and the limitations imposed by political reality. With
some noteworthy exceptions, he attempted to take them into ac-
count during his political career.

Among the other merits of Professor Johnson's article one should
notice particularly the way in which he considers all the facets of
the man, and the skill with which Johnson uses Guizot to illu-
minate the period as a whole.

All the statesmen and politicians of nineteenth-century France need
to be reconsidered; it is doubtful whether any deserves reconsideration more than Guizot. Neither historians nor history have been
fair towards him. He was a man who achieved eminence in many
different ways, as a journalist, a historian, an educationalist, a
diplomat, a writer on theological matters, an administrator of the
French Protestant church and one of the great orators of France,
as well as being a political leader. "J'ai eu trois vies," he once
wrote to Madame Lenormant, "une littéraire, une politique et une
religieuse. J'espère qu'il y a eu harmonie entre les trois et que
l'harmonie sera claire." [1] But his wish has not been met. If his
historical work, the histories of civilization in Europe and in
France or the history of the English Revolution, is remembered,
or if, more rarely, his various meditations on Christianity are recalled, they are rarely associated with his career as a politician or as
a minister. He is invariably thought of as a politician whose intellectual preoccupations are not to be set against his outstanding
characteristic, which is that of failure. At best therefore Guizot
is thought of as a superior mediocrity, a dull dog, a man whose
importance is only grudgingly admitted, so that an English historian has recently written of "the strange preponderance of M.
Guizot" with reference to the period of the restoration; at worst
Guizot is thought to typify class oppression and corruption, and
by his deliberate perversion of parliamentary institutions and de-

---

[1] Guizot to Madame Lenormant (a niece of Mme. Récamier and widow of
the director of the Catholic review *Le correspondant*), October 1, 1865.
Lettres à M. et Mme. Lenormant: Les années de retraite de M. Guizot.
Paris, 1902, p. 245.

liberate encouragement of middle-class egoism, he is still considered, as he was once called, "le mauvais génie de la bourgeoisie française." [2] It seems therefore true to say that Guizot has suffered more than the customary depreciation of most nineteenth-century intellectuals whose positions have been undermined by the changing perspective of historical and religious enquiry. There seems to be a general supposition that behind his eloquence and industry there lay a fundamental incapacity, and that behind his austere exterior there was even a certain dishonesty.

These suppositions have persisted, although many legends about Guizot have been exploded. It has for a long time been known that the phrase "enrichissez-vous" could only be thought of as an example of political immorality when removed from its context, which was either "enrichissez-vous par le travail et par l'épargne," an exhortation to which no one could have taken exception, or an appeal to the Chamber to better the moral and material conditions of France, which was equally far from having any sinister implications.[3] It has also been clear from Guizot's correspondence with intimate friends, much of which has been published, that he was far from being the distant and disagreeable Huguenot so frequently presented in the textbooks, but was instead a man of great warmth of personality, capable of inspiring and of experiencing deep affection.[4] It has been evident too for some time that the charge that Guizot maintained himself in power by corrupt elec-

[2] MRS. IRENE COLLINS in *History* (February 1961), 20; PILLON and RENOUVIER in *Le critique philosophique* (September 24, 1874).

[3] For a discussion of the "enrichissez-vous" phrase see *L'Intermédiaire des chercheurs et des curieux*. XL (1899), 869–70. For Guizot's speech in the Chamber of Deputies on March 1, 1843, see GUIZOT, *Histoire parlementaire de France*. Paris, 1864, vol. IV, p. 68.

[4] Guizot's daughter Mme. Conrad de Witt edited two volumes, *Monsieur Guizot dans sa famille et avec ses amis*. Paris, 1880, and *Lettres de Monsieur Guizot à sa famille et à ses amis*. Paris, 1884. *Lettres à M. et Mme. Lenormant* and *François Guizot et Madame Laure de Gasparin*, ANDRÉ GAYOT, ed., Paris, 1934, contain many letters which changed people's opinions about Guizot. On the letters to Mme. de Gasparin the critic Émile Henriot wrote, "Nous croyions avoir affaire à un mort, exsangue et figé, momifié dans ses principes comme un pharaon dans ses bandelettes: et quelques pages d'écriture, o merveille! le rendent soudain à la vie et nous permettent d'approcher l'homme, infiniment digne d'estime et de sympathie, malgré ses fautes et son échec." *Le Temps,* October 27, 1931. Although Guizot's correspondence with the Princess Lieven has never been published in full (Monsieur Jean Schlumberger tells me that he is preparing an edition) some of his letters have been published by Ernest Daudet, *Une ambassadrice du siècle dernier*. Paris, 1903.

tions and packed parliaments needs to be modified. Not only have historians been content with slight evidence and the conviction that there existed examples of corruption although they could not cite them,[5] but they have also supposed that there is only one ideal form of parliamentary government, by which the French system of the 1840's must be judged. Guizot himself commented on the fact that although all his government's papers had fallen into the hands of his opponents after 1848, little was found to confirm the two charges which had been made most frequently against him, those of corrupting parliamentary life and of pursuing a timid foreign policy.[6] Yet in spite of this knowledge, the conventional picture of Guizot both as a man and as a statesman has tended to persist.

In this tendency, historians are following in the tradition of Guizot's contemporaries, many of whom were continually hostile to him. They sought to belittle him by suggesting that he was of no importance, "un homme de carton-pierre," or "un télégraphe" worked either by Louis-Philippe or by de Broglie; they suggested that he was unpatriotic and emphasized his pro-English sentiment by calling him "Sir Guizot" or "Lord Guizot"; they recalled his mission to the exiled Louis XVIII at Ghent in 1815, when he had supposedly betrayed his country by giving constitutional advice to the king at a time when France was being invaded; they attacked his personal character, making him out to be "une nature maigre, jaune, soucieuse, retatinée, étrangère à tous les côtés riants et gracieux de l'existence," clinging to office out of an arid love of power.[7] It is true to say that Guizot was never popular and this is undoubtedly a fact of some importance. In 1848, for example, his unpopularity helps to explain why the opposition was so determined to get rid of him and why many conservatives were reluctant to defend his government. There were moments when he succeeded in creating enthusiasm, as when, along with Victor Cousin and Villemain, he was one of the great lecturers of the university, one of what Sainte-Beuve called "les trois régents de

[5] E.g., JEAN DAUTRY, 1818 et la IIe République. Paris, 1947, 2nd ed., p. 48.

[6] Guizot to Lord Aberdeen, April 26, 1852, in DOUGLAS JOHNSON, Guizot et Lord Aberdeen en 1852. Revue d'Histoire Moderne et Contemporaine (January–March 1958), 65.

[7] HIPPOLYTE CASTILLE, Les hommes et les mœurs en France sous le règne de Louis-Philippe. Paris, 1853, p. 33; MARCELLE, Guizot et Napoléon. Paris, s.d.; L'Histoire peu française de Lord F. Guizot, organe des intérêts anglais dans le cabinet et ministre des étrangers en France. Paris, 1842; A. J. DE MARNAY, D'une chute à l'autre. Paris, new ed. 1880, p. 281.

la jeunesse." There were times when he was treated with great respect, as when he received Lacordaire at the Académie Française in 1861, or when he intervened in the Protestant Synod of 1872. And towards the end of his life many people admired "l'illustre solitaire du Val Richer," working incessantly in his house near to Lisieux, apparently untroubled by the reverses of fortune. Yet this was not popularity, as Guizot himself realized. In one of his rare complaints he said to his co-religionist Jules Pédézert, "On n'a jamais voulu me rendre cette justice que j'étais bon." [8]

A new insight has recently been given into this unpopularity by the publication of the memoirs of Charles de Rémusat, who knew Guizot extremely well and who for several years was his closest colleague.[9] The portrait which Rémusat draws of Guizot is severe, and in particular he stresses this unpopularity. According to Rémusat, nobody liked Guizot. Louis-Philippe, Casimir Périer, Talleyrand, Duchâtel, the center groups of the Chamber, and even his friend de Broglie, in his rather distinguished way, are all represented by Rémusat as finding Guizot in some way or other unlikeable. Rémusat even suggests that Guizot's unpopularity was great enough to lead some people (including Thiers) to suppose that he would be booed at his reception to the Académie Française (to which, incidentally, he had been elected unopposed) in 1836. All this repeats and magnifies the sort of remark which is to be found in Sainte-Beuve's *Mes Poisons,* that Guizot had "dans sa personne une raideur désagréable et qui offense, quelque chose d'essentiellement antipathique." [10] But whereas *Mes Poisons* can be dismissed as an accumulation of secret malice, Rémusat, by the detail of his narrative and by his knowledge of events, has to be considered seriously.

Yet it is difficult to believe that Guizot could have been so unpopular and still capable of remaining a minister and even of becoming chief minister. In judging Rémusat's account, one has to remember what he himself was during the restoration and the July Monarchy. He was a journalist who was often without a newspaper, a deputy without any consistent following in the Chamber, a minister for only a few unsuccessful months, a thinker who had few positive ideas and an author who was, after all, only "un peu

[8] JULES PÉDÉZERT, *Guizot.* Paris, 1874, p. 11.
[9] CHARLES DE RÉMUSAT, *Mémoires de ma vie,* Ch. Pouthas, ed., Paris, 1958–60. Three volumes have so far been published.
[10] SAINTE-BEUVE, *Mes Poisons.* Paris, 1926, p. 67.

auteur." He had given himself the appearance of being important by assiduously cultivating the sources of power, and as a would-be constructor of ministries he had made himself into a go-between. It is natural that he should have sought to stress the importance of all these activities, and it is clear that his portrait of Guizot does just that. For Guizot is presented as having essentially only one loyal friend, Rémusat. That he succeeded at all, in spite of the dislike that surrounded him, could only be because of the indispensable qualities of that friend. Viewed in this light, Rémusat's descriptions of Guizot are less convincing than might at first sight appear.

But whilst Rémusat's authority needs to be questioned, or at least examined critically, it would be unwise to reject everything that he, and his contemporaries, said about Guizot. There is one anecdote told by Rémusat which is particularly interesting and which perhaps helps one to understand how misunderstandings have grown up concerning Guizot. On the day on which Guizot's first wife, Pauline de Meulan (herself a distinguished writer and educationalist), died, in 1827, Rémusat was present in Guizot's house. When Guizot joined the members of his family and Rémusat to tell them that death had taken place, he stayed with them for only a few minutes; then turning to his nieces he said, "Allons-nous habiller," meaning that they should put on their mourning. There was no doubt, and Rémusat never doubted, that Guizot was deeply moved by his wife's death, and there was no hypocrisy in his mourning. Yet his anxiety to be seen in mourning was undoubtedly affectation, even if it were the affectation of a sincere sentiment. This incident therefore reveals a certain gaucherie in human relations which one must appreciate if one is to understand Guizot. He was always anxious to compose a public countenance which was severe and correct. It was this public countenance which was disliked and which one must try to penetrate.

Guizot's connections with the pastors of the Protestant Église du Désert (both his grandfather and one of his great-uncles were pastors), his birth in the Protestant center of Nîmes and his unusually cosmopolitan education in Geneva, which must have been one of the few parts of imperial France where it was possible to study foreign languages and literature, were particularly significant. They emphasized an un-French side to his character which made him always somewhat remote from the French scene. As a young man, living after 1805 in Paris, he showed no interest in the military ceremonies of the capital or in the military prowess of the empire. At a time of intense French nationalism he was mainly preoccupied with foreign literature; he was a journalist, but Pauline de Meulan, with whom he collaborated in writing for *Le publiciste,* claimed that he had no knowledge of the public for whom he was writing. Under the empire he became an intellectual when the government had no use for intellectuals, with the restoration he was a journalist and professor when the government was attacking both the press and the university, with the July Monarchy he was a minister and an upholder of the established order at a time when it was both facile and modish to be amongst the critics and opponents of this society. If one considers his Protestantism, then one has to notice how far he was from being at ease amongst many of his co-religionists and how he always possessed an admiration for Catholicism which was not generally shared by them. Yet at the same time his writings suggest that he never understood the Catholic church as an institution or the Catholic religion as a faith. In all these ways, and in others, he was continually resisting movements of opinion within France, frequently at odds with general opinion in the country. As foreign minister he never understood the enthusiasm that existed in France for Mehemet Ali and the Egyptian cause during 1840, as he never understood the excitement over the British and French disagreement in Tahiti and the hatred engendered by the British missionary Pritchard who opposed the French protectorate, while he was completely surprised by the indignation aroused by the "right of search" agreements, which would have allowed British warships to stop French vessels suspected of taking part in the slave trade. "Je ne suis pas un grand soldat comme Thiers" he once wrote jocularly to Duchâtel, but he never understood that Thiers's bellicose gestures gave him a certain popularity, however much they may have merited ridicule.[11] In short, as a politician who did not understand the nature of public enthusiasms, he seems to have had many of the characteristics of a foreigner amongst the French. It is noticeable that Ernest Renan contrasted Guizot to Cousin and Villemain, not finding his talent to be particularly French,[12]

[11] Guizot to Duchâtel (undated) in the *Duchâtel Papers.* Archives nationales, Paris, 2 A.P. 8. This note might well have been written after the military review of 26 September 1830.
[12] ERNEST RENAN. *Essais de morale et de critique.* Paris, 2nd ed. 1860, p. 57.

and that Guizot was particularly attracted towards publications such as the *Revue des Deux Mondes* which were read by "le public européen" rather than being confined to France.

Yet there were some advantages in being "un-French." Some of the most impressive political intellects of France have been those of untypical Frenchmen, who have either had an unorthodox preparation for politics or a "foreign" approach to national questions. It might be that this very detachment in the long run causes such a politician to be isolated and to make mistakes, but at the same time it often enables him to look with greater clarity on a situation with which he feels less involved. However, one should not think of Guizot's "separateness" as only important so far as politics was concerned. Perhaps the outstanding feature of his career was the continuity of his activities.

In 1814 Guizot, then professor of modern history at the university of Paris, accompanied his colleague, the philosopher Royer-Collard, to the Ministry of the Interior, becoming secretary-general to the ministry when the abbé de Montesquiou was minister. The Hundred Days caused Guizot to quit this position and return to his university teaching, but after Waterloo he resumed administrative functions, first at the Ministry of Justice and later at the Conseil d'État. It was in 1820 that the victories of more violent liberals and the assassination of the duc de Berri provoked a political reaction which removed Guizot from his position as a ministerial adviser. He then concentrated on his university lectures, the subject of which was the "Origins of Representative Government." In 1822 Villèle stopped the lectures, and Guizot concentrated on his writing and began his study of seventeenth-century English history. The coming to power of Martignac restored him to the university and to the success of his lectures on civilization, whilst the society *Aide-toi le ciel t'aidera,* which prepared for the elections, recalled him to more active politics. When, in the 1840's, matters of international diplomacy began to be particularly important, Guizot himself became a diplomat (being ambassador in London from February to October 1840) and a specialist in foreign affairs. Eighteen forty-eight was a repetition of 1814 and 1822. Once events had interrupted his political career, and he had made his escape to London, Guizot simply resumed his study of the English Revolution where he had earlier abandoned it. When in the 1860's, partly no doubt for political reasons, there was a strong movement towards religious writing and discussion, Guizot followed in the fashion and began to publish works which were concerned with Christian doctrine and belief. Thus when one form of activity was stopped he turned to another. He was never reduced to idleness and he was never silenced.

But this was not simply an example of industry; it was also a demonstration of consistency. He always believed that the issues of the day could only be understood if they were considered within their intellectual framework. Nineteenth-century France was distinguished by its confusion of problems and ideas and by the great uncertainties which hung over it. It was necessary therefore to find the pattern within the complexity, to distinguish the different tendencies and to understand the nature of the contradictory forces. Intellectually Guizot was always trying to stabilize and fix things which were constantly in motion, and it was in fulfilling this function that his "un-French" remoteness from the scene was a source of strength to him.

It is this which distinguishes him as a political thinker. The famous "canapé des doctrinaires" which emerged in 1817 was to be distinguished from such groups as the "réunion Piet" or the groups which met at Laffitte's or Ternaux's, because it was not so much a tactical pressure-group as a doctrinal pressure-group. The "doctrinaires" sought to move French politics out of the routine of nostalgia, emotion and ad hoc reasoning into which it had fallen since the revolution, and they wanted to elucidate principles which would be a guide to action. More than any of the other "doctrinaires," Guizot emphasized the need for politicians to understand the principles and laws on which society was based, to work out a theory of society and a theory of institutions. He believed that politics, like history, could not avoid becoming philosophical, and he was severe in his criticism of those politicians who had but one opinion, which was "se méfier de toutes les opinions, passer entre elles, glaner quelque chose sur chacune, pendre ici de quoi répondre là, là de quoi répondre ici, et se composer ainsi chaque jour une sagesse qui suffise à la nécessité du moment." [13] As a historian Guizot not only believed that a

[13] GUIZOT, *Des moyens de gouvernement et d'opposition dans l'état actuel de la France.* Paris, 1821, p. 45. Pasquier was the politician whom Guizot gave as an illustration of this "tact politique." Pasquier was said never to have forgiven him, an example of Guizot's undoubted ability to make enemies.

knowledge of history was desirable in so far as it gratified man's imagination and his desire for knowledge, but he also and more particularly thought of history as having a function to perform in society. "Chez un peuple curieux et instruit de son histoire," he wrote in his *Mémoires,* "on est presque assuré de trouver le jugement plus sain et plus équitable, même sur ses affaires présentes, ses conditions de progrès et ses chances d'avenir." [14] In a divided society the appeal was to history. Guizot was not a rationalist, trying to devise institutions by reflection only, or trying to find formulae sufficiently abstract to be accepted by everyone: he thought historically and he sought to write history so as to discover the general and hidden fact which lay enveloped beneath all the external facts. As he put it,

> Quand les évenements sont une fois consommés, quand ils sont devenus de l'histoire, ce qui importe, ce que l'homme cherche surtout, ce sont les faits généraux, l'enchaînement des causes et des effets. C'est là, pour ainsi dire la portion immortelle de l'histoire, celle à laquelle toutes les générations ont besoin d'assister pour comprendre le passé et pour se comprendre elle-mêmes. Le besoin de généralité, de résultat rationnel, est le plus puissant et le plus glorieux de tous les besoins intellectuels . . .[15]

History, that is to say, must make sense.

Both politics and history continually brought Guizot to consider man's moral state, his conception of himself and of God; and he sometimes went beyond the normal scope of the rational political thinker and historian when he sought to chase the riddle of human life and instincts, and when he became preoccupied with "le mal inhérent à notre nature . . . l'ennemi que nous portons en nous." [16] Christianity too had to be understood in terms of certain permanent principles. The dogmas of Christianity gave value to its precepts. The fundamental dogmas had therefore to be separated from those that were only secondary. When Guizot read the successful English publication *Ecce Homo* (which was published anonymously but which was later known to have been written by Sir John Seeley) he found a great deal to admire. He introduced the work to French readers and translated certain

[14] GUIZOT, *Mémoires pour servir à l'histoire de mon temps.* Paris, 1858–67, vol. III, p. 171.
[15] GUIZOT, *Histoire de la civilisation en Europe.* Paris, 1848 ed., pp. 324–25.
[16] GUIZOT, *L'Église et la société chrétienne en 1861.* Paris, 1861, p. 259.

chapters, but he differed from Seeley in so far as the latter had attempted to study the life but not the theology of Christ.[17] For Guizot this was a mutilation of the subject. If Seeley produced a moral approach to Christ, as Strauss had produced the rational *Leben Jesu* and Renan the imaginative *Vie de Jésus,* Guizot insisted on the doctrinal approach, the elucidation of "le principe Chrétien." [18]

In his treatment of educational matters, both in the early period of his career when he edited the *Annales de l'Éducation* (1810–14) and in the years when he was minister for Public Instruction (1832–37, with interruptions), as well as in his approach to international diplomacy, Guizot was equally skillful in elucidating principles of action. In this intellectual effort one can see that from his beginnings under the empire to his contribution to Protestant affairs under the Third Republic, when a confession of faith was elaborated, Guizot's work forms a whole. It is this that explains his long eminence, his "strange preponderance." Possessing as he did great gifts as a writer and orator, his major contribution was to construct an intellectual system around the issues affecting French society. In this way he made himself indispensable, one might almost say unavoidable. He gave a distinction and a sense of purpose to activities which were otherwise without them. Policies which were the day-to-day affairs of an uninspired governing class, could be placed by Guizot in the movement of world history. Whilst educational matters tended to be part of a sterile quarrel between the church and the university, Guizot was sufficiently remote to try to determine the place of education in a modern society. Whilst foreign affairs were surrounded by an unthinking excitement, Guizot stood apart and insisted on finding a foreign policy appropriate to French interests and resources. He could turn the researches of scholars into illuminating generalizations, as he could elevate the uneasiness of orthodox Protestants into the definition of doctrinal authority. It is of course true that he sometimes lost his detachment and forgot that his role was to indicate decisions according to principles. Thus between 1840 and 1848 he often allowed himself to be

[17] GUIZOT, *Méditation sur la religion chrétienne dans ses rapports avec l'état actuel des sociétés et des esprits.* Paris, 1868, pp. 227 ff.
[18] See particularly GUIZOT, *Méditations sur l'essence de la religion chrétienne.* Paris, 1864.

controlled by an uncertain parliamentary majority so as to become inactive and to magnify the difficulties of legislation. During the same period, as minister for foreign affairs, he sometimes forgot the principles of policy, became unduly bound up with personalities and, like many French ministers, over-nervous of diplomatic movements directed against him. However, since Guizot was primarily distinguished by his intellectual system, it is by this that he should be judged.

It possessed three major weaknesses. Firstly, there was obviously a strain in being both an intellectual and a practical man of affairs. Too often the principles which were elucidated were those which were convenient. In France it was evident that the return of the Bourbons and the provision of the Charter had both been largely accidental. If these sources of authority had been established only accidentally, then how could their authority be accepted on principle? A theory of sovereignty had to be worked out. There were two rival schools: there were those who placed sovereignty in a monarch, and there were those who placed it in the people. In practical terms this was the conflict between Louis XVIII returning to France because he was the rightful king, and the Napoleonic Senate claiming that they invited him to accept their constitution. In 1814 this conflict had been avoided rather than resolved and, if it was not to recur, then some theoretical solution had to be found. Guizot was one of those who rejected both theories and who presented a third, stating that sovereignty existed nowhere on earth. He maintained that no one man, no group of men, nor all men together could claim to possess the rightful sovereignty of a state or nation. The only rightful sovereignty was that of justice, truth and reason, and the task of political science was to discover which form of government could best attain this sovereignty. Guizot believed that representative government was the form of government best suited to this task.

It is evident that this theory, which recurs at various times in Guizot's work but which was most clearly expressed during the restoration,[19] was an attempt to resolve a particular dilemma. The

[19] See FREDERICK ANCILLON, *De la souveraineté et des formes de gouvernement,* translated with critical notes by Guizot. Paris, 1816; GUIZOT, *Histoire des origines du gouvernement représentatif.* Paris, 1851, the text of his 1820–22 lectures. After 1822 Guizot started to write a refutation of Rousseau. This was never completed but the portion of it published in *Le Globe,* November 25, 1826, is concerned with sovereignty.

denial of sovereignty meant in practice the denial of any supremacy in the state. French society was too complex for there to be any single source of authority; the state should be a multiplicity of powers working in harmony rather than the entrenchment of any one particular power. As a theory, Guizot's sovereignty of reason was subtle rather than profound and most resembles a form of expertise. It ignored any idea of individual rights; it was a theory of representative government but not a theory of representation; it was a counter-system rather than a system. But, above all, since the best government was the government which governed most justly, government was an affair for experts rather than the product of a particular society. There is thus a distinction between government and society. Guizot himself noted this phenomenon in France, writing in 1852: "Il y a deux Frances, celle des classes politiques et celle des classes populaires. Elles ne se connaissent pas du tout et agissent chacune pour son compte, sans se soucier l'une de l'autre." [20] Yet he never seemed to see that such a situation was in keeping with his own theories. In much the same way, Guizot saw the upper middle class as playing a political role in the state without reference to its economic interests.

French Protestants have always had to face the problem of deciding whether they should affirm their position by emphasizing the differences between them and other Frenchmen, or consolidate it by stressing their resemblances to other Frenchmen. Guizot, as a statesman anxious to reduce the differences within French society, always followed the latter course, and since he consistently tried to minimize the differences between Protestants and Catholics and to stress the beliefs that united them, he took a particular view of Protestantism, both historically and theologically. He looked for a doctrinal minimum which would be enough to unite believers against unbelievers, and thus provide a bulwark against rationalism and revolution. Therefore in his attempt to define Christian doctrine he was careful to avoid issues which promised difficulties, such as the Trinity, free enquiry, or baptismal regeneration. In this way his theology was incomplete, but all the same his position was radically different from that of his Protestant opponents who confronted him at the pastoral conferences and at the synod. The Athanase Coquerels, father and son, Timothée Colani, Felix

[20] Guizot to Piscatory, March 7, 1852. *Lettres à sa famille et à ses amis,* pp. 332 ff.

Pécaut and their associates thought above all of Protestantism as in practical rather than doctrinal danger. They viewed their church as a collection of people. They wanted this church to grow and to convert other people; they wanted a church which could resist invading Catholicism and which would save the scattered rural communities. For them a declaration of faith would divide the church and would present immense practical difficulties since each Protestant congregation contained many different variations of faith. They were moved by "l'instinct de vivre" in a way which was alien to Guizot. As a politician he could not afford to think in proselytizing terms and his thought was too closely allied to particular conditions. In some respects he was, in the shrewd words of Albert de Broglie, "trop français pour être tout à fait Protestant." [21]

One could give further examples of the way in which Guizot's thought was limited by practical considerations. His educational policy, particularly the law of 1833 which founded the system of primary education, was of great importance. Yet it is noticeable that he did not think of education as creating a new society; he thought only of maintaining the society which already existed. He created an ensemble of primary education consisting of the *école primaire,* the *école primaire supérieure,* and the departmental training college for primary teachers; in 1836 he tried unsuccessfully to create a system of secondary schools. But he never considered any system whereby the two could be joined. Similarly he did very little for the education of girls, which might have brought about social change. Because he was concerned with the France that existed rather than with some ideal state his thought was bound to be conservative.

The second major weakness in Guizot's intellectual system was that it was eclectic or, as it was sometimes called, "syncretic." He pointed out that with the restoration of the Bourbons, for the first time since 1792 the France of the *ancien régime* and the France of the revolution could meet in conditions of liberty. He accepted both the past and the present in order that what was good in both the *ancien régime* and the revolution might be maintained, and what was bad in both be eliminated. The Charter was for Guizot

[21]ALBERT DE BROGLIE, Le Christianisme et la société. *Revue des Deux Mondes* (February 1, 1869), 531.

a drawing together of the achievements of history, it was a climax to French development.

This view of affairs enabled Guizot to accept the simultaneous existence of a legitimate monarch, the outstanding characteristic of the *ancien régime,* of a restricted form of parliamentary government, the outstanding feature of the early, constitutional revolution, and of a centralized administrative system which had been perfected under Napoleon. Unlike Royer-Collard, he did not believe that the aristocracy had ceased to exist. After it had in 1815 accepted the loss of its privileges, and in 1830 the fall of the Bourbons, it could still play a vital part in French affairs. "Je suis grand partisan de la race des country-gentlemen" he once wrote to Sainte–Aulaire.[22] As minister for public instruction, he refused to accept any of the exclusive principles which had dominated primary education in the past. He claimed that he took what was good from past systems and called upon all the resources of French society when he made the supervisory authorities the state (through the minister, the prefects and the university), the local authorities (through the municipal and departmental notabilities) and the church (through the local curé). In matters of secondary education his projected law of 1836, and the other projects put forward under his supervision by Villemain and Salvandy, all refused to make a choice between the church and the university, just as in diplomatic matters Guizot refused any exclusive alliances. The *entente cordiale* before the Spanish marriages was never intended to affect his relations with the northern powers (Aberdeen's brother, Sir Robert Gordon, was frequently concerned about French advances to Vienna at this time), and the *rapprochement* with Metternich after the marriages was never intended to replace collaboration with England in a number of different questions (such as Cracow, the River Plate, the Sonderbund). As the historian of civilization Guizot believed that the eclectic character of European civilization was its outstanding characteristic; no single element had been dominant, all the principles of social organization had borne fruit, whether theocratic, monarchical, aristocratic or democratic. Rome provided municipal institutions and the idea of law; the Christian church provided moral influence; the Germanic invaders brought with them the

[22] Guizot to Sainte-Aulaire, March 11, 1842. *Guizot Papers* in Archives nationales, 42 A.P. 8.

modern spirit of liberty as well as the bond between a leader and his followers which became feudalism. Guizot saw this variety of forces as responsible for the distinctive diversity of European civilization. At the end of his life the declaration of faith presented to the synod in 1872 as a summary of "the great Christian facts" was especially eclectic. Colani, one of its opponents, said, "Vous voulez faire une part à la Bible et une part à la critique, une part à l'esprit de vos pères et une part à l'esprit moderne." [23]

Eclecticism was, of course, natural in the circumstances of the nineteenth century. It was particularly appropriate to the conditions of France. But it nevertheless represented a great intellectual and practical weakness. Guizot, for example, ignored the suggestions which had been made by Mallet du Pan in earlier years, and by de Tocqueville in his own time, that an electoral system was incompatible with a centralized administrative system. He preferred to accept both and he told Brougham that the influence of the administration on electoral matters in France was comparable to the influence of the aristocracy in England.[24] Guizot accepted, in the same way, the hostility between priest and schoolteacher over primary school matters; he made no attempt to solve the problem, he refused to intervene in favor of either party, he simply hoped that the hostility would diminish rather than grow. Eclecticism saps any sense of reform or of creation. New developments cannot easily be appreciated; the past obscures the present. Above all, this eclectic strain in Guizot's thought meant that he had no ideal. It was this that young men found most unsatisfying in the July Monarchy. One recalls Ernest Renan's words, when he wrote, "Je ne me figure pas comment on rebâtira, sans les anciens rêves, les assises d'une vie noble et heureuse." [25]

But perhaps the greatest weakness of Guizot's thought was that, at a time when thought was becoming increasingly social, he based his theories and generalizations concerning human nature upon a

[23] EUGÈNE BERSIER, Histoire du synod général de l'église réformée de France. Paris, 1872, vol. I, p. 264.
[24] Guizot to Brougham, July 14, 1856. Brougham Papers, University College Library, London. After the 1846 elections Duvergier de Hauranne told Thiers that he was beginning to wonder whether an electoral system could work within the French administrative system. Duvergier de Hauranne to Thiers, August 5, 1846. Thiers Papers, Bibliothèque nationale, MSS., Nouvelles Acquisitions, 20617.
[25] ERNEST RENAN, Preface to L'Avenir de la science in Oeuvres complètes. Henriette Psichari, ed., Paris, s.d., vol. III, pp. 726–27.

hypothetical individual man. This is most clear in his historical work when he stresses the importance of "vraisemblances morales" in judging both theories and evidence. Montesquieu's ideas on territorial property and the nature of benefices are unacceptable to Guizot because man has a natural tendency to settle and to become the perpetual owner of land. Pelagianism has to be seen, not merely in fifth-century terms, but as a part of man's nature and a recurrent phenomenon in European history. The English republic has to be understood against a background of men who were reverent of law and devoted to the monarchy, because men wish to attach themselves to principles which are perpetual. Throughout his historical work Guizot assumes that there are certain self-evident truths. He believes that men have a natural tendency to elevate themselves to a sphere superior to their own, that they are shocked by the spectacle of disorder, that they only accept a superior if there is a legitimate reason why this superiority should exist. In his political thought, when he dealt with man's desire to have institutions which linked him to the past or with the individual's approach to sovereignty, in his religious thought, particularly when stressing man's devotion to the supernatural, there are similar, basic assumptions. Even in diplomatic affairs this method of reasoning is evident. Over the Swiss crisis of 1847, for example, Guizot is convinced that the Swiss population would turn away from extremism only when it had experienced civil war, because human nature needed such experience to reinforce its natural tendencies.

Thus at the heart of Guizot's reasoning there is much that is vague and instinctive; he proceeds too readily from assumption to assumption. It is therefore not surprising to find Guizot as baffled as anyone by the spectacle of divided France, telling Lord Aberdeen that it was "la lutte des vestes contre les habits, les casquettes contre les chapeaux," telling J. W. Croker that "La France est un malade à la fois impatient et fatigué . . . qui tantôt s'agite à toute risque pour échapper à sa souffrance, tantôt demande qu'on ne le remue pas et qu'on le laisse comme il est de peur de souffrir encore davantage." [26] And while other public men could afford their moments of incomprehension, Guizot could not. His mission

---

[26] Guizot to Aberdeen, July 28, 1849, *Aberdeen Papers,* British Museum, Add. MSS. 43, 134; Guizot to Croker, July 24, 1851, *Croker Papers,* Add. MSS. 41, 128.

was to understand and to explain; when he failed to do so he had little else to offer. In politics he could do little more than hope that the possessing classes would not be too egoistical and that the poorer classes would not be envious; he had nothing to offer but a warning about pride. In history he could not put forward any satisfactory explanations for change and development. In religious matters he had no answer to give to those who believed that the days of confession of faith were over, and to those who were moving towards a new conception of the supernatural.

It can of course be said that to explain Guizot's failure in terms of his intellectual inadequacies, rather than in terms of personal shortcomings, is only to change the emphasis. He remains a failure. This of course is true, but one might quote Guizot's own remark, made in 1861: "De nos jours, qui n'est pas tombé?" he asked.[27] In fairness to Guizot there are certain things which must be added. It may well be that his political thought was lacking in force, but at all events it gains in stature when compared to the various types of sentiment which masqueraded as theory within the French political world during his lifetime. The difficulties of governing France, like the difficulties of economic development in France, are to be largely explained by a varied social structure and by a historical development which had created new divisions and intensified old ones. In this situation, as Guizot believed, there was no single or self-evident way in which representative government could be organized. It has sometimes been said that there was no essential difference between Guizot and Thiers during the July Monarchy, and the royalist leader, Berryer, later recalled how, in the days of their rivalry, each had "la prétention de jouer diversement le même air." [28] Yet in fact there was an essential difference. Whilst Thiers acted from day to day, observing the situation attentively, and always taking every opportunity to increase his support and to make himself more "ministrable," Guizot, as one can see from his speeches and letters, tried to justify his government in terms of principle and to make his leadership an intellectual leadership.

It was during the July Monarchy that France began to resemble a modern state and that the government began to provide the equipment necessary for economic development. In this, the

[27] *Mémoires, op. cit.,* vol. IV, p. 289.
[28] Berryer to Brougham, June 12, 1859. *Brougham Papers.*

period from 1840 to 1848 is of vital importance, and if one considers the very heavy expenditure incurred by the government in those years, it is ironical to think how they were accused of doing nothing ("Rien, rien, rien" as one of their critics put it in a phrase which has echoed through the textbooks). When one remembers the law of 1833 on primary education, the freedom of the press, the importance and vitality of the parliamentary debates, and the way in which the whole period was alive with intellectual speculation, it seems inappropriate to dismiss the "liberalism" of Guizot as a sham. In foreign policy, whilst the opposition indulged in emotions and struck appealing attitudes, Guizot's policy was always reasonable and usually realistic. When one remembers the excitement caused by French policy in Tahiti, when the British government protested against the expulsion of the Reverend Mr. Pritchard and the French opposition protested against Guizot's supposed subservience to England, one can only agree with Guizot's remark to Brougham, "Pour que la guerre sortît de là, il faudrait que les fous fussent devenus les maîtres ou que les sages fussent devenus fous." [29] Without going into the wearisome details of the Spanish marriages it would seem that it was Palmerston rather than Guizot who lost his sense of proportion over the affair. Guizot expressed his astonishment that the marriage of the youngest son of the French king to the younger sister of the Spanish queen taking place simultaneously with the marriage of the Spanish queen to a Spanish nobleman, should give rise to indignation in England; he was convinced that there was nothing certain or predictable in Spanish affairs and he saw no reason why the estrangement between England and France should be permanent. The historian shares his astonishment and history confirms his conviction.

When considering Guizot it is also only fair to recall that Augustin Thierry wrote that there had been no progress in the study of the history of France until the appearance of *Essais sur l'histoire de France* and of *L'Histoire de la civilisation française;* then, with these books by Guizot, Thierry wrote, "le progrès éclate de toutes parts." [30] To many Englishmen it was remarkable that such a scholar, who was also a prominent politician, could fill a ministerial post devoted to public instruction, could, by direct

[29] Guizot to Brougham, August 30, 1844. *Brougham Papers.*
[30] AUGUSTIN THIERRY, *Considérations sur l'histoire de France. Oeuvres.* Paris, 1878, vol. VII, p. 190.

action, lead an assault on illiteracy and could, by the same direct action, further the cause of erudition and learning. They found it not only a remarkable state of affairs, they thought it a highly desirable one. Finally, although Guizot's attempt to discover the essence of Christianity earned him much criticism, yet it must be said that as so often in his life he was simply stating an unpalatable truth. However much Christians attempt to modernize Christianity and adapt it to new conditions, there are certain doctrinal claims which they cannot surrender and there is a point beyond which they cannot go if what is specific to Christianity is not to disappear. It was typical of Guizot that he should have seen this, and equally typical that he should have sought to explain the situation.

Guizot can be compared to many French statesmen. He has some resemblances to Mounier, the old constitutionalist, to de Tocqueville, to Emile Ollivier, and to certain politicians of the Third Republic. Yet it remains true that none of these men, however admirable they were in particular ways, possess anything like the diversity of talents or the consistent determination which were Guizot's. In every respect he was, as Sainte-Beuve put it, "un homme considérable dont il y a tant à dire."

5.

Liberalism in Nineteenth-Century Europe

Irene Collins

❋❋❋

EDITORIAL NOTE: *Mrs. Collins addresses herself to the broad sweep of European liberalism through the nineteenth century. Such a wide-ranging essay must gloss over some details and complexities, but her general assessment is well-balanced and sound. She attempts to define political liberalism and suggests some of its national varieties. The common ground for all varieties of liberalism, she argues, is the pursuit of "free institutions." Liberals everywhere attempted to construct media through which various sorts of freedom might be realized. Areas of liberal concern varied from equality before the law (except for women and workers) and freedom of expression to parliamentary constitutionalism and a qualified drive for the abolition of social privilege. While the foundations for the Liberal Era (what Mrs. Collins would call the "institutional" victory) had generally been laid by 1870, the question of translating form into substance remained. Mrs. Collins argues that victorious liberalism had a tired, jaded quality, that its bargains with power and tradition were too extensive, and that liberalism entered the twentieth century ill-prepared to cope with the coming political whirlwinds.*

Her argument, while set in precise, traditional political terms, is refreshingly broad. She never really ventures into the broader questions of the economic and social foundations of political issues, but she has a sense of the movement of ideas, of the interplay of thought and institutions, and of the shifting substance of liberal doctrine as the century progressed. Here there is at least one problem. I believe that Mrs. Collins draws an overly sharp distinction between liberals and democrats; the dividing lines are easier to draw in specific than in general cases. English radicals, generally although not always democrats, developed much if not most of English liberal ideology. By the 1860's, English Liberals were moving inexorably towards democracy, although one of their ablest spokesmen, Robert Lowe, pleaded against it. Many shared Lowe's fears, but after the advent of urban democracy in 1867, they concurred in his dictum, "We must educate our masters." Of course, the framework of "free institutions" had been developed far earlier in the century. Liberals in Spain or Portugal, on the other hand, worked for far narrower objectives with considerably less success. The Iberian peninsula proved generally hostile to Liberals and liberalism.

Mrs. Collins points to but does not define a more basic liberal dilemma: the conflict between quality and quantity. Jacobins trumpeted "Liberty, Equality, Fraternity" during the French Revolution, and the rhetoric, purged of subversive undertones, was a nineteenth-century Liberal battle cry. Equality and Fraternity were presumed to derive from Liberty, an assumption which broke down in practice. The last century and a half unfortunately testify to the impossibility of achieving equality without some restrictions on liberty. This poses a problem to which the conventional answer is evasion. Does the Liberal demand some measure of self-help? Must the individual work for his personal emancipation? Or does political liberalism imply the artificial elevation of those socially less fortunate through state intervention? In the later nineteenth century the efforts to resolve this quandary revealed that some basic liberal assumptions were wrong. The workingman of the newly-founded German Empire was offered an option of liberty or security. Like most modern democrats, he opted for the latter.

With problems as difficult as the irreconcilability of quality and quantity, or the conflicting claims of liberalism and nationalism, there was an understandably growing gap during the nineteenth century between liberal promise and performance. Here Mrs. Collins offers an exclusively political answer that leaves too much unexplained. Max Hartwell and Asa Briggs suggest aspects of the economic and social context of the Liberal world and help to define factors which conditioned political decisions, even elements which ideologues attempted to rationalize. Seen another way, Robert Kann and Douglas Johnson used Metternich and Guizot to assess the aspirations and achievements of the first post-Napoleonic generation. Irene Collins and Douglas Johnson disagree in their assessment of Guizot, but they concur in a broader and more important point—the contrast between the Liberal ideals of the restoration and the vulgar jobbery and pursuit of self-interest that characterized the Liberals in power during the July Monarchy.

The anti-clericalism of liberalism is a subtle but pervasive theme. Mrs. Collins stresses its paramount importance in Italy, although a conflict of secular interests sharpened spiritual and intellectual animosity. Raymond Grew, in a later essay (chapter 9), suggests other more profound problems about liberalism in the Risorgimento. There are times when Mrs. Collins casts the liberal net too wide. French thinkers like Lamennais were principally concerned with detaching the church from its traditional alliance with the dying cause of Bourbon monarchy. They wished to cut away the sources of anti-clericalism but were by no means, as Mrs. Collins suggests, politically liberal. But Mrs. Collins has the principal argument right. The hostility of the Roman Catholic church to liberalism, formally proclaimed by Pope Pius IX in the Syllabus of Errors (1864), deprived Liberals of much moral weight among those very social elements to which they sought to appeal. It required, for example, a sort of doublethink for a good Belgian Catholic to be a Liberal. In Italy the lasting effects of the Risorgimento were crucial. The church refused to acknowledge the existence of the Italian state for the better part of three quarters of a century. For years the papacy demanded, to no avail, that Catholics work for the restoration of papal territories. When the church finally came to terms with the state in 1929, it was with Mussolini's Fascism, not Cavour's liberalism.

I

The term "liberal," meaning a type of political opinion, was new in the nineteenth century. The word itself was not new, but hitherto it had been used to describe a type of education, or to describe a man of generous inclinations—a liberal, open-handed fellow. The political term "liberal" was coined in Spain and was first widely used with reference to the Spanish rebels of 1820. This was an unfortunate beginning for it, since the Spanish rebels were looked down upon by respectable people in Europe; and the term "liberal" consequently came to be regarded as a term of abuse. It was used as such by the French royalists of the restoration period, who referred to their opponents on the left of the Chamber as "liberal" in order to imply that they were a disreputable lot. In England the term was at first usually used in its French or in its Spanish form, and we hear from the 1820's scathing references to "English *libéraux*" or "English *liberales*." It was not until the middle of the century that the term was really accepted in England as English and respectable; but once it had been accepted it got itself thoroughly well dug in, and from the sixties onwards it took on a very specialized meaning. "Liberal" in England came to mean purely and simply a member of Mr. Gladstone's party.

On the continent of Europe the term never had such a specialized meaning, except perhaps in Belgium. In most other countries of Europe it was never applied solely to the members of one particular party. Indeed, it was often used to describe at one and the same time men who were vigorously opposing each other on political platforms. When Englishmen wanted to refer to a French liberal they usually chose M. Guizot, who seemed a fairly near approach to their own Mr. Gladstone; but the French not only gave the name liberal to Guizot and the members of his group; they gave it also to Thiers, who was the bitterest opponent of Guizot, and they gave it at the same time to Odilon Barrot, who led a political party in opposition to both Guizot and Thiers. In Italy the name liberal was given in the 1840's to writers who advocated a federation of Italian states under the presidency of the pope, and to writers who urged that Italy should fall into step behind the king of Piedmont.

What was there in common between the motley group of students, merchants, and soldiers who made the liberal revolution in Spain in 1820, and an experienced French politician like Guizot? Or between the sophisticated liberal aristocrats of Naples who despised the brutal rule of King Ferdinand I, and the German professors and lawyers who sat in the Frankfurt Assembly in 1848 and tried to make a united Germany? That they had something in common was realized at least by the opponents of liberalism. Metternich knew a liberal when he met with one, whatever guise the man appeared under. To embrace all the variations of liberalism throughout the century a complicated definition would be required, yet liberals themselves, certainly up to 1860 or 1870, saw nothing complicated in their creed. Whatever twists and turns were demanded of them by circumstances, they held at heart a simple faith: a belief that progress, leading to final perfection, could be achieved by means of free institutions. The liberals of nineteenth-century Europe were not exclusively dreamers and theorists. Liberalism drew its staunchest supporters from businessmen, technicians, and men of the hardworking professions; competent men of sound common sense who applied themselves in a businesslike fashion to the tasks which came to hand. But in liberalism even in its most prosaic forms there was always an idealistic element. The inspiration behind liberalism was not a sense of duty, or a feeling for the inevitable, or a love of tidiness and efficiency, though all were present to some degree, but the vision of an ideal society. The vision was not strictly speaking a Utopia, an unattainable dream world: it was a vision which liberals believed could be translated into reality, and by a known method. Perfection was to be reached by means of free institutions.

Liberals in practice often betrayed their ideal and often behaved in a manner unworthy of men pursuing an ideal. The French liberals who had talked so much of an ideal society in the 1820's, when they got into power in the 1840's spent much of their time speculating in railway shares for their own financial profit and filling government offices with their own relatives and friends. This kind of behavior made it easy for Karl Marx to condemn most liberals as insincere and to present their talk of an ideal society as a cloak for selfish ambition. More recently the liberals of the Frankfurt Assembly of 1848 have been singled out for especial condemnation by historians because, after all their talk of freedom, they displayed their greatest energy in an attempt to bring Posen and Bohemia into United Germany by force and against the wishes of the people living there. But it is possible to believe sincerely in an ideal and yet to fall short of that ideal in one's behavior, and neither Karl Marx nor sceptical historians of a later date have put forward conclusive reasons for condemning liberals as hypocrites when they proclaimed that free institutions could and would result in progress; progress in all spheres, material and spiritual; progress leading to a perfect society to be enjoyed by all men, of all classes, creeds, and nations. When liberals lost sight of this vision, as many did in the closing years of the century, they lost the spirit with which liberals in former days had battled joyously against outnumbering enemies.

Liberals from time to time and from place to place differed as to what they meant by "free institutions." The young liberal advisers of Alexander I of Russia, with little hope of making headway against the diehard Russian aristocracy, were content that the czar should begin with a reformed council of state and leave the idea of a constitution to be considered in the far-distant future. Guizot in France in the 1840's thought that the revolution of 1830 had established all the free institutions that Frenchmen could possibly require for their progress towards perfection. Cavour in

Italy in the 1850's worked to establish a form of government very much like that to be found in England at the time of Sir Robert Peel, though he was prepared to envisage the lower classes playing more part in politics as their education advanced. Many liberals, particularly in the early years of the century, had only vague notions concerning the form which free institutions ought to take; hence the adoption, by both Spanish and Neapolitan liberals in 1820, of the abortive Spanish constitution of 1812, a concoction produced from the many French constitutions of the revolutionary period and hardly applicable to the circumstances prevailing in southern Europe. None of the liberals believed that the free institutions which they advocated in themselves constituted a perfect state. They were merely the framework within which men would have the best opportunity to advance towards perfection. When Guizot in 1847 insisted that no further reform was needed in France he was not trying to say that France was already perfect, but merely that the essential framework had been established. He was no doubt over-sanguine in his hopes, but his opponents were wrong when they accused him of being completely blind to the suffering going on around him.

Often liberals had to concentrate on achieving some immediate object which they regarded as the first step on the road to freedom. Thus the liberals in Vienna in 1848 agitated for the dismissal of the chancellor Metternich; the Belgian liberals after 1815 worked for the separation of Belgium from the Dutch crown; the Italian and German liberals worked for national unity. But it must not be forgotten that their further aim was to set up free institutions. It was this higher aim which distinguished the nationalism of the German liberals of 1848 from the nationalism of Bismarck, who did not fulfill the aims of 1848, as he is sometimes credited with doing, so much as denature and destroy them. It was this higher aim, too, which distinguished the making of United Italy by Cavour from the making of United Germany by Bismarck. If Cavour's methods were sometimes regrettably like those of Bismarck, his final aim was fundamentally different; he worked for a freedom which Bismarck never understood.

After 1815, liberals in Europe tended to look to France for a shining example of freedom, and for support in their own struggles. After 1830 they ceased to do so. The result of the 1830 revolution in France profoundly disappointed liberals elsewhere in Europe.

The aim of the new French king, Louis-Philippe, seemed to be solely to kick down the revolutionary ladder by which he had risen, and to dissociate himself and France from revolutionary movements anywhere in Europe. In their disappointment, liberals elsewhere in Europe learnt in time to turn away from France and to look rather to their own efforts. Oddly enough, they learnt to do this from men whom we cannot count as belonging to the liberal cause. German liberals learnt from the works of Hegel to think that Germany was destined to play the leading role in Europe, and in 1848 we find them urging that Germany, not France, should give the shining example to Europe. Italian liberals learnt to stand on their own feet from Mazzini, the democrat. That Italy must help herself, and that each nation must fulfill its own destiny, was the most potent part of Mazzini's teaching; it was the message which caused Metternich to describe Mazzini as the most dangerous man in Europe. Only after 1848 did Italian liberals unlearn the lesson and turn again to France, under Louis Napoleon, for active help. Louis Napoleon restored some of France's prestige among European liberals by his two earliest exploits in foreign policy—his intervention in the Crimean War, which discredited Russian autocracy by revealing its military weakness, and his help to Cavour in driving the Austrians out of Lombardy. His incentive in European politics was romantic rather than liberal, however, and at home he sapped the strength of liberalism by giving the French people more material benefits than they had ever received from the freer governments of earlier years.

It is nevertheless to France that we usually look for expositions of liberal theory. French liberals had some experience of government at their command; they were not silenced, except for brief intervals, by censorship laws; they did not have to concentrate their energies in a nationalistic movement; they were in a better position than most for theorizing. In the early years of the nineteenth century we find many French liberals urgently stressing the point that liberalism was a new creed. They could not deny that men in former times had worked for liberty, but they contended that the liberty which had been seen in ancient Greece and Rome, and even the liberty understood in the French Revolution, was entirely different from the liberty which would appear in the modern world. This anxiety to show that a break had been made with the past arose from an anxiety to deny all connection with the excesses of the French Revolution. Most people in France and indeed in Europe dreaded a recurrence of the turmoil and bloodshed of the revolution, and most liberals felt obliged to fight these memories of the revolution as their worst enemies. When Benjamin Constant, in a speech before a learned society in Paris in 1819, condemned the liberty of the ancient world as subjecting the individual to the community, he was clearly thinking of the Jacobins, and his elaborate argument on this occasion was really in the same category as the impassioned claim which he made to the French voters in the next election: "We do not want any revolutions!"

This denial of the past put French liberals in sharp contrast to English liberals, who liked to trace their descent in unbroken line as far back as Magna Carta. The English liberals' fondness for the past was to French liberals a sign that the English, successful though they were in the practice of parliamentary government, did not really understand the nature of liberty. What the Englishman wanted, said the French, was not liberty, but a collection of liberties; not freedom for everybody, but privileges for everybody. Yet the French owed a great deal to the past which some of them denied so vigorously; especially to the recent past. The real origin of their creed lay in the philosophy of the eighteenth century, known as the Enlightenment. From the Enlightenment, and especially from Rousseau, came the belief that man can on earth and by his own efforts achieve perfection; because man is born good, and given the right surroundings, he will grow in goodness. From the Enlightenment, too, came the belief that the right surroundings consist of free institutions. From the Enlightenment, the belief that the fight for a perfect state of happiness on earth must be waged, cannot be neglected, because it is the whole object of man's life on earth. Man has been born with intelligence and talents so that he can advance at least a few steps in the right direction and benefit others who come after him. All these older ideas were to be found at the heart of the so-called "new" liberalism; but they had to be stated in a new form. For one thing, they had to be extricated from all talk of "reason." There was a popular assumption in the nineteenth century, wrong but no less powerful, that the "reason" of the eighteenth century had been cold and hard and heartless, allowing no room for faith and feeling, and the early nineteenth century, which was an emotional age, would have nothing to do with it. The old idea of liberty had also to be dissociated from "equality." "Liberty, equality, fraternity" had been the motto of 1789, but the revolution had shown that talk of equality led to demands which lovers of liberty were not always ready to concede.

For restating the old beliefs in a new form, Europe was indebted to a group of French liberals called the *doctrinaires.* The group deserves to be better known by historians than it has been hitherto. The politicians of the group sat on the left-center of the French Chamber in the teens and twenties of the century; amongst them was the philosopher Royer-Collard, whose long dissertations upon the *juste milieu* taught liberals how to reinterpret the French Revolution. The chief publicists of the group were Guizot and Charles de Rémusat, and the members met socially in the salon of the Duchesse de Broglie. From their writings and speeches we can formulate a statement which might well have come from any liberal in Europe at any time later in the century. The individual can best achieve his own welfare through the welfare of all. No individual can know what is the welfare of all, so some political system must be devised which allows the voice of each individual to be heard. Essential features of such a political system are: a freely elected parliament to deliberate upon the laws; a ministry dependent on that parliament, to carry out the laws; a judicature entirely independent of other branches of government, to deal with offenders against the laws; freedom of speech, freedom of religion, freedom from arbitrary arrest, freedom for the individual to enter any trade or profession according to his ability, freedom for the individual to accumulate property and to possess it in safety. In this way the individual can find his fullest expression and will be able to grow in that essential goodness which leads to perfection.

An important difference between this conception of liberty and those of the eighteenth century lies in the origin which it attributes to individual freedom. Most eighteenth-century philosophers had favored the idea that the individual possessed natural rights which were quite independent of the state and which the state was obliged to recognize. This idea, expressed in the American Bill of Rights of 1776 and the Declaration of the Rights of Man preceding the first French constitution of 1791, had been a powerful weapon in the destruction of the personal privileges so well known to the ancien régime; but it had also contained the seeds of endless revolution. If freedom belongs to nature and not to the state, government institutions must be reduced to a minimum so that natural law can flourish: an anarchical idea which seemed to the liberals of the nineteenth century more conducive to chaos than to liberty. They favored, rather, Rousseau's conception of civil liberty. The individual has no rights in nature; he merely has claims, which might in nature be thwarted by the claims of other individuals. These claims become rights only when they are recognized by society, and when the state guarantees to each individual the liberty which does not conflict with the liberty of others. The belief in natural rights was to have some lingerings in the nineteenth century. From it came the belief, prevalent in the many disturbances of the 1820's, that the mere publication of a "paper" constitution guaranteeing men's rights would suffice to achieve liberty, regardless of tradition and social background; from it, too, came the tendency among many liberals to regard the state as the inevitable enemy of the individual. But the clearest thinkers discarded it from the beginning.

Another difference is the emphasis on the individual rather than on the people. It is in the individual rather than in the people that the goodness which will lead to perfection is to be found. The French Revolution had shown that "the people" is something different from a sum total of individuals, and in the nineteenth century, references to "the people" came from democrats rather than from liberals. The idea of "the sovereignty of the people" could not be discarded altogether, because it was needed as a guarantee against assumptions of sovereignty by the monarch, but henceforth sovereignty of the people was to be recognized as limited by liberty of the individual. Royer-Collard's invocation of "the sovereignty of reason," which he believed resided in a sphere above the conflicting interests of individuals, was rejected by most liberals as leading back to Rousseau's doctrine of the general will. Respectability was a craving by no means confined to Victorian England, and it was with a creed shorn of all elements that had come to be regarded as disreputable that European liberals made their attack upon the old order.

II

If liberalism had been only an attack upon the old order, its task would have been difficult enough. The old order was by no means as decrepit as liberals liked to pretend, for the absolute monarchs controlled the armed forces of their realms, and they had learnt, from Napoleon, to extend their bureaucracies and to equip themselves with police forces and spy services. Many people had a vested interest in the maintenance of the old regime—a factor whose importance was demonstrated very clearly in the collapse of the 1848 revolutions in Austria. The theory of legitimacy, with which Metternich tried to bolster up absolute monarchy in western Europe, was not very impressive, but Russian czars continued to derive strength and zeal from their belief in the divine right of kings, and their sense of a mission to Europe led Alexander I in the 1820's and Nicholas I in 1849 to offer their services in defense of the old order in western Europe. This was not the whole of the problem, however. Despotism was sometimes of a new order, as in the case of Napoleon III and Bismarck. Napoleon III's "caesarian democracy" had a wide appeal in France, whilst Bismarck's stand against the Prussian parliament in the early sixties seemed justified by the ever-growing success of his nationalist campaign.

Moreover, liberals felt obliged all along to take action against another new creed: democracy. Democracy, like liberalism, had had its origin in the philosophy of the eighteenth century, and the two had developed side by side for a time, but they had parted company during the French Revolution. The democratic ideal—that all political power should belong to the people—seemed to the liberals to spell tyranny rather than liberty. They believed that it would lead to the tyranny of the mass over the individual and of the majority over the minority, and as proof they pointed to the example of Jacobinism during the French Revolution. Jacobinism was hardly a fair trial of democracy, but nineteenth-century liberals were too near to it to admit that, or perhaps even to see it. Jacobinism had shown them all the worst features of democracy, and consequently they not only hated democracy but feared it, with a fear that could very easily turn to sheer panic, as it did in France after the rising of the workers in June 1848. The fear of democracy brought with it other fears; amongst them the fear of revolution. Liberals always remembered that Jacobinism had come to the fore as the result of a revolution prolonged beyond its original aims; and though the liberals made many revolutions during the nineteenth century, they always tried to stop their revolutions after the initial stages. This was one of the most noticeable features of the revolutions of 1848. As soon as free institutions had been established, and sometimes when they had merely been promised, the liberals began forming National Guards and taking other security measures, lest the populace should begin to make demands which had not been included in the original program.

The fear of democracy also brought with it the fear of republicanism. A republic, in which not only the parliament but the president was elected by the people, would encourage too much mass intervention in politics, and the president would be too much under the influence of the majority opinion which had carried him into office. The liberals wished to destroy absolute monarchy in Europe, but most of them dared not go the whole way and destroy monarchy entirely. They recognized the value of kings as centers of loyalty, as permanent heads of society, as defenders of government institutions against popular attack. What they really wanted to do was to persuade the old absolute monarchs of Europe to grant parliaments and other free institutions and then help in defending them. This was a much more difficult task than an attack on monarchy, because it meant trying to cooperate with kings who were never enthusiastic about the cause and who could seldom be relied upon to stick to it even if they were driven to join it in moments of weakness. Liberals were again and again let down by the monarchs with whom they were trying to cooperate, but most of them persevered, even when the monarch in question was as stupid as Victor Emmanuel II of Piedmont. Austrian liberals, in spite of their betrayal by the Emperor Ferdinand in 1848, threw in their lot with the new Emperor Francis Joseph and imagined, in the 1860's, that they could bribe him into granting free institutions by supporting the claims of his dynasty to rule Greater Germany. French liberals between 1814 and 1870 tried three kings and an emperor in the attempt to achieve the permanent head which they thought so necessary to a constitutional regime, and when they were finally driven in the 1870's, by the obstinacy of the Bourbon pretender, to accept a republic, they consoled themselves by making it as little like a republic as an unmonarchical state could be.

An obvious move in the struggle against democracy was for liberals to cling to a limited franchise. The Italian Moderates of the 1840's and 1850's could easily defend such a policy in a country where large numbers of the population were illiterate, but the task was more difficult for Guizot in France, where radical orators claimed that the electoral law of 1831 excluded from the franchise many millions of bourgeois who had all the education necessary to understand the use of a vote. To all attacks Guizot replied that freedom could not be improved upon merely by increasing the number of voters—an argument which gained some support from the events of a later age, when extensions of the franchise brought with them methods of electioneering little in keeping with liberal ideas of the supremacy of the individual. Unfortunately, Guizot and his supporters used weapons even less justifiable than a limited franchise: they curtailed two of their own dearest freedoms, liberty of the press and liberty of association, so anxious were they to prevent democratic leaders from appealing to the public. It is more to the credit of German liberals in the post-1870 period that they refused to pass penal legislation against the Social Democrats, although this refusal worked towards their own downfall. In Italy the struggle between liberalism and democracy crystallized, in the middle years of the century, into the struggle between Cavour on the one hand and Mazzini and Garibaldi on the other. Cavour saw Mazzini as a demagogue and dictator combined, a man who would stir the masses to action and then dominate them in their ignorance; whilst Garibaldi, with his irresponsible guerilla activities and his extraordinary sympathy for the depressed peasantry of southern Italy, could hardly fail to jeopardize the parliamentary state which Cavour was patiently founding on the middle-class society of the north. In the dramatic year of 1860, which afterwards ranked as the pinnacle of Cavour's liberal achievement, Mazzini remained under sentence of death from the Piedmontese government, and Cavour did all he could to prevent Garibaldi's expedition to Sicily.

Liberals always spoke of democracy as a disreputable force, springing from all the worst passions of mankind. In French middle-class homes in the early nineteenth century the words democracy and republic were not considered suitable for use before the children. Democrats, on the other hand, presented liberalism as a selfish creed, shrouded in a lot of talk about freedom for everybody, but in actual fact designed to put power and privileges into the hands of the middle classes. This was a powerful argument because it could be supported by fact. French liberal governments during the July Monarchy failed in eighteen years to pass a single measure of social reform. They claimed that social legislation demanded too much activity from the state; and French liberalism never produced a group like the English Benthamites whose ideas on the duties of the state could act as a corrective to exaggerated notions of laissez-faire. When Guizot refused to introduce so much as a poor law, democrats hastened to the conclusion that here was liberalism in its true colors. One French liberal, Alexis de Tocqueville, believed that this was not liberalism in its true colors, but liberalism in the hands of unimaginative men, and in 1848 he urged the deputies to mend their ways before it was too late; but he entirely failed to convince them of the urgency of the situation. At this point matters were complicated by the events of the 1848 revolution in France. The demands put forward by the workers during the months from February to June 1848 were so excessive that property-owners began to fear for the safety of private property. Shopkeepers could not sell anything because people preferred to keep their property in cash lest they should have to flee the country; and as late as 1851 farmers were cutting down their corn before it was ripe lest at any moment their fields should be seized and divided into strips amongst the workers. After this panic, any political party which wanted to keep middle-class votes had to promise the protection of property and had to keep off any social reform which might in the smallest way strike at the interests of property owners. Social reform on the continent became almost exclusively the property of the democrats, and socialism and democracy allied against liberalism increasingly as the century proceeded. Consequently liberalism was regarded by many people as a conservative creed, even as an outworn creed, long before it had finished its attack on the old order in Europe.

Meanwhile liberals had had other enemies to face. The most insidious enemy, in the early years of the century, was romanticism. Amongst the origins of romanticism lay a desire to free the individual mind and heart from the cold intellectualism of eighteenth-century reason, and in consequence a romantic outlook on life was sometimes combined with liberal views on politics. This was the case with Benjamin Constant in France, with Stein in Prussia, and at a later date with the brothers Gagern, who played so important a part in the German revolution of 1848. More often, however, romanticism in politics looked back upon the past, which it saw through rose-colored spectacles as an age of faith and feeling and chivalry. Liberals in France quickly saw the dangers of these views, and most of them promptly attacked romanticism in all its forms. French liberal newspapers in the teens and twenties hotly defended classical literature against romantic literature; hostile criticisms of romantic poetry were given front-page importance, and an energetic liberal journalist, Armand Carrel, threatened to challenge Victor Hugo to a duel over the interpretation of a passage in Bossuet. The romantics, meanwhile, ranged themselves on the side of the restored monarchy, and encouraged Charles X to squeeze every ounce of power for himself out of the constitutional settlement of 1814. They encouraged him in romantic displays such as the return to the ancient form of coronation at Rheims, and touching for the king's evil, and many young romantics joined a secret society, the Knights of the Faith, whose double object was to restore Frenchmen to more faith and feeling and to restore absolute monarchy.

Elsewhere in Europe the antipathy between liberalism and romanticism was not so clearly demonstrated. Romanticism, for all its strange manifestations, sprang from generous sentiments, and the men who took to it were often ready to plunge into self-sacrifice on behalf of the oppressed. Hence romantics were to be found fighting on the side of the Greeks in the War of Independence and in similar exploits which caused them to be confused in the popular mind with the liberals. Metternich added to the confusion by persecuting both with equal vigor, since to him the fanatical young men who insisted on a return to chivalry seemed just as dangerous to the established order as the more ponderous gentlemen who asked for parliamentary institutions. But romanticism and liberalism were nevertheless distinct in essence, and more often than not mutually hostile, and in one sphere at any rate romanticism did great harm to the liberal cause. This was in Germany, where the movement for national unity had far more romanticism than liberalism in it from the beginning. The student societies which Metternich persecuted were inspired by romantic aims of uniting Germany so that she might return to her past greatness, rather than by liberal aims of uniting her so that the freedom of the individual might triumph. Whilst it is possible to find some liberalism in Germany in the early years of the century, liberalism did not really begin to get any sort of hold there until the 1840's, and even then many liberals mistakenly believed the romanticism of Frederick William IV of Prussia to be compatible with their own views. When the Frankfurt Assembly met in 1848 few people in Germany understood the liberal as distinct from the nationalist aspect of the Assembly's aims, and the Assembly was afterwards criticized for having spent too much time in pursuit of free institutions instead of trying to achieve German unity by hook or by crook.

The leading place amongst the opponents of liberalism must be given, however, to the Roman Catholic church. The opposition of the church appeared on two fronts, one practical and Italian, the other theoretical and European, and it lasted throughout the century.

In Italy, liberalism meant nationalism, for there seemed to be no hope of getting rid of the baleful influence of Austria, and the despotism of the petty princes of Italy, without some form of national unity. Nationalism in its most obvious form would mean the church losing its lands in central Italy, and at the beginning of the nineteenth century the pope still regarded the possession of these lands as necessary to the independence and hence to the spiritual authority of the church. Nationalism was thus made to look like an attack not merely on the church's temporal possessions, but on its spiritual power. In the 1840's a group of nationalist writers headed by Gioberti tried to solve the dilemma by suggesting that Italy need not become a unitary state; she could form a confederation, each state keeping its own ruler and each uniting with the others under some form of federal government. The proposal won a large number of adherents in Italy, but Mazzini and other radicals spurned it from the beginning as worse than useless to true nationalists, and it eventually collapsed in 1848 from its failure to cope with the Austrian problem. Theoretically speaking, Austria could have been allowed to keep Lombardy-Venetia and rule it as part of a new Italian confederation, but few Italian nationalists would consider any such proposal. The Austrians must be driven out of Italy, and when the pope declined, as he needs must, to countenance any such movement, the initiative passed to Piedmont. Cavour began modernizing the Piedmontese state ready to play its part in the freeing of North Italy, and some of his earliest measures consisted of a serious reduction in the secular power of the church, but he had no intention of attacking the spiritual power of the church. Nor had he any intention of doing so in 1859 and 1860, when events drove him to annex the greater part of the Papal States. Cavour offered to Pius IX proposals for a settlement very similar to those accepted at a later date by Leo XIII, but Pius would have nothing to do with them. Italian unity had to be achieved in direct opposition to the wishes of the church and by actually taking arms against her; and even when United Italy was an accomplished fact, Pius IX continued to demonstrate his hostility to the creation. This made many difficulties for the new Italian kingdom, which had a hard enough task anyway to win and hold the loyalty of the mass of the Italian people. It also made clear to liberals everywhere in Europe that Pius IX had dissociated the church from what they regarded as liberalism's finest achievement.

Behind the Italian conflict lay a conflict of ideas which was of European significance. Liberalism undeniably contained many beliefs which were contrary to the teaching of the church. The belief that man is born good, that his progress is inevitable, that he can by his own efforts reach perfection on earth—all these were contrary to the church's teaching on original sin, on salvation through Christ, and on the sovereignty of God over earth and heaven. But there were other aspects of liberalism. A courageous French priest, Lamennais, tried to persuade his fellow churchmen that liberalism should be accepted and encouraged by the church because it sprang from instincts which were truly Christian: from the desire to recognize the dignity of man born in the image of God, and from the desire to allow men the free use of the faculties given them by God. The French bishops were not convinced, and in November 1831 Lamennais journeyed to Rome, seeking a pronouncement from Pope Gregory XVI in favor of his views. Gregory at first temporized, and Lamennais returned to France in a hopeful frame of mind, but before he had actually reached France he received from the pope an encyclical letter whose content amounted to a complete rejection of all that he had urged. In fairness to Gregory, one can show that he could hardly have done otherwise. It is not the duty of the pope to keep abreast of prophets like Lamennais so much as to see that the flock stays within the fold, and liberalism at this time contained much that was likely to lead the ordinary man astray. One can show, too, that the responsibility for the encyclical rests as much, if not more, with Lamennais as with Gregory. For more than a year Gregory had turned a blind eye to the newspaper which Lamennais was publishing in France, and Lamennais should have been content to be tolerated. The encyclical *Mirari vos* made clear for the first time that liberalism, in spite of its many good qualities, could find no accommodation in the most spacious of all churches. Some fourteen years later liberals hoped for accommodation from a new pope, Pius IX, who was said to have liberal sympathies, but their hopes were founded on an illusion. Pius IX carried out a few reforms in the Papal States, but this was because he was a kind-hearted man and a well-meaning ruler, not because he was a liberal. He allowed liberals in Italy to acclaim him as their leader, but this was because he was too inexperienced of the world to know what liberalism implied. When he discovered that liberalism contained elements of which he could not approve he turned against it in all its forms. In 1864 he denounced liberalism outright, along with pantheism, rationalism, indifferentism, socialism, communism, secret societies and Bible societies, as one of the errors of the age; ending his declaration with the pronouncement that it was a damnable error to suggest that the pope could or should reconcile himself to liberty, progress, and recent civilization. Fortunately for liberalism, the Catholic mind rose to the occasion, and large numbers of Frenchmen and Italians, Belgians and Spaniards convinced themselves, by a triumph of adaptation, that they could obey the pope whilst remaining liberal. Nevertheless, the opposition of the Catholic church deprived liberalism of much moral force, and continued to harm the liberal cause in Europe to the last years of the century.

III

By 1870 the countries of western Europe had obtained something like the free institutions for which liberals had fought since the beginning of the century, and Europe entered upon what historians have called "the liberal era." Free institutions had never been regarded as an end in themselves, however; they were merely the essential beginning, and the time had now come to demonstrate to the world, and especially to those parts of Europe, notably Russia, which remained under despotic governments, that free institutions resulted in progress. Unfortunately the free institutions were by no means firmly founded, and the defense of them against enemies, old and new, might easily prove a task which allowed little room for progress.

Each country presented its own problems. In the Hapsburg Empire, transformed by the "compromise" of 1867 into the dual state of Austria-Hungary and ruled according to two separate constitutions, the maintenance of parliamentary government depended on the ability of the liberals to solve the age-old problem of conflicting national claims. In Austria the franchise was limited and organized in such a way as to debar the Czechs from any effective part in political life, and although the hostility which this provoked amongst the Czechs was a serious drag on the new constitutional regime, the liberals dared not try to allay it by extending the franchise. Any concession to the Czechs would have resulted in a policy to obtain similar rights for the Slavs in Hungary, and this would have reduced the power of the Magyars, who alone were strong enough to frighten Francis Joseph into keeping the constitutional settlement of 1867. The inability of the liberals to move towards any solution of the Czech problem, combined with the shock which the economic crisis of 1873 gave to their system of laissez-faire, gradually weakened their popularity even amongst the Austrian Germans, whose interests they were most likely to promote. Francis Joseph grew angry with them when they opposed his occupation of Bosnia-Herzegovina in 1878, and in the general election of the following year he used his influence to bring about the defeat of their candidates. The liberals never again, to the end of the century, achieved a majority in the parliament. For the next fourteen years they saw the conservative prime minister Taaffe making a mockery of parliamentary institutions, but their own policy of clinging to a narrow franchise and to an economic policy of laissez-faire which paid exclusive attention to upper middle-class interests failed to find wide enough support to enable them to put up any effective resistance. When the threat from the growing radical party caused Francis Joseph to dismiss Taaffe in 1893, the liberals could form a government only by allying with conservative groups, and the failure of their coalitions to pursue any effective policy either at home or abroad ended what little patience Francis Joseph had had with the constitutional system. By 1900 he had ceased to obey the most fundamental rules of the constitution, and the liberals were incapable of gathering sufficient strength to oppose his renewed absolutism.

In the new kingdom of Italy the liberal policy of Cavour devolved in 1860 upon the party of the right, which controlled the destinies of the country for the next sixteen years. The members of the party were faced with the difficult task of assimilating into the parliamentary system the states of central and southern Italy which Cavour had not thought ripe for parliamentary government and which he annexed to his northern kingdom only because he was driven to do so by the activities of Garibaldi. The difficulty of the task was not lessened by the fact that the right underestimated it. With the exception of Minghetti, the leading members of the right had no direct knowledge of the central and southern provinces, and the traditions of the Risorgimento had not taught them to pay any attention to the social and agrarian problems of the peasantry. Obliged, in view of the high percentage of illiteracy amongst the Italian people, to keep to a narrow franchise which gave more votes to the northern provinces than to the rest of the country, the right could hardly have escaped the accusation of dictatorship; but at least the dictatorship ought to have been used to raise the level of wealth and education amongst the mass of the people and thus to pave the way for the extension of political rights. Instead it was used primarily to enhance the greatness of the new kingdom in the eyes of the other powers of Europe. The discontent which prevailed in the south provided a fertile field for radical propaganda, and in 1876 the government of the right fell before that of the left. Extension of the franchise inevitably followed, and the results soon showed how little of liberal ideals the mass of the population had imbibed. The new voters were unable to understand their rights except as a means of obtaining corresponding benefits, and this tempted politicians into a system of patronage which quickly discredited parliamentary life. An outward respect for civil liberty and for constitutional forms preserved a façade of liberalism, and this concealed the decadence of the ruling class and the political ignorance of the masses to the end of the century, but it could hardly survive the disintegrating forces which came upon the country in later years.

In the new German Reich the constitution of 1871 established a parliament elected by universal suffrage and an imperial chancellor who must depend on parliament to pass the budget. The task of the liberals was to give these institutions more meaning than Bismarck intended them to have. A parliament elected by universal suffrage was more likely to prove a bulwark of authoritarianism than of liberalism, as had been proved in France during the Second

Empire; and even if the electorate gave its loyalty to liberal ideals the parliament would have difficulty in making its influence felt upon ministers who were responsible only to the emperor. In other words, the constitution was a doubtful concession to liberalism, and German liberals, far from being now in control of the political situation, were faced with a despotic power stronger than the despotisms of the early nineteenth century: stronger because it could claim brilliant achievements both at home and abroad, because it was administratively efficient, and because it appeared more forceful and progressive than a liberal creed connected in people's minds with the failures of 1848. Under these circumstances many liberals—indeed the majority of liberal politicians in Germany—saw no prospect of success in opposing Bismarck, and they joined those Prussian liberals who, in 1866, had rallied to Bismarck's support and called themselves the National Liberal Party.

The party contained some of the leading politicians in Germany —Lasker, Forckenbeck, Twesten, and Unruh, who had opposed Bismarck in the Prussian parliament in the early sixties; Bennigsen and Miquel who had led the liberal opposition in Hanover. Miquel announced, "The time for ideals is past, and the duty of politicians is to ask not for what is desirable, but for what is attainable." Yet the National Liberals were not wholly deserting their ideals when they joined Bismarck, nor even suspending them until happier times. Since the unfortunate experiences of 1848 many German liberals had come to distrust what they regarded as "French" views on the proper position and function of parliament in the state. They turned back to the teaching of Hegel and Kant, and from this they imbibed a juridical concept of the state, defining liberty as consisting of legal rights granted by the state to the individual, and used by the individual in such a way as to prevent any encroachment from above or below. In England the common law had been given a place almost equal to that of parliament in the defense of individual freedom; and German liberals, obsessed by the insecurity which seemed to result from complete supremacy of the legislature, were ready to place more faith in the rule of law than in the rule of parliament. This kind of liberty, expounded in the second half of the nineteenth century by Gneist, Laband, Meyer, and Jellinek, might well be found in the political system established by Bismarck, which brought an element of self-government into the administration and allowed the parliament to exercise critical functions. The chief danger was that Bismarck might one day destroy the parliament which he had granted in 1871 as a grudging concession to liberal opinion, and thus place the rule of law in jeopardy. To guard against this danger the National Liberals opposed all Bismarck's attempts to make himself financially independent of parliament. Their success in this field proved to be their undoing, for Bismarck soon tired of allies so lacking in docility. In 1878–79, using to the full his remarkable gifts as a propagandist and political tactician, he destroyed their popularity with the electorate by making them appear disloyal to the emperor, broke their political party by dividing them on the subject of protection, and discarded their alliance in favor of one with the Catholic Center party. Bismarck's reliance on conservative groups during the 1880's accelerated the growth of social democracy, and it was with this force, which liberals had always distrusted, that the future of parliamentary institutions in Germany lay at the end of the century.

Even France, with its older tradition of parliamentary government, was no easy field for the liberals after 1870. The Third Republic began its career under the taint of national dishonor and social repression—the acceptance of the humiliating peace terms offered by Bismarck, and the suppression of the Commune. The fear of Jacobinism, which had broken out in Paris during the Franco-Prussian War, and the fear of Communism, which most Frenchmen wrongly believed to have been responsible for the Commune, would have forced a conservative policy on future governments whether they had wanted it or not, and for twenty years vigorous advances either in foreign policy or in social legislation were out of the question. Left-wing groups, which combined democratic and socialistic views with intense patriotism, were likely to become increasingly hostile to a liberal republic which seemed no different, in essentials, from the July Monarchy. In an attempt to give the republic wider support the veteran liberal Thiers allied with the radical Gambetta in the elections of 1876, and the so-called "opportunist" program which resulted from this alliance was carried out energetically by the governments of the 1880's. Its main features were the extension of political rights and the establishment of free, secular, and compulsory education: there was a notable lack of any attention to reform of a purely social nature. In other words, liberalism compounded with democracy but refused to make any concession to the socialism with which democracy had been connected since the days of Louis Blanc. This refusal, along with an equally firm refusal to adopt a policy of revenge against Germany, provoked the dangerous outbreak of caesarism which took place in the name of Boulanger in the years 1886–89. Discredited further by the Panama scandal and the Dreyfus affair, the opportunist groups were obliged to give way in the last years of the century to the radical ministry of Waldeck-Rousseau. From this time onwards the republic underwent a much larger infusion of democracy and socialism than liberals would once have thought compatible with freedom of the individual.

Behind these failures, and similar failures elsewhere, lay an increasing doubt as to the efficacy of free institutions to achieve progress. In the early years of the century, when liberals had talked of the need to free the individual so that he could advance towards perfection, the meaning of progress had had a predominantly moral content; but by 1870 philosophy and its allied studies had surrendered pride of place to the exact sciences, and progress came to mean an increasing mastery over the physical universe and an increasing possession of the material benefits which this mastery afforded. These benefits could only be acquired by the individual if he had wealth. The middle classes settled down to the accumulation of wealth with all the hope and determination which they had once put into politics, and in the era of economic expansion which followed on the creation of the new nation-states they prospered. But economic prosperity now depended to a large extent on national security and power, and governments were often led into foreign policies little in keeping with the ideals of a liberal state.

At the same time, increasing industrialization brought the growth of urban proletariats anxious to obtain their share in the benefits which they saw around them. Their share did not come to them automatically, as Guizot had thought it would, by the mere force of circumstances; perhaps because the middle classes were more selfish than Guizot had believed, but more certainly because the new economic structure was more impersonal and more complicated than Guizot could ever have envisaged. Radical politicians urged that a reasonable standard of living for the workers could only be obtained by social legislation, but liberal politicians in the 1870's and 1880's held out against such demands, as Gladstone held out against Joseph Chamberlain in England. They gave as their reason their unwillingness to encroach on freedom of the individual, but opponents accused them of selfish class interest, and side by side the two ideas gained ground, that liberalism was a middle-class creed and that the interests of the middle class and the lower class were incompatible. Revolutionary socialism of one kind and another, inspired by Marx, Bakunin, and Blanqui, enjoyed a brief vogue amongst advanced politicians in most of the countries of western Europe in the 1870's. In time, however, the development of workingmen's associations and trades unions gave rise to a class of workmen skilled in leadership, trained in workers' politics, and accustomed to negotiating—a working-class intelligentsia, which took over the function performed earlier in the century by the middle-class intelligentsia and acted as a connecting link between the middle and the lower classes. Workmen were persuaded by these new leaders that nothing was to be gained by violence and that everything was to be gained by using the machinery of free speech and free association. By the 1890's there had appeared in most countries a parliamentary socialism of a type which had been developing slowly in England since the days of the Chartists. To this new socialism and its "minimum programs" liberal politicians felt obliged to make some concessions, telling themselves that they could do so without danger to parliamentary institutions. But concessions to socialism implied an amount of state activity which liberals of an earlier generation would not have countenanced, and the inescapable inference was that liberalism could only cater to the demands of the lower classes by sacrificing its own principles.

In one country of Europe the sacrifice called for seemed to be too great to be contemplated. This was in Russia, which proved to be the scene of liberalism's greatest failure. Very early in the nineteenth century Czar Alexander I had been attracted to liberal ideas, only to conclude that they were inapplicable in a country where large parts of the population remained under serfdom. Alexander II, more for reasons of state than for any liberal purpose, had emancipated the serfs in 1861, but had failed to assimilate them into the rest of society. The peasants remained a class apart, uneducated, inexperienced, incapable of concerted action to improve their own welfare, and with grievances which demanded attention on every ground of justice and humanity. Victorian doctrines of self-help were hardly applicable; the problem could only be answered by state intervention of a kind and on a scale which seemed to have little in keeping with liberal principles. The small liberal groups which appeared in the Duma of 1906, Russia's first national parliament, had no answer to suggest. They refused to support the proposal by the democratic "Cadet" group, for the expropriation of land; and the field was thus left open for extremist elements of every kind.

By the end of the nineteenth century liberalism was a jaded force compared with what it had been in earlier years. Compromises with enemies old and new had shrouded its meaning, and other political parties, owing much in their origin to liberalism, but inimical to its existence as a political force, had obtained a wider electoral appeal. Optimism remained high, but it was insecurely founded and could not survive the disappointments following on 1918. The inevitability of progress, whether moral or material, appeared then to have been a delusion, and perfection had so far eluded men's grasp as to have passed beyond their hopes. Liberals still aimed at freeing the individual, but not in the certainty that he would achieve perfection so much as in the belief that freedom would enable him to do the best for himself and others in a difficult and unpredictable world. Liberalism had thus put aside many of the idealistic beliefs which had caused Karl Marx to ridicule it and the Catholic church to denounce it, but in doing so it had lost much of its vigor. It was in a prevailing mood of doubt and despondency that liberalism faced, in the twentieth century, the two greatest threats it had yet seen—the rise of power politics in Germany and of Communism in Russia.

6.

Nationality and Liberty

Lewis B. Namier

✤✤

EDITORIAL NOTE: *Sir Lewis Namier considers the mid-century crisis of liberalism in this essay. The 1820's and 1830's were decades of extraordinary intellectual ferment. Political philosophers developed their creeds confident that the inevitable fall of the old order must herald victory for their principles. The central European revolutions of 1848 were jointly inspired by demands for liberty and for nationality; they were presumed to be interrelated. But British and French liberalism, from which central European notions of liberty derived, had developed within predefined national units. British nationalism was territorial, and in France linguistic and territorial nationality approximately coincided. The nationalism that emerged in the nineteenth century was linguistic, and the tribal or racial patterns of central and eastern Europe bore little relation to real estate holdings. There could be no liberal resolution of the question of nationality. Nationalism might be subordinated or ignored. It might triumph over liberalism. The simultaneous attainment of liberty and nationality was impossible. Centuries of migration and conquest had hopelessly confused the linguistic map. Germans (and linguistic nationalism was peculiarly although not uniquely German) dominated the central European plain. They also controlled all urban areas of the Hapsburg Empire (to be urban was to be German)and lived in colonies or pockets as far afield as the Caucasus, the central Balkans, and northern Italy.*

This problem was compounded by the master nationalities which had, or claimed to have, histories, and the peasant or subject nationalities, which did not. Germans, Italians, Poles, and Hungarians could assert more or less valid historical claims to an independent political past. Czechs, Croats, Slovenes, Ruthenes, and a myriad of other peoples—the subject nationalities—also attempted, often with more art than substance, to justify their national existence. The conflict, as is evident, was both political and social.

Subject and master nationalities could realize their claims only at the expense of each other. Both subject and master nationalities, moreover, could only realize their goals at the expense of the existing dynastic states and the traditional concept of nations as property. The German Confederation, the Austrian Empire, the Russian Empire, and the Ottoman Empire were each dynastic, supra-national political organizations. Each was to fall before the onslaught of the national principle and, as Robert Kann has indicated in his reappraisal of Metternich, the victory of nationalism, master or subject, has produced neither domestic nor international concord. Many contemporaries recognized the complexity of the problem and hoped to work through established political forms. Francis Palacky, the Czech spokesman for subject nationalities, told the Slav Congress at Prague in 1848 that if Austria did not exist, it would be necessary to create her. But his appeal to the Hapsburgs went unheeded. There was always a social as well as a political issue at stake, and it was beyond the capacity of a reactionary dynasty to make common cause against upstart master nationalities with the radical democracy of the subject nationalities.

Namier holds that linguistic nationalism won. It destroyed or warped constitutional growth. Irene Collins earlier discussed the abuse of liberal institutions and intentions by such leaders of the Hapsburg Empire as Count Taaffe. The German Liberals, frustrated in their quest for unification by consent through the Frankfurt Parliament of 1848, and defeated by Bismarck in the Prussian constitutional crisis of the 1860's, surrendered their principles, moved toward political quietism, and contented themselves with economic advance and administrative reform.

On one point there can be no disagreement. The revolutions of 1848 were crucial for central European liberalism. Liberal leaders in Germany, Austria, and Italy determined to bargain with power rather than risk social revolution. The radical dictators of 1848, Mazzini and Kossuth, provided inspiration at home and abroad but enjoyed little political success: their example was often admired but not emulated. The Liberal members of the Frankfurt parliament had no more luck and less common sense. The two real powers in the German Confederation, Austria and Prussia, were preoccupied with revolutions in Vienna and Berlin. Moreover, real questions of power were at stake in those revolutions. The Liberal parliamentarians at Frankfurt, with the powers otherwise occupied, found Germany a power vacuum which they were unable and unwilling to fill. Once the revolutions in Vienna and Berlin were defeated, Prussian troops appeared to chase the Frankfurt Liberals back to the relative safety of journals and lecture halls.

In a sense the Liberals of central Europe were captivated by power because they were so incapable of employing it. Radicals and democrats invoked the masses, albeit in a condescending manner, but the masses proved disinterested. The Radicals sought other formulae and new slogans; the German Liberals never forgot their humiliation. Next time they would be on the winning side. Central European Liberals learned from 1848 to appreciate power. Again the social implications of a political question helped to tip the balance. The question was ultimately decided by linguistic national interests. Since the power of the masses, democracy, implied releasing the subject nationalities, the Liberal master nationalities felt themselves left with no choice.

Liberty was claimed in 1848 for the individual and liberty for nations, and a natural, wellnigh intrinsic connection was assumed between the two; to be consummated—so the theory ran—in a peaceful fellowship of free nations. But there was a deeper antinomy between constitutional development in most of the states concerned, and the postulates of the new national movements. Individual and civic liberty requires a stable, uncontested political framework: internal freedom is best secured where the communal consciousness coincides with the territory of the state, that is, where nationality is territorial in character and the existing frontiers do not give rise to claims by, or against, neighbors. But the politically minded cannot feel truly free except in a state which they acknowledge as their own, and in which they are acknowledged as indigenous: that is, in their own national state; and the nationalisms which in 1848 entered the political arena, and held it during the next one hundred years, were primarily linguistic. "The sole idea now fruitful and powerful in Europe is the idea of national liberty; the worship of principle has begun," wrote Mazzini in 1832.[1] And further: "The nation is the universality of the citizens speaking the same tongue."[2] Territorial nationality is essentially conservative, for it is the product of a long historical development; nationalisms which place the emphasis on language almost invariably seek change, since no existing satiated community singles out one principle for its basis—the demand that the state should be coextensive with linguistic nationality was an internationally revolutionary

[1] *Life and Writings* (1864), vol. I, p. 147.
[2] *Ibid.*, vol. I, p. 167.

postulate which, seeing that nations are seldom linguistically seg-
regated, proved destructive both of constitutional growth and of
international peace. National feeling was hailed in 1848 as a great
and noble force which was to have regenerated Europe, and is
denounced today as an obsession which has brought ruin upon her:
but from the outset it was the expression of social and political
maladjustment, and has since been at least as much the vehicle as
the source of destructive passions.

I

The British and Swiss concepts of nationality are primarily territorial: it is the state which has created the nationality, and not
vice versa. A historical process, operating within a geographically
determined framework, has produced a British island nationality
which comprises the English, Scots, and Welsh, and to which
Ulster adheres; and neither within the island, nor in the English-
speaking world outside, could language be the criterion of nationality, or else Scotland and Wales would each be split internally,
while, for instance, Irishmen and Americans would have to count
as "English." Liberty and self-government have molded the territorial nation of Britain, and given content to its communal nationality. The political life of the British island community centers
in its parliament at Westminster, which represents men rooted in
British soil. This is a territorial, and not a tribal, assembly; it was
for centuries the representation of freeholders and householders, of
men with a share in their native land; and "every blade of grass
in Great Britain" was said to be represented in it. Bound to the
soil of Britain, it is limited to it: by now the British parliament
does not claim authority over communities even of British origin
and English speech once they are rooted in other soil. And so close
is the nexus between territory and nationality in English law that
a child of whatever parentage if born under the British flag can
claim British nationality. Indeed, the English language lacks a
word to describe a "nationality" distinct from, or contrasted with,
the citizenship derived from territory and state; and the meaningless term of "race" is often used for what in continental languages
is covered by "nationality."

The island character of Britain and the "genius" of its people
are acclaimed as factors which have produced that rare entity, a
real, and not merely nominal, territorial nationality. But the argu-

ment must not be pressed too far: for in the adjoining island a
similar mixture of Celt, Anglo-Saxon, and Norman has failed to
evolve an Irish territorial nationality. Even unity of language has
failed to bring its inhabitants together; and now the political dis-
sonance has resulted in a deliberate and laborious attempt to revive
linguistic separateness. The geographical factor is obvious also in
the rise and development of the Swiss nationality, yet the frontiers
of Switzerland are by no means preordained, nor amenable to a
strict rational explanation. Undisputed territory has rendered possible the growth of orderly self-government and of civil liberty,
which in turn has heightened the national consciousness and co-
herence of the community: so that any desire for territorial expansion, still more for merging into another state, is completely
absent. In and even before 1848, the most far-sighted among the
German nationalists desiring a union of all Germans, feared the
growth of civic liberty and self-government in the separate German
states as liable to consolidate and crystallize them, and thereby to
hinder unification. Fichte wrote:[3] "One might say: gradually a
German nation will come to be. But how can the conception of
one nation arise at all? (Nor was Greece ever united. What prevented it? Answer: the single state prematurely grown solid)."[4]
Men cannot fit themselves into a new nation "once a communal
existence [*das Volkseyn*] has entered their natural existence and
consciousness." All men desire civil liberty, and mutual understanding and trust between representatives and represented is the
basis of national life: "Therefore a people can no longer be reformed, or added to another, once it has started steadily to progress
towards a free constitution."

II

The Germans, more than any other European nation, had emptied
the territorial state of communal contents and converted it into
sheer dynastic property; and they brought forth dynasties without
roots or substance, ready to rule over any country or people. The
denationalized state with an unpolitical population was the product of German political incapacity and deadness, and of German
administrative efficiency. The Hapsburg monarchy, an almost

[3] Politische Fragmente aus den Jahren 1807 und 1813. *Werke,* vol. VII,
p. 549.
[4] *der schon zu feste Einzelstaat.*

unique phenomenon in history, rooted in the German hereditary provinces, the *Erbländer,* yet seemingly unrelated to any land or people, unrestricted in its acquisitive ambitions and singularly successful, variegated and ever changeable, was private dynastic domain, and so were the innumerable German pygmy states, too small to rank as political entities. Even Prussia, a military and administrative organization turned state, was ready to absorb territory and population of any language or race. In such dynastic proprietary or organizational creations German and non-German provinces were frequently yoked together, while the German dynasties and bureaucracies of Vienna, Berlin, and St. Petersburg encouraged fresh German settlements in non-German lands, adding considerably to the residue left by earlier, medieval, migrations. Lastly, Hapsburg non-national territorialism extended the contradiction between nationality and state to other parts of Europe, especially to Italy; and when in 1848 the demand arose for national liberty and self-determination, it was against the Hapsburgs that it was primarily directed.

The highest forms of communal life became the basis of west European nationalisms, the myth of the barbaric horde that of German nationalism.

> Nationalism in the West was based upon a nationality which was the product of social and political factors [writes Professor Hans Kohn[5]] ; nationalism in Germany did not find its justification in a rational societal conception, it found it in the "natural" fact of a community, held together . . . by traditional ties of kinship and status. German nationalism substituted for the legal and rational concept of "citizenship" the infinitely vaguer concept of "folk," which, first discovered by the German humanists, was fully developed by Herder and the German romanticists.

With roots which "seemed to reach into the dark soil of primitive times," that concept "lent itself more easily to the embroideries of imagination and the excitations of emotion." Moreover, the Germans transferred "to the field of society and nationalism" Rousseau's ethical and cultural antithesis between the primitive and artificial.

They established a distinction between state and nation: they regarded the state as a mechanical and juridical construction,

[5] *The Idea of Nationalism* (1946), p. 331.

the artificial product of historical accidents, while they believed
the nation to be the work of nature, and therefore something
sacred, eternal, organic, carrying a deeper justification than
works of men.[6]

Here it was not the state which molded nationality, but a pre-
existent nationality which postulated a state. The German concept
of nationality is linguistic and "racial," rather than political and
territorial, and it finds its final expression in the doctrine of the
Volksdeutsche which claims that anyone of German "race" and
language owes allegiance, first and foremost, to his German Fatherland, of whatever other state such an *Ausland-Deutscher* may
claim to be a citizen. Nor is that idea a mere Nazi invention: for
instance, in the Frankfurt parliament of 1848 the suggestion was
made that Germans resident in Paris should be represented in it;
this patently absurd and impossible proposal received no support,
yet it is symptomatic of certain trends in German thought that it
should have been made at all. And though no other European nation has gone the same length as the Germans, the German concept
of nationality, largely through the influence which German political formations and deformities had on central and eastern
Europe, has become dominant on the continent.

III

The French monarchy was based on territory with a common literary language and a national culture and consciousness; the elements of a rich nationality were present, but the welding force of
active civic development was wanting; and no synthesis was
reached between the power of the state, the growing influence of
Paris, and the vigorous life of the provinces. The final unification
of France was achieved not through an organic growth preserving
the historical individuality of the component parts but in the cata-
clysm of the great revolution: by abstract thought setting out to
build on a non-historical basis. A new principle of unity was found
in the community of men declared free and equal; the liberty of
the individual and his rights were placed in the forefront, yet he
was completely integrated into the sovereign nation. The emphasis
in the concept of nationality was shifted from the land to the people; the component countries and populations were merged into

[6] *Ibid.,* p. 249.

the republic, one and indivisible: *la patrie* became a dogma and a principle. To the French people, coincident with the territory of its state, was ascribed a non-territorial and a-historical existence: it was as if the French nation had shaken off the bonds of locality and time, and taken wing.

> In the words of Siéyès [writes Lord Acton,[7]] it was no longer France, but some unknown country to which the nation was transported. . . . The idea of the sovereignty of the people, uncontrolled by the past, gave birth to the idea of nationality independent of the political influence of history. . . . Every effaceable trace and relic of national history was carefully wiped away—the system of administration, the physical divisions of the country, the classes of society, the corporations, the weights and measures, the calendar.

Here was a break in historical continuity which has left deep rifts in the nation; and the French, passionately attached both to nationality and liberty, have to this day failed to evolve political forms that would provide the consensus and stability which these two require. But so dazzling in its spiritual magnificence was the opening of the new era, so convincing intellectually the argument, so powerful the surge of the movement, and so generous and universal was the message of the revolution, that men were slow in perceiving the losses which were suffered even in the realm of ideas. From the French Revolution dates the active rise of modern nationalism with some of its most dangerous features: of a mass movement centralizing and leveling, dynamic and ruthless, akin in nature to the horde.

It was the agrarian movement that rendered invincible the French Revolution of 1789 and the Russian of 1917, but it was the cities which supplied these two revolutions with their ideology and their striking force; and a metropolitan population is the common denominator of the nation detached from its lands. Michelet, himself a Parisian, extolled Paris as "the great and complete symbol" of France formed into one city.

> The genius of Paris is a most complex and at the same time the highest form of France. It might seem that something which

[7] In his essay on Nationality, published in the *Home and Foreign Review* (July 1862); reprinted in *The History of Freedom and other Essays* (1909), pp. 277-78.

resulted from the destruction of all local spirit, of all regionalism, must be something that is purely negative. It is not so: of all the negations of material, local, particular ideas results a living generality, a positive thing, a life force.[8]

Indeed, Michelet rejoiced at the rapid effacement of the "French provincial distinctions" (*nos provincialités françaises*).

That sacrifice of the diverse interior nationalities to the great nationality which comprises them, undoubtedly strengthens the latter. . . . It was at the moment when France suppressed within herself the diverging French countries that she proclaimed her high and original revelation.[9]

And he reached the significant conclusion that "nations will endure . . . if they do not take thought to suppress the towns, in which the nationalities have condensed their self-expression" (*ont résumé leur génie*).[10] Rousseau, on the contrary, "hated the great metropolitan capitals which seemed to him to destroy the individuality of nations." [11] "It is in the distant provinces," he wrote, ". . . where the inhabitants move about less, and experience fewer changes of fortune and status, that the genius and customs (*le génie et les moeurs*) of a nation have to be studied. "Yet the contradiction between Rousseau and Michelet is more apparent than real, for they were speaking about different things: Michelet had in mind the modern nationalist movements, now so curiously alike all the world over, while Rousseau thought of the distinct contents of each nationality.

IV

For men rooted in the soil there is, as a rule, a hierarchy of allegiances: to their village community or estate, to their district, to their "country" [12]—for them the nation is of a naturally federal structure. Traditional beliefs and hereditary ties persist; class and the way of living determine alignments; things are individual and concrete in the village or the small, old-fashioned town. But in

[8] Quoted after HANS KOHN, *Prophets and Peoples* (1946), p. 53.
[9] MICHELET, *Le Peuple* (1946), p. 286.
[10] *Ibid.*, p. 288.
[11] KOHN, *The Idea of Nationalism*, p. 254.
[12] In France *pays* is used to this day for various provinces; in eighteenth-century England, "country" was still frequently used for "county."

the great modern cities men grow anonymous, become ciphers, and are regimented; thinking becomes more abstract and is forced into generalizations; inherited beliefs are shaken and old ties are broken; there is a void, uncertainty, and hidden fear which man tries to master by rational thought. He starts by proudly asserting the rights of the abstract average individual freed from the bondage of tradition, and then integrates him into the crowd, a collective personality, which unloads itself in mass movements. The mass is the refuge of the uprooted individual; and disintegration of spiritual values is as potent a process as the splitting of the atom: it releases demonic forces which burst all dams. The program may be social revolution, or national revolution, or both; the aim may be to right wrongs or to sweep away stultifying encumbrances; the result can be liberation, but it can hardly be liberty which is founded on restraint and not on force, even if genuine idealism guides it. "Whenever a single definite object is made the supreme end of the state," wrote Lord Acton,[13] "be it the advantage of a class, the safety or the power of the country, or the support of any speculative idea, the state becomes for the time absolute. Liberty alone demands for its realization the limitation of the public authority. . . ." Liberty is the fruit of slow growth in a stable society; is based on respect for the rights of the individual, deeply embedded in the life and habits of the community; is in its origin an aristocratic idea: of the self-conscious individual, certain of himself and his position, and therefore perfectly at ease. It spreads when every man's house becomes "his castle": yet he must have a house and be safely rooted.

In 1848 the political insufficiency of the existing states of central and east-central Europe was rendered even more glaring by a peak period in intellectual development. Cultural entities were forming which transcended meaningless frontiers or disrupted territorial agglomerations. British political practice and French revolutionary doctrine provided the runways for the new movements, and the work of the Napoleonic period, uncompleted or reversed, their starting-points; while the Metternich regime, negative and uncreative, had hollowed out still further the forms which it endeavored to maintain, for it had impeded within them the growth of an active political life such as is apt to evolve nationality even within accidental territorial frameworks. The conception of dy-

[13] *Op. cit.,* p. 288.

nastic property in states was of feudal origin and derived from property in land: it fitted into the ideology of a community whose relations and connections were bound up with the soil. But it no longer made sense in urban communities: and it was these, with their strong educated class and their new proletariat, which were now coming to the fore. The uprooted individual becomes conscious of his personal rights, rational rather than traditional; and so does the crowd detached from the soil. There is a profound difference between a king of France and an emperor or king of the French—but what if the territorial term does not even correspond to a human aggregate?

The first logical inference of individual liberty and popular sovereignty is the claim to national self-determination: "One hardly knows what any division of the human race should be free to do, if not to determine with which of the various collective bodies of human beings they choose to associate themselves," wrote J. S. Mill in 1861.[14] And he rightly concluded that "it is in general a necessary condition of free institutions, that the boundaries of governments should coincide in the main with those of nationalities." [15] Liberty and nationality, especially when opposed to the concept of dynastic property in states, seemed therefore to be concordant ideas. The national movements demanded the union of nations disrupted between dynastic domains, and the independence of other nations engulfed in dynastic empires. It was taken for granted that representative and responsible government would be practiced by the sovereign nations, with full guarantees of the rights of the individual; and it was hopefully assumed that no free people would ever attack another people. The problem of the territorial squaring of intersecting national circles did not as yet vex the minds of the theoretical exponents of the creed of nationality.

V

A foremost position among the prophets of nationality is due to Mazzini, a man outstanding for spiritual integrity and single-minded devotion to the cause he preached. A sincere lover of liberty, he believed in the rights and dignity of man, in the "law of progress," and the joint destiny of humanity; and he adhered

[14] *Considerations on Representative Government,* p. 289.
[15] *Ibid.,* pp. 291–92.

passionately to the tenets and postulates of a truly humanitarian liberalism. "Liberty is sacred, as the individual is sacred." "Without liberty there is no true morality." And on what principle can an association of free men be founded except on "that of the rights of the individual?" Yet he never wearied of contrasting the age which had placed rights in the forefront with the new age centered on duty—the doctrine of individualism with that of nationality. "The epoch of *individuality* is concluded"; it has been "replaced by the epoch of the peoples"; "the question of nationalities is destined to give its name to the century." "Individuality" was "a doctrine useful perhaps . . . in securing the exercise of some personal rights, but impotent to found nationality or association"; and "it is the duty of reformers to initiate the epoch of association. Collective man is omnipotent upon the earth he treads." Mazzini yearned for a collective life which would reveal itself "in regular and progressive development, similar to the gradual evolution of vegetation in the new world, wherein the separate trees continue to mingle their branches, until they form the gigantic unity of the forest." Even art, "vital art," must be a collective performance, inspired by the collective purpose and serving it. He was prepared to subordinate the entire life of the community to a political aim—thus Young Italy was "to comprehend all the various manifestations of national life in one sole conception, and direct . . . them all . . . towards one sole aim, the emancipation of our country and its brotherhood with free nations." He saw Europe being transformed "into vast and united masses."

Mazzini himself said that his heart was stronger than his head; and the moral fervor, purity of purpose, and religious sincerity which pervade his writings—words of faith and action rather than of thought—were apt to conceal from contemporaries how deficient his teachings were in substance correlated to everyday reality, and what dangerous germs they contained. National self-glorification and claims to moral superiority were of their core: which entails a measure of depreciation of other peoples, and is not conducive to international comity. Nor are self-conscious apostles of an exalted creed easy to work with at home. Liberty calls for sanity, a modicum of scepticism, and tolerance: a man must be prepared to believe that he may be mistaken, if he is to treat others as equals. Mazzini was not; he had faith and was intolerant of "opinions"; his aim was action which ill accords with doubt. He retained his contempt of the "moderates" even after the goal of a united Italy had been achieved by them; and he never showed real understanding for the nature of parliamentary government, which rests on a good many seeming absurdities but so far has proved the most efficient system for safeguarding civic liberty.

Mazzini claimed for Italy a position of primacy in the world, and assigned to her a unique mission. There was "a void, a want in Europe"; "no power of initiative" existed in any of its peoples; a "regenerate Italy" could alone initiate a new and superior life and unity among them. Twice before has the world been united by Rome, imperial and papal; and the tradition of those two epochs bears witness to a further mission.

> Why should not a new Rome, the Rome of the Italian people . . . arise to create a third and still vaster unity; to link together and harmonize earth and heaven, right and duty; and utter, not to individuals but to peoples, the great word Association—to make known to free men and equals their mission here below?

But first, Italy had to be reconstituted "as one independent sovereign nation of free men and equals"; and the basis was to be republican and unitarian, not monarchical and federal.

> Because without unity, there is no true nation.
> Because without unity, there is no real strength; and Italy surrounded as she is by powerful, united, and jealous nations, has need of strength before all things.
> Because federalism, by reducing her to the political impotence of Switzerland, would necessarily place her under the influence of one of the neighboring nations.

Mazzini insisted that the first thing was "to put an end to our servile subjection to French influence," intellectual as much as political; and he seemed hardly aware of how much his "unitarian" program was a response, both defensive and imitative, to the national France of the great revolution. "I could wish," he wrote in 1861, "that all the artificial territorial divisions now existing were transformed into simple sections and circumscriptions."

"Young Italy," when he started organizing it in 1831, was to be the instrument of Italy's regeneration: it was to be "neither a sect nor a party but a faith and an apostolate"; and the emphasis was not on numbers but on the homogeneous character of the movement. "I still believe," he wrote on another occasion, "that next to the capacity of rightly leading, the greatest merit consists in knowing how and when to follow." During the period which might elapse before the movement achieved "the complete liberation of Italian soil," it would have to be directed "by a provisional dictatorial power, concentrated in the hands of a small number of men."

The banner of Young Italy was to bear "on the one side the words—*Liberty, Equality, Humanity;* and on the other—*Unity, Independence.*" What is it we want?" wrote Mazzini in 1832.

> We demand to exist. We demand a name. We desire to make our country powerful and respected, free and happy . . .
> In other words, we demand independence, unity and liberty, for ourselves and for our fellow-countrymen.
> . . . All are agreed in the cry of *Out with the foreigner.*

The same process of unification Mazzini desired for other nations. He saw the future "arousing extinct peoples, uniting divided races, proceeding by masses, and making individuals the mere stepping-stones to their ascent." "To reconstruct the map of Europe . . . in accordance with the special mission assigned to each people by geographical, ethnographical, and historical conditions, was the first step necessary for all." "Lasting liberty can only be achieved and maintained in Europe by strong and compact nations, equally balanced in power."

Here was real vision of the future though not of its dangers, and high idealism not devoid of elements which have since become dominant in nationalist movements. He wanted to see his country "powerful and respected," not merely free and secure: "the political impotence of Switzerland" would not have been acceptable to his feelings. His conscious thought turned towards humanity and embraced the whole; but when stigmatizing an answer given in 1831 by the provisional government of Bologna, he says that they spoke "like foreign barbarians." He disliked Italy's two neighbors, France and Austria; his demand of an equal balance in Europe was directed against the French "instinct of domination," and his program of redrawing the map of Europe against Austria's survival. He spoke of "the special mission assigned to each people," but would hardly have endorsed those claimed by the nations themselves: they might not have left the "mission Italy is destined to accomplish towards humanity" quite as great as Mazzini conceived it.

For in the romantic era the prophets of each nation found that it was destined to play the noblest part. "La patrie, ma patrie peut seule sauver le monde," wrote Michelet in 1846. The history of all the nations was "mutilated," that of France alone was "complete": "avec elle, vous sauvez le monde." But France, after some experience in the redeeming of nations, knew that such attempts do not necessarily earn the love of those to be "saved." "Children, children," wrote Michelet, "I say to you: ascend a mountain, provided it is sufficiently high; look to the four winds, and you will see nothing but enemies." [16] Poland "the Christ among the Nations" was at the time the doctrine of Polish Messianism propounded by her greatest poet, Mickiewicz; all the other nations were described as worshipping false gods who were no gods, while the Poles alone were "from first to last faithful to the God of their fathers." [17] Russia as "the God-bearing nation" was the creed of her most inspired writers from Khomiakov to Dostoyevsky, coupled with contempt for the "decaying West" (which did not impair their admiration for its achievements). Fichte, one of the discoverers of *Germanentum,* found that the Germans alone were a real nation, *ein Urvolk,* speaking a living language—the other languages were "dead in their roots," mere echoes. He thus apostrophized the Germans in 1808: "Of all the modern nations it is you who carry most clearly the germ of human perfection, and it is your mission to develop it. Should this perish in you, all hope of humanity for salvation from the depths of its evils will perish with you." [18] And the much applauded poetaster Geibel, wrote in 1861 on "Germany's Calling":

Und es mag am deutschen Wesen
Einmal noch die Welt genesen!

Thus every nation was exalted above the rest: compensatory dreams of grandeur dreamt by suffering or afflicted nations and uprooted individuals—immature, comparable to the daydreams of

[16] *Le Peuple,* p. 35.
[17] *Ksiegi narodu polskiego i pielgrzymstwa polskiego* (1832).
[18] *Reden an die deutsche Nation* (1808).

adolescents. Nations unified, regenerated, or resurrected, have since proved to be in no way better than other nations—there is a limit to miracles even in Wonderland, as Alice discovered when she ate cake. And what remains after the idealistic gilt of nationalism has worn off is the claim to superiority, hence to dominion.

VI

The impact of France on Europe during the revolutionary and Napoleonic periods was the chief political factor in the arousing of its nationalisms. In France, united even before 1789, the process of revolutionary transformation had released forces which deluged Europe: a nation welded into an ideological entity, and freed from the bonds of territory and tradition, offered a spectacle of power of which the nature, cost, and consequences men did not as yet probe, but which evoked the wonder, envy, and fear of its neighbors. The Germans, superior in number to the French, and the Italians, not very much inferior, realized to what disadvantage they were put through the political fragmentation of their countries. Napoleon himself started the work of territorial "rationalization" in both; and the fall of many governments and the frequent redistribution of territory "deprived the political settlement of the dignity of permanence"—"tradition and prescription," writes Lord Acton, "ceased to be guardians of authority." In Italy most of the previous states were reestablished in 1815, but the foreign origin of so many of the rulers and the foreign support on which they relied, the foreign occupation of Lombardy and Venetia, and the oppressive character of most of the governments rendered the territorial divisions even more galling. Genoa was merged into Piedmont; and one wonders how much this may have contributed to Mazzini's "unitarianism"—if his native city had still been the glorious ancient republic, would he have wished to wipe out its identity? But after it had been placed under a dynasty strange to it, was it not more reasonable to go the whole length in national unification? In his "General Instructions for Members of Young Italy" he used against a monarchical constitution for a united Italy the argument that "while the populations of the various Italian states would cheerfully unite in the name of a principle which would give no umbrage to local ambition, they would not willingly submit to be governed by a man—the offspring of one of those states."

In Germany the territorial resettlement of the Napoleonic period was much more extensive and more permanent. More than two hundred small principalities, ecclesiastical states, and free cities were incorporated in the big and middle-sized states whose character was thereby changed very considerably. After the Rhineland and Westphalia had in 1815 been included in Prussia, the Roman Catholics came to form more than one-third of her population; the inclusion of Franconia and the Palatinate in Bavaria raised the proportion of her Protestants to over one-fourth of the whole; in Baden, originally a Protestant country, the Roman Catholics now formed two-thirds of the population, and in Würtemberg one-third. The west-German Roman Catholics felt no affection for the Hohenzollerns, nor the Protestants, say, of Nuremberg for the Wittelsbachs, etc. And both in 1814–15 and in 1848, the small mediatized princes or Knights of the Empire were among the foremost champions of a united Germany: Stein, the Gagerns, Leiningen, and Chlodwig zu Hohenlohe-Schillingsfürst are outstanding examples. Men whose old territorial rights had been extinguished, or whose allegiance had been changed, wished to see all territorial rights merged in a Great Germany: in 1848 *Stock-Preussen* or *Alt-Bayern* showed a high degree of *Partikularismus* (local territorial consciousness), especially in the rural districts, but the newly acquired provinces clamored for German national unity, the Roman Catholics hoping for a Hapsburg Empire, and the Protestants for one under the Hohenzollerns. The territorial shufflings and reshufflings in the Napoleonic period and at the Congress of Vienna facilitated the rise of a movement for a united Germany.

"The German people wanted a strong and free state: this is the content of the German revolution of 1848–49," writes its historian, Veit Valentin, in the first volume of his work;[19] but by the time he reached the second, "free" dropped out: "The strong national Reich was the foremost aim of the German revolution."[20] And while Mazzini's counterpart to the watchwords of the French Revolution was *Independence, Unity, Liberty,* that of the German revolution of 1848 was *Einheit, Freiheit, und Macht* ("Unity, Freedom, and Power"); which was soon abbreviated to *Einheit und Macht*. Bassermann, one of the foremost leaders of

[19] *Geschichte der deutschen Revolution von 1848–49,* vol. I, p. 246.
[20] *Ibid.,* vol. II, p. 31.

the southwestern Liberals and chairman of the Constitutional Committee, said in the National Assembly on February 16, 1849: "If I knew the unity and future greatness of Germany were to be attained through a temporary renunciation of all the freedoms (*sämmtlicher Freiheitsrechte*), I should be the first to submit to such a dictatorship." And Stremayr, an Austrian member of the left, said on October 27, 1848: "Were Slavia to offer me freedom, and Germania to put me in chains, I would still follow Germany, for I am convinced that a united Germany will lead me to freedom." Thus the emphasis was on nationality rather than on liberty, and even where liberty was placed in the forefront, it was not always for its own sake but rather as the means for realizing the overriding purpose of national unification. As dynastic interests and rivalries were the main obstacle, and it was not possible to square them by negotiation or compromise, national unity could have been easiest achieved in a German republic, one and indivisible; and even to the moderates the doctrine of a joint German national sovereignty, superior to the claims of dynasties and constituent states, supplied the basis for their endeavors to achieve unity. But everywhere "the German revolution stopped at the steps to the thrones"; and not one dynasty was overthrown. Indeed, again for the sake of unity some republicans considered it necessary to renounce their program: "I desire German unity," wrote Heinrich Simon, a leader of the left, in April 1848, "but it would be impossible if in a few places the republic was now proclaimed."

Aggrieved national feelings were perhaps the greatest and most universal force behind the revolution of 1848. Here are two passages from the oath to be taken by members of Young Italy:[21]

> By the blush that rises to my brow when I stand before citizens of other lands, to know that I have no rights of citizenship, no country and no national flag . . .
> By the memory of our former greatness, and the sense of our present degradation . . .

And Prince Chlodwig zu Hohenlohe-Schillingsfürst wrote in December 1847:[22]

[21] MAZZINI, *Life and Writings,* vol. I, p. 111.
[22] *Denkwürdigkeiten des Fürsten Chlodwig zu Hohenlohe-Schillingsfürst,* F. Curtius, ed. (1906), vol. I, p. 38.

One reason for dissatisfaction is universal in Germany, and every thinking German feels it deeply and painfully. It is the nullity [*Nullität*] of Germany vis-à-vis of other states. . . . It is sad and humiliating not to be able to say proudly abroad: "I am a German," not to see the German flag flying on ships, nor find a consul, but to have to say: "I am a Kurhesse, Darmstädter, Bückeburger, my Fatherland was once a great, powerful country, but is now split into thirty-eight fragments."

And a memorandum presented on October 19, 1848 by the radical minority on the Constitutional Committee (including H. Simon and Robert Blum) declared that the German revolution had been provoked as much by the princes suppressing popular freedom as by their "failing to unite with a view to establishing Germany's power." Germany's *Macht* was a concern of the left no less than of the center and right.

The longing for German unity was strongest where the state could not endue its educated and semi-educated classes with a "consciousness of power" (*Machtbewusstsein*), which is the German substitute for freedom, as the organized violence of war is the German version of revolution: a commutation of particular importance in a study of liberty and nationality, many other nationalisms having since developed along similar lines. Southwestern, western, and central Germany were most solidly behind the endeavors of the Frankfurt assembly: these were regions of small or middle-sized states and of disaffected provinces, where the most extensive territorial reshuffles and transfers of allegiance had occurred, and where the impact of France—the influence of French ideas, and the fear of a new French invasion—was felt most acutely. Austria and Prussia, or even Bavaria and Hanover, had developed a "state consciousness" (*Staatsbewusstsein*), the territorial nationality of "subjects"; but their "nationality" being of dynastic or organizational origin, and not based on a free communal life, was as acquisitive as the dynasty or organization which had created the state.[23] Yet, their territorial ambitions being more realistic (they had existing states for basis), were moderate when compared with the formless, unmeasured, visionary pan-

[23] The German language has no word to describe the "nationality" of the separate states, and in 1848 the term employed for those territorial nationalities was *Stämme,* which means "tribes" and was originally employed for the Franks, Swabians, Saxons, etc. To attach it to territorial formations, some of as recent origin as 1815, is rather comic.

Germanism of more or less stateless Germans: most of the extravagant German claims of the two world wars were raised and applauded by the "freedom-loving" *idéologues* of the Frankfurt parliament of 1848.

"What is the German's Fatherland?" The Frankfurt assembly, being the parliament not of an existing state but of one to be created, had to decide the question. And a double, contradictory answer was given: *Was deutsch spricht, soll deutsch werden* ("Whatever speaks German, shall become German"), and *Was deutsch ist, soll deutsch bleiben* ("Whatever is German, shall remain German"). Thus linguistic claims were combined with another set based on history and the *status possidendi,* and each in detail was further garnished and extended—strategy, geography, the presumed wish or interest of some "inferior" race, or the "needs" of German expansion supplying the arguments. Even the linguistic test, *wie weit die deutsche Zunge klingt* (as far as the German language resounds) was indefinite, for it was left open how many Germans had to speak at the top of their voices for the claim to be established. Poland, martyred, partitioned Poland, the victim of Czarism, enjoyed quite exceptional popularity with the exponents of liberty and nationality in 1848; and the Frankfurt pre-parliament started off with a resolution declaring the dismemberment of Poland a "shameful wrong," and her restoration "a sacred duty of the German nation": but at no time did it occur to anyone that the Polish-speaking districts of West Prussia and Upper Silesia were due to the Poles, while in Posnania, recognized as Polish, a demarcation line was drawn between German and Polish districts which, after several consecutive corrections each favoring the Germans, gave the Poles less than one-fourth of a province in which they formed two-thirds of the population.

Even less liberal was the attitude of the Frankfurt parliament concerning Trieste and the Trentino. Schuselka, a leader of the left, thus defended the *Territorialpolitik* of the national assembly in July 1848: "Such must be our basis, for a great nation requires space (*Raum*) to fulfill its world destiny (*Weltberuf*), and I would rather die a thousand times than, for instance, renounce Trieste because they speak Italian." Don Giovanni a Prato, a leading figure in the Trentino, had, against the opinion of the Trentino émigrés who had left with the Lombard *insorti,* persuaded the population to take part in the elections to the Frankfurt parliament in the hope of having the national claims of the Trentino endorsed by it:[24] he left Frankfurt in December 1848 a deeply disappointed man. (Giovanni de Pretis, Count Festi,[25] and G. Vettorazzi had done so before him.)

When the Czechs, under Palacky's leadership, refused to send representatives to the German national assembly, their refusal produced a storm of indignation among the Frankfurt "Liberals": it was described as "a direct challenge to the territorial integrity of Germany," and their absence as in no way affecting the right of the assembly to legislate for the Czech provinces. There was unanimity in condemning any possible claim of so-called "a-historic" nations to an independent national existence. Heinrich von Gagern, an outstanding personality who dominated as no one else the Frankfurt parliament, thus defined on October 26, 1848 Germany's "task in the East": "to include as satellites nations on the Danube which have neither a call nor a claim to independence." And Wilhelm Jordan, one of the first on the left to translate his political radicalism into ultra-nationalist terms, spoke on June 20, 1848 of "the attempts of puny nationalities [*Nationalitätchen*] to found their own lives in our midst, and like parasites to destroy ours." Even Marx and Engels admitted the right only of "the great European nations" to "a separate and independent national existence," but not of "those numerous small relics of peoples" which have been (or should have been) absorbed by the "more powerful nations." But as they did not deny that right to the Magyars, who were hardly equal in number to the Czechs, and much inferior to the Yugoslavs and Rumans, one must presume that, unconsciously, these German middle-class prophets of class-war assigned the privilege of nationhood to peoples with a well-developed upper and middle class, and denied it to such as consisted almost entirely of "a-historical" peasants and workmen.

VII

The linguistic nationalism of the Germans, through its lore and example as well as through its impact, in turn stimulated the growth of linguistic nationalisms among their eastern neighbors, especially in the Hapsburg monarchy. But as Austria's *Staatsidee* was territorial, the Czech or Slovene cultural revival, so long as

[24] See M. MANFRONI, *Don Giovanni a Prato* (1920), pp. 50–51.
[25] See LIVIO MARCHETT, *Il Trentino nel Risorgimento* (1913).

it remained a-political, received lenient, or even friendly, treatment from the dynasty and the feudal aristocracy, whose territorial concepts it did not as yet contravene. "There is no such thing as an Austrian patriotism," declared a speaker in the Hungarian parliament in 1848. "It is as unthinkable as a specific patriotism on the various estates of Prince Esterhazy." Wherein he was wrong: every territorial unit is capable of developing a specific patriotism[26] in those truly rooted in it; which non-territorial mass-formations may, however, in time cut across, overshadow, or even destroy. "Patriotism" need not be one of "storm and stress"; there can be also a patriotism interested in what exists, and desirous of preserving it: such conservative sentiment, of varying intensity, gathers round every existing territorial formation.

The nationalities of the Hapsburg monarchy, barring the Italians and Serbs, all had, at one time or another, some interest of their own in its survival, developing accordingly their specific type of "Austrian patriotism." This was strongest and most permanent among the Austrian Germans: German was the official language of the monarchy, they held the central position within it, supplied the largest proportion of administrative officials and army officers, and felt as if they were partners of the dynasty—even a democracy is apt to assume the role or inheritance of its late rulers.[27] But the fact that the Hapsburg monarchy tended to show tolerance to nationalities which did not threaten its territorial integrity, even in 1848 very much sharpened the hostility to it of the extremer German nationalists, especially in the Czech provinces, and en-hanced their desire to break up the monarchy and engulf its western provinces in a united Germany, which would enable them to crush completely the Czech national movement: a program openly avowed in the Frankfurt parliament. Naturally the danger of such inclusion made the Czechs wish for Austria's survival: they de-veloped the idea of "Austro-Slavism" of the Hapsburg monarchy reconstructed on a Slav basis. This program enjoyed the support

---

[26] An amusing example of "estate patriotism," amazing in its inhumanity, occurs in Bismarck's early correspondence. On April 9, 1845, at a time of great floods, he wrote to his sister: "I am proud to be able to report that my rivulet [*Nebenfluss*], the Zampel, has drowned a carrier and his horse" (see HORST KOHL, *Bismarckbriefe.* 7th ed. (1898), pp. 24–25).

[27] When in 1536 the citizens of Geneva drove out the Bishop and the Vidomne, they cried with joy, "Nous sommes princes," and proceeded to rule in an autocratic manner thirty surrounding villages.

of a great many aristocrats who were of very mixed national origin and talked at home German or French, but developed a Bohemian territorial nationality, favored the Czech national movement (as dynasties, whatever their origin, assume the nationality of the country over which they rule), and demanded within the framework of the Hapsburg monarchy, autonomy for the Czech provinces, expecting to maintain their own primacy in the provincial self-government. When the Czech national movement assumed during the next fifty years a markedly democratic character, the Bohemian territorial nationalism of the magnates steeply declined.

The Magyars were at all times opposed to a federalist reconstruction of the Hapsburg monarchy which would have conceded territorial or linguistic rights to any of the "subject" races, since freedom for the Czechs (the nearest kinsmen of the Slovaks), the Yugoslavs, the Ruthenes, or the Rumans in Austria, would have encouraged parallel movements in Hungary; and the Magyars, who insisted on Hungary's right to an independent state existence, within that state insisted on their own absolute dominion over Slavs and Rumans. They were bitterly hostile to the concept of a *Gesammtmonarchie* (a monarchy embracing all Hapsburg dominions) upheld by the Vienna centralists, for which these tried to enlist the support of Hungary's subject races. Yet while all Magyars were united in the defense of Hungary's constitutional rights and territorial integrity, the views on how best to secure them ranged from those of nationalists even more *enragé* than Kossuth, to those of the Old-Hungarian magnates who on a conservative basis wished to arrive at a compromise with the dynasty and the Vienna court; and the less radical a group was politically the more tolerant it was as a rule towards the non-Magyar nationalities of Hungary: an early example of conflict between nationality and liberty, and, in the case of Kossuth, of a spurious reputation for liberalism.

In 1848 most of the Poles were hostile to the Hapsburgs and the Vienna government. They still expected an early restoration of a free and united Poland; in 1846 they had experienced the catastrophe of the West Galician *jacquerie* in which Polish peasants, incited by Austrian officials, turned on the Polish gentry as these were about to start an insurrection of a national and, in fact, democratic, character; and in East Galicia they were faced by an alliance of the Vienna Government with the Ruthene peasants on a socially and nationally anti-Polish basis. But even then there was a group of Polish aristocrats and conservatives who aimed at a cooperation with the Hapsburgs such as was established afterwards. And while the Poles continued to suffer persecution under Russia and Prussia, in Austria they attained a privileged position, enjoying after 1867 self-government and dominion over the Ruthenes. Consequently during the fifty years preceding World War I, they developed a remarkable Austrian patriotism.

The Slovenes, Croats, Rumans, Slovaks, and Ruthenes or Ukrainians in various periods developed varying degrees of pro-Austrian feeling; but in time all these Austrian "patriotisms" were disappointed, barring that of the "partners" of the dynasty. No civic territorial nationality could unite the different nationalities of Austria-Hungary, for such community is possible only between linguistic groups acknowledging each other as equals, whereas the Germans, Magyars, and Poles claimed cultural, social, and political superiority over those on whom they looked down as "a-historic" subject races, not entitled to an independent national existence. The Compromise of 1867 resulted in a division of the Hapsburg dominions into three distinct domains: Western Austria of the Germans—approximately the territory which in 1848 these had wanted to see included in the Frankfurt parliament; Hungary of the Magyars; and Galicia, which in 1919–20 the Poles managed to carry over entire into the restored Poland against the armed opposition of the Ruthenes.

VIII

In 1789 two nations on the European continent, Poland and Hungary, could look back to an unbroken tradition of parliamentary government, with a concomitant territorial nationality and a high degree of personal liberty for their citizens; these, however, in contrast to England, were of a single estate or caste: the gentry, a very numerous body comprising about one-tenth of the population, yet an exclusive, privileged class. Towards the end of the Middle Ages, under the impact of German aggression or infiltration, the Poles had developed an early form of conscious linguistic nationality. But in their own subsequent expansion to the east they changed their concept of nationality: Poland and Lithuania, consti-

tutionally united, became a gentry-republic (under elected kings),
based not on a common language or religion but on caste: the
gentry-nation spoke Polish, White and Little Russian, and Lith-
uanian; in some western and northern districts also German and
Swedish; and it comprised even Moslem Tartars, Armenians, and
baptized Jews. Citizenship depended on being of the gentry, or
being received into it. In Poland, in the sixteenth century, the
official language was Latin, in Lithuania it was White Russian;
and the Greek Orthodox and Protestants together may at one
time have equalled in number the Roman Catholics. But gradually, across Reformation and Counter-Reformation and the Uniat
Church, the overwhelming majority of the gentry joined Rome,
and with Polish superseding Latin as the literary language, became
Polonized. Similarly in Hungary the gentry-class was of very
mixed national extraction, and its nationality was originally territorial rather than linguistic; the language of state and parliament
was Latin, and so remained till the nineteenth century, when a
growing Magyar linguistic nationalism transformed the nature of
the Hungarian state.

Had the landed gentry of the non-Polish or non-Magyar provinces remained united to the peasants in language and religion, the
territorial nationality of the two realms might possibly have been
capable of modern development and readjustments, and might consequently have survived. But when the deep cleavage of the agrarian problem became exacerbated by differences in language and
religion, a joint territorial nationality became utterly impossible:
Poland and Hungary could claim their historic frontiers only so
long as the peasant masses did not count politically. Consequently
the modern Polish and Magyar nationalisms, which were no
longer those of "single-class" communities but which none the less
aspired to taking over the territorial inheritance of the gentry-
nations, were driven into hopeless contradictions and manœuvres.
In 1848 these two nations were looked upon as foremost champions
of liberty and nationality: they had had within their historic frontiers a fuller and freer political life than most continental nations,
and therefore a stronger civic consciousness and patriotism; and
now they were fighting the despots of the Holy Alliance to re-
establish those free and independent communities; that these had
in the meantime become social anachronisms and could not be re-

built on modern foundations, was realized by very few among the men of 1848 in western and central Europe, and was never acknowledged.

IX

The revolution of 1848 was urban in its character and ideology. It started in the capitals, spread to other towns, and was directed or turned to account by the urban middle-class intelligentsia. The countryside remained indifferent or hostile, or, if revolutionary, pursued aims extraneous and alien to the distinctive purposes of that year. In France it was Paris which made the February Revolution without encountering any active opposition from the provinces; but the June Days and the presidential election of December 1848 disclosed the social conservatism of the peasantry. In Italy the peasants gave no support to the liberal and national revolution which remained entirely urban, while in Sicily and Naples the rural movement bore a purely agrarian character. In northern Germany the countryside was almost entirely conservative, far more so than appeared in the April elections, and Prussian Junkers, like Bismarck, chafed to lead their peasants against Berlin. F. Th. Vischer, a Würtemberger who in the Frankfurt parliament belonged to the left, wrote to a friend on May 28, 1848: "Here are Pomeranians and East Prussians, some of them hefty fellows with the best will who say that if we proceed too sharply, we shall provoke a reaction not from the government but from the provinces. . . . A German Vendée." [28] And there was more than one potential Vendée in Germany; while revolutionary agrarian movements—in Silesia, Baden, Würtemberg, or Hesse—threatened to result in *jacqueries,* but were completely indifferent to national or constitutional ideas. In the Hapsburg monarchy there was a strong peasant movement but again of a purely agrarian character: the leaders in the Austrian parliament clearly realized that once the peasant was freed from the remainders of servitude and from feudal rights and dues, and was given his land, he would turn reactionary. On the whole governments and oppositions alike avoided appealing to the peasants, a dark, incalculable force which, if roused, could not easily be directed or mastered. Thus neither

[28] ENGELHAAF, ed., Achtzehn Briefe aus der Paulskirche. *Deutsche Revue* (1909).

the landed classes nor the peasants had a share in determining the character of the revolution of 1848 which used to be described as "the awakening of the Peoples."

X

The year 1848 marks, for good or evil, the opening of the era of linguistic nationalisms shaping mass personalities and producing their inevitable conflicts: a nation which bases its unity on language cannot easily renounce groups of co-nationals intermingled with those of the neighboring nation; and an alien minority within the state, or an intensely coveted *terra irredenta,* are both likely to distort the life of the nation, and impair the growth of its civic liberty. The alien community within the disputed borderland, hostile to the state and possibly plotting against it, provokes repressions which are apt to abase the standards of government; while fellow-countrymen across the border awaiting liberation keep up international tensions, which again are destructive of a free civic life. Moreover, the strongly knitted mass formations of the neo-horde are based on positive feelings which keep the nation together; but the negative feelings, which have to be suppressed within the group, turn with increased virulence against "the stranger in our midst," or against the neighbor. Freedom is safest in the self-contained community with a territorial nationality; and where this has not by some miracle or the grace of God grown up spontaneously, it might perhaps best be secured by a transfer of populations. But it serves no purpose to expostulate with history: *on ne fait pas le procès aux révolutions,* nor to any other historical phenomena.

7.

Crimea: the War That Would Not Boil

A. J. P. Taylor

❖❖❖

EDITORIAL NOTE: *The revolutions of 1848 were the first decisive events in the maturation of liberalism, but an external event, the Crimean War, reinforced the lesson. The Crimean War was ostensibly an outgrowth of the Eastern Question—the problem of the decline of the Ottoman Empire and the interest of the European powers in the region. There are areas of historical enquiry where the closer one examines a problem the less sense it makes. The Crimean War is one of them. While there have been many studies of the problem in this graveyard of graduate students and historical imagination, there remain those involved and unpronounceable treaties; the preposterous squabbles about the key to the front door of the church of the Nativity, with Latin and Greek monks bludgeoning one another; and the endless series of crises, gigantic bluffs, and occasional sharp military confrontations. Dyspeptic professors can always crush the enthusiastic student with, "Now, Mr. Jones, what do you know about the treaty of Kutchuk Kainardji?"*

A. J. P. Taylor is not content with the traditional obfuscation of the problem, but then Taylor is ever ready to develop a striking argument and never shies away from controversy. He argues that the basic error lies in viewing the Crimean War as an installment of the Eastern Question. Traditionalists see it, complete in itself, as an instance of the tragic breakdown of diplomacy leading to a peripheral and indecisive war. With courage worthy of the Light Brigade, but with more good sense, Taylor charges the guns of traditional historical interpretation. He pointedly suggests that both the meaning of the Crimean War and the lack of it, a charming paradox, are understood only when we make it part of the European question. The Crimean War turned out to be Europe's war to exclude Russia. The European radicals wanted another, more decisive war. Had Prussia and Austria joined, it would have been Europe's war to destroy Russia, the guardian of reactionary Europe and leader of the counter-revolution in 1848.

The war proved to be the opening of the Liberal bargain with power. Subsequent essays treat these compromises in detail. The elimination of Russia from Europe for twenty years was the decisive result of an indecisive confrontation, and Russia's exile permitted the unification of Germany and Italy, the construction of "liberal" states which could withstand the pressure of France or Russia for European hegemony. This resolution of the European, not the Eastern, question appeared at the time to be a sound Liberal compromise. The national principle was both released and controlled in central Europe: popular institutions constructed, but hemmed in by reasonable constraints.

John Bright, with ponderous Victorian wit, called the Crimean War "a crime"; most historians have presented it as a bewildering series of diplomatic and military blunders. With the experience of the last few years to enlighten us, we should do better: we know that the diplomatic tangles since 1945, which may seem bewildering to the future historian, conceal the reality of "the cold war." The Crimean War was the cold war in an earlier phase. Two world systems, mutually uncomprehending, lurched against each other, each convinced of its defensive good faith. The struggle between them was fought in a ragged way at the edges. Both sides shrank from the head-on collision which would have produced a war to remake the world—Russia from lack of strength, the Western powers from lack of conviction. Though the Crimean War seemed indecisive, great decisions followed from it. Without it neither Germany nor Italy could have been united; without it Europe would never have known "the liberal era," that halcyon age which ended in 1914 and which, for centuries to come, men will regard as "normal times," just as the barbarians looked back to the peace and security of Augustan Rome.

The Crimean War is often treated in England as a war over the Eastern Question, a war to secure the route to India, and thus a rehearsal for Disraeli's "peace with honor" campaign in 1878. This is to err both in time and place. The war had little or nothing to do with the security of India. The Suez Canal was not built; the overland route catered for a few travelers in a hurry; for that matter Russia's land-route to India was still in the future. The Crimean War was fought for essentially European considerations—against Russia rather than in favor of Turkey. It was fought for the sake of the balance of power and for "the liberties of Europe"; more positively, it aimed to substitute diplomacy by agreement, the Concert of Europe, for the settlement of affairs at the dictation of a single great power. Disraeli was a consistent disciple of Metternich when he criticized the Crimean War and yet opposed Russia in 1878: the Crimean War had general altruistic motives, the crisis of 1878 was caused solely by the defense of imperial interests. In other words, 1878 was a Tory affair; the Crimean War, with all its muddle, sprang from Whig principles, the last fling of a dying party.

British policy in the Near East had not been consistently anti-Russian before the Crimean War, though it became so afterwards. Canning, for instance, cooperated with Russia throughout the Greek War of Independence; and though Palmerston thought of working with France against Russia in the Near East in 1833, he ended up by working with Russia against France in 1839 and 1840. Throughout the eighteen-forties, and indeed until the beginning of 1853, British suspicions were turned against France both at Constantinople and in Egypt; and Great Britain and Russia often made common cause in resisting French encroachment. Nor can there be an easy dividing line in their attitude to the Ottoman Empire, as though Russia wanted to break it up and Great Britain wished to preserve it. Both powers found it a convenience; and both powers doubted its capacity to survive. Their difference was in timing, not in judgment of the situation.

The British attitude to Russia was very different when it came to Europe; hence the Crimean War makes sense only with a European background. Ever since 1815 British statesmen had been obsessed with the thought that, if France ceased to dominate Europe, Russia would take her place; as Napoleon had said, in fifty years all Europe would be either republican or Cossack. Hence Castlereagh's rather absurd alliance with France and Austria in January 1815; hence Canning's calling in of a New World to redress the balance of the Old (though the New World did not respond to his invitation); hence Palmerston's welcome to the July Monarchy in France and his Quadruple Alliance with Spain and Portugal as well in 1834. This was one side of British policy: to maintain France as a great power and yet to keep her harmless—

just strong enough to check Russia's domination without reviving the same taste in herself. The other element in British policy was to develop the independence of central Europe, so that it could hold its own against both Cossacks and republicans without constant alarms or war. This was what was meant by the favorite description of Prussia and Austria as Great Britain's "natural allies": they were serving the purposes of British policy without any effort on the British side. Curiously enough, Metternich and Palmerston, who were supposed to hate each other so much, were pursuing exactly the same aims and served each other's needs. So long as the "Metternich system" worked, central Europe was independent of both France and Russia; and the balance of power in Europe freed Great Britain from European commitments.

The revolutions of 1848 ended this finely drawn policy. The fall of Metternich was a disaster to the British position; and it was little consolation to make out that he had fallen because of his refusal to take British advice. The revolutions of 1848 seemed to make France more powerful than before; to weaken Prussia; and to threaten Austria with elimination from the ranks of the great powers. Europe would become either republican or Cossack. Though this bitter saying was not at once fulfilled, it seemed at most postponed. On the one side, France emerged from the revolutionary year under the rule of a new Bonaparte, inescapably committed to the overthrow of the treaties of 1815 and almost as much to the restoration of French domination in Europe. On the other, the revolutions in central Europe—in Germany, in Italy and in Hungary—were defeated only with Russian backing; so far as Hungary went, only with Russian military aid. By 1850, Francis Joseph of Austria and Frederick William IV of Prussia seemed to be Russian dependents, subservient not only from ideological similarity, but from their inability to hold their monarchical power except with Russian support. The Holy Alliance was the Cominform of Kings.

The defeat of the revolutions of 1848 with Russian aid had a profound effect on British public opinion. Before 1848 fear of Russia had been a diplomat's calculation; there had been no "Russian bogey." After 1848 British liberals picked up the habit of continental radicals and began to regard Russia as the tyrant of Europe. War against Russia was regarded as the preliminary to any radical success elsewhere. The old diplomatic apprehension of Russia now seemed tepid and halfhearted. In radical circles, for instance, it was common doctrine that Palmerston was in Russian pay; the proof was found in his reluctance to launch the great European "war of liberation." This theory can be found worked out in the essays which Karl Marx wrote on *The Eastern Question*; he learnt it from the pro-Turk lunatic, Urquhart. Except among radicals and exiles, fear of France still predominated in England until the spring of 1853. Indeed, belief that the British were more apprehensive about Belgium than about Turkey was one of the factors which led Czar Nicholas to act so carelessly and so provocatively in May 1853, when the war crisis first began to stir.

There was, of course, another and more obvious cause of Russian confidence. A coalition ministry had been formed in England at the end of 1852 under Lord Aberdeen; and Aberdeen, though a free trader, was an old-fashioned Tory. He had no sympathy with radical hostility to Russia; great confidence in the czar's good faith; and great distrust of Napoleon III. If Aberdeen had had his way there would have been no Crimean War. Russia would have strengthened her position in Turkey, consolidated her reactionary hold over Europe; and Great Britain would have consoled herself by taking Egypt. This would have been a reasonable, though not an idealistic, solution; hence the later regrets of Lord Salisbury, a reasonable man without ideals, that it was not adopted. It could only have been adopted by a purely Tory cabinet; and from such a cabinet Aberdeen was barred by his free-trade doctrines. Instead, he was saddled with Whig colleagues, Palmerston and Russell, who were both in their way friendly to France and who both, without yet distrusting the czar, wished to draw a sharp line against any new Russian advance. Russell had been prime minister; Palmerston was going to be. They were both pretty clear that a firm line against Russia would be a winning card in the game for public favor which they were playing against each other. Here too, if Palmerston and Russell had had their way, there would have been no war. The czar would have stepped aside from the Eastern Question before his prestige was involved and waited for a more favorable opportunity. Perhaps even, as we go on dreaming nowadays, Russian despotism would have saved everyone the trouble of a war by crumbling from within. It was this mixture of conciliation always too grudging and firmness always too late which, on the British side, produced the Crimean War.

There was, however, another principal in the war, one often forgotten in British and even in Russian accounts. Neither the czar nor the British government wanted war; Napoleon III did. Not necessarily the Crimean War as it worked itself out, but a war which would disrupt the existing structure of Europe. Thus Great Britain became involved in war in order to preserve the balance of power and to defend the liberties of Europe; Napoleon III pushed into war in order to overthrow the balance of power and to clear the way for French domination. After all, it is a simple calculation that if the allies of a great war fall out the defeated party will come into his own. In 1853 the calculation was made in Paris; now* it is made in every German village. The Crimean War was not a good war from Napoleon III's point of view; a war in Poland, in Italy, or on the Rhine, would have been much better. But it was better than no war at all. On the other hand, Napoleon III had learnt from his uncle's failure—had learnt, that is, in the scrappy, illogical way, in which men use the past to prop up their own prejudices. Napoleon III supposed, though wrongly, that his uncle's great mistake had been to quarrel with England; his key to success was therefore to be the British alliance, and the Crimean War was welcome to him in that it gave him this alliance. In the long run, however, Napoleon III did no better with the British alliance than his uncle had done without it—unless it is better to die in Chislehurst than at St. Helena.

By the summer of 1853 France, Russia and Great Britain were all tugging themselves into war in their different ways. The czar, though with no deep-laid plans for encroaching on Turkey, had grown too confident; regarding Prussia and Austria as his satellites, he supposed that he could display his prestige at Constantinople without risk. When this proved mistaken, he—like the Russians generally when they are challenged—felt genuinely threatened with aggression; and in Russian eyes the Crimean War was a defensive war. The British government, though also without deep-laid plans, would not allow the czar's claims and, in their anxiety to win the alliance of France, often acted more firmly than Napoleon III expected or desired. Napoleon, on his side, wanted to shake Russia's prestige and to build up his own; but most of all, he wanted to keep in step with the British, who, with the same motive, con-

* Written in 1952 [Ed.].

stantly quickened the pace until the two fleets tumbled into the Black Sea more to prove mutual good faith and enthusiasm as allies than to oppose Russia. As a matter of fact, when the British and French fleets entered the Black Sea at the end of 1853, the Crimean War, not yet started, had already been won so far as the original causes of war, or excuses for it, were concerned. That is, the czar was quite prepared to drop his immediate claims on Turkey, once it became clear that England and France intended to resist them. This did not satisfy the Western allies. With their public opinion roused and their resources mobilized, what they wanted was a decision, not merely the withdrawal of the present Russian demands. The problem of the Crimean War, never solved, lay here. The Russians had dropped their demands because the British and French fleets had entered the Black Sea. How could the renewal of these demands be prevented when the British and French fleets went away again?

The problem had two sides, military and diplomatic. The military problem was, how to get at the Russians, in order to inflict on them the defeat which would make them accept the terms needed for Europe's security? The diplomatic problem was, what were the terms which should be imposed on the Russians when they were defeated? The two problems were mixed up throughout the war. Sometimes the allies tried to devise terms which would make a defeat of the Russians unnecessary; sometimes they dreamt of a defeat so decisive as to spare them the trouble of devising terms. At bottom the problem was insoluble. The Western powers could not alone inflict on Russia a decisive and lasting defeat; nor, even were she defeated, could they devise terms which would ensure against a renewal of her expansion. It would have been a different matter if Austria and Prussia, the states of central Europe, could have been drawn into the war. Hence the real decision of the Crimean War came from the two Germanic powers when they decided to stay out of it. Austria and Prussia were "the third force." Their persistence in this line of policy both caused the Crimean War and led to its being indecisive. Until the beginning of 1854 the czar had regarded them as reliable satellite states, dependent on his support. As soon, however, as he depended on their support, they ceased to be satellites. He could no longer keep France out of the Near East by a threat from Prussia on the Rhine and from Austria in Italy.

The Western powers imagined that "the third force" had come over to their side and that a full-scale defeat of Russia was in sight. Certainly a coalition of all the great powers of Europe against Russia would have excluded her from Europe, might even have destroyed her as a great power. Poland would have been restored, Turkey secured; Louis Napoleon would have become master of Europe. This was an outcome more unwelcome to Prussia and Austria even than Russian domination of Turkey. Whereas the Western powers wanted a decision, the central powers wanted no decision; and they got their way. Prussia had the great advantage that she was indifferent to the affairs of the Near East, though concerned with the general European balance. Hence her neutrality was genuinely impartial. Her only aim, which seemed craven enough, was to ensure that no fighting took place on Prussian soil. This no doubt benefited Russia and won her gratitude; but since Prussia did not promise anything to the Western powers, she did not disappoint them either. When the war ended, Prussia was not at first invited to the Peace Congress at Paris. This seemed a humiliation; later events showed the enormous gains to be won from keeping out of other people's quarrels. Any contemporary statesman who wishes to reap the advantages of the third course should study the policy of Prussia during the Crimean War.

Austrian policy is equally instructive: it shows the disadvantages of a neutrality which offends both sides. Whereas Prussia was neutral from indifference, Austria was neutral from being too deeply committed. She had her own grounds for opposing Russia. Russia's control of the mouth of the Danube, where her troops had established themselves in 1853, cut one of Austria's main economic arteries with the outer world. Thus the practical aim of Austrian policy was to get Russia out of Rumania and to get herself in. But there were complicating factors. If Austria entered the war on the side of the Western powers, she would bear the brunt of the fighting; worse, an allied victory, expelling Russia from Europe, would make Napoleon III supreme and thus clear the way for the national principle. Austria would win Rumania at too high a price if she lost her Italian lands, the symbol of her imperial greatness. Yet, apart from her anxiety about Rumania, Austria dared not favor Russia nor even keep a resolute neutrality, for fear that Napoleon III would explode Italy against her. As a result Austria followed the worst of all policies. She offended the czar by refusing to promise a secure neutrality; she offended the Western powers by refusing to go to war. She pressed her alliance on England and France in order to conciliate them; she failed to operate it and left them more estranged than before. Neutrality, like virtue, has its merits if maintained inviolate; it can also be sold for a high price. The one impossible thing is to be up for auction and to remain virtuous at the same time.

The first stage of the Crimean War was the stage when the Western powers imagined that "the third force" could be drawn into the war and a real decision thus produced. This stage lasted until the summer of 1854, by which time Prussian neutrality was certain and Austrian belligerence uncertain. The Crimean War, in the strict sense of the term, followed—the war with all its blunders and muddles which perplexed contemporaries and baffled posterity. Yet the confusion had a simple cause—how could the allies get at Russia when the great neutral buffer of central Europe was interposed between them? The allies had hoped that the Russians would obligingly remain in Rumania in order that they might be defeated there; instead the Russians withdrew from Rumania in July 1854. In their perplexity the allies decided on Sebastopol, the Russian naval base in the Crimea, which was supposed to be vulnerable to an amphibious operation. As a matter of fact, it took nearly a year's fighting and the mobilization of armies on a continental scale for this amphibious operation to succeed.

It takes two to make a war. Russian strength in the Near East lay in her proximity; her strength in the European balance lay in her army. Her naval power in the Black Sea was a secondary affair; and it could always be checked if the British and French fleets, or even the British fleet alone, passed the Straits. If the Russians had abandoned Sebastopol and sealed off the Crimea, the western allies would have scored a success of prestige; but Russia would have been no weaker than before. The allies would have cruised undisturbed in the Black Sea until their position became ridiculous; they would then have retired, and Russia's pressure on Turkey could have been resumed. But autocratic monarchies also have their prestige. The czar did not grasp that if the allies failed to defeat him, he had won; whereas, whatever efforts he made at Sebastopol, he could not defeat the allies. Russia's military strength lies in withdrawal; but this has always to be imposed upon her by her enemies, instead of being a conscious choice. Alexander I fought Napoleon at Austerlitz and even wanted to fight on the frontier in 1812; Stalin was only saved from catastrophe on the frontier in 1941 by being caught unprepared. In the Crimean War, the czar obligingly provided the maritime powers with the battlefield which they could never have found for themselves. Instead of being withdrawn, the Russian armies in Sebastopol were reinforced; and Russia exhausted herself for the sake of the maritime powers. The allies lamented that they had not taken Sebastopol by a *coup de main* when they landed in 1854; if they had, there would have been no Crimean War and nothing would have been achieved at all. For the essence of war is not to take this point or that, but to destroy, or at least to weaken, the military strength of the enemy. This was accomplished by the year's fighting in front of Sebastopol. The Russian armies were greatly weakened; Russia's military prestige lessened; most of all, Russia's economic resources were intolerably strained. It took Russia a generation to recover from the effort of the Crimean War; and in this generation Europe was remade without Russian interference.

The defeat of the Russian armies, and the weakening of Russian power, were the real result of the Crimean War; but this was a result too vague to satisfy the victorious allies. Their victory had to be translated into a treaty of peace; yet they had no clear idea what this treaty should contain. As on other occasions, the Western powers knew what they were fighting against, not what they were fighting for. They were fighting against Russia; and their real wish was that Russia should cease to exist or—what amounts to the same thing—become a modest and satisfied member of an Anglo-French world. Napoleon III was prepared to accept the logic of this wish. When Sebastopol fell, he proposed to the British government a program which would sweep Russia from Europe and destroy her as a great power—the program of full national reconstruction, especially of Poland, which would incidentally make France supreme in Europe. The British government had the exactly opposite aim: they had wished to destroy Russian supremacy in Europe without putting French supremacy in its place. Yet on the other hand they were the more eager of the two to continue the war until a "decision" had been reached. A characteristic compromise followed. Each accepted the other's negative: the war was brought to an end, without any positive war-aims being drawn up.

This is not to say that the Crimean War accomplished nothing, nor even that the Treaty of Paris contained nothing of moment. Apart from the weakening of Russian power, which could not be put into a treaty, the Crimean War had two achievements, one which lasted for nearly eighty years, the other for fifteen years. The more permanent outcome, as things go in international affairs, was the independence of Rumania, freeing the mouths of the Danube from either Russian or Austrian control. The Russian army had withdrawn in July 1854; the Austrian army had taken its place, and the Austrians had hoped to annex Rumania. But they would not pay the French price, which was to give up Italy; therefore they had to withdraw in their turn, and Rumania became a genuinely independent state, a buffer between Russian interests and those of central Europe, until the time of Stalin and Hitler.

The more prized achievement of the Treaty of Paris was the "neutralization" of the Black Sea. Russia was forbidden to maintain a fleet in the Black Sea, or to rebuild her naval arsenals; it is true that the same restrictions were imposed on Turkey, but since the Turks could maintain a fleet in the Sea of Marmora they could always dominate the Black Sea in time of war. The neutralization clauses of the Treaty of Paris were a rehearsal for the demilitarization of the Rhineland in the Treaty of Versailles, and equally futile. Either Russia accepted them because she feared England and France; in that case she would repudiate them when she ceased to fear England or France. Alternatively Russia accepted them because she had changed her ways and given up aggression against Turkey; in that case they were unnecessary. The British and French would not keep their fleets in the Black Sea indefinitely; they were not even sure that they would remain indefinitely on good terms. Hence they tried to make the Russians promise that they would continue to behave as though the allied fleets were still in the Black Sea when in fact they had been long withdrawn. A treaty of peace can only define the conditions of the present; it cannot bind the future. This the Russians demonstrated fifteen years later, when they repudiated the Black Sea clauses of the Treaty of Paris. The British doctrine of the sanctity of treaties was upheld only by the pious pretence of a conference in London, at which the powers, to no one's surprise, confirmed what Russia had already done. The neutralization clauses taught a lesson which was ignored in 1919: if you wish to perpetuate a military victory, you must perpetuate the balance of forces which produced that victory.

The Crimean War was, in short, a war that did not come off, a war without a decision. But that was itself the decision. Though Russian strength was not broken, Russian influence in Europe was lessened. Though French prestige was increased, France did not become dominant in Europe. Napoleon III thought he had freed his hands in order to remodel Italy and Germany to his own taste; it turned out that Italy and Germany had freed their own hands to remodel themselves against him. Cavour and Bismarck, not Napoleon III, were the real victors of the Crimean War. If there were a moral to be drawn from the Crimean War which might apply to the present, it would be this: in a war between Russia and the west, it is the powers which keep out who will be the real gainers. Last time it gave Prussia mastery of Germany.

For the British, the Crimean War, though superficially inconclusive, was less of a disappointment than it was to Napoleon III. They had set out to lessen Russian power; and they had succeeded. Later on, they imagined that they had intended to give Turkey the chance of reforming herself; and were correspondingly embittered when no reform followed. Nevertheless, the Crimean War brought real gains to the British. The balance of power in Europe was strengthened, not overthrown; and Great Britain did not need to intervene in a continental war for sixty years thereafter. Two generations of peace are something to be thankful for; it is more than we have had in our lifetime.

8.

The Myth of Napoleon III

Theodore Zeldin

✤✤✤

EDITORIAL NOTE: *Napoleon III has suffered Guizot's fate and for some of the same reasons. It is difficult to conceive of two more different personalities, but they shared one quality: both were liberal failures. The Liberal Empire, that experiment in plebiscitarian democracy constructed on the wreckage of the revolution of 1848, proved a failure and collapsed unmourned in 1870, a casualty of the Franco-Prussian war. Napoleon was likeable—a gay blade and a good horseman who had some germs of political and social philosophy. But he has never escaped the appellation of the frivolous political adventurer. Napoleon III was in part the victim of his uncle; the great Napoleon had done great things, while he, by contrast, was always* Napoléon le petit. *There was something artificial about the regime from the beginning. When Napoleon III moved into the Tuileries, the staff found that the gold plate had disappeared during the revolutions of 1848. Government economy precluded replacement, so the newly-developed technique of electroplating, so popular among the arriviste bourgeoisie, was employed. It provided the necessary sparkle, but certainly not substance. Like the palace plate, there were liberal representative institutions which also had no meaning. Opinion was regulated, parliament hamstrung. Elections, as in the Orleanist days, were rigged. Plebiscites proclaimed assent but offered no alternatives.*

Ironically for a man attempting to run his state with a public relations approach, Napoleon had a bad press from the start. It was easy to criticize the beaten man at Sedan, but he had always had intelligent critics. Bismarck called him "the sphinx without a secret," and the label has stuck. Charles Seignebos (a republican) and Pierre de la Gorce (a royalist) who wrote the great histories of the period, left permanent scars on the Liberal Empire and the Napoleonic reputation. The rehabilitation of Napoleon III is a relatively recent phenomenon. Students of Napoleonic ideas have found a strikingly modern and convivial ring to his pronounce-

ments. Nor did it escape revisionist notice that the only Frenchman to travel to Napoleon's funeral in exile was a trade union representative. Perhaps, some began to reason, Napoleon had attempted to break through the over-rigid social structure and the violent oscillation in French politics between revolution and reaction. Albert Guérard began the disinterment of the good Napoleon III. Lynn Case, Roger Williams, and Theodore Zeldin have continued the process, but the restoration has not been without challenge. Sir Lewis Namier, with his eye on the twentieth century, called Napoleon III "the first mountebank dictator," and argued a forceful case. A. J. P. Taylor substantially endorsed Bismarck's tart verdict. More recently, Alan Spitzer, while unwilling to go as far as Namier and Taylor, found Napoleon's regime "meretricious." "If the imperial system anticipated any aspect of the twentieth century," he argues, "it is the tendency to conduct foreign affairs as a branch of domestic public relations and to beg many difficult alternatives of policy formulation by doublethink, self-deception, and cant." [1]

Zeldin, who has thoroughly examined the structure and operation of Liberal Empire politics, slights the disastrous, adventuring foreign policy of Napoleon III and concentrates on his domestic achievements. He believes that Napoleon was, among other things, the one man capable of cutting through local hostilities and traditional discord. Only he could have ended (or evaded) the republican-royalist feud. And, Zeldin argues, he was more successful as a Liberal conciliator than most historians acknowledge. Whatever the merits of the argument, Napoleon was destroyed by mistakes in domestic and foreign policy that, whatever one may say in his defense, were of his own making.

"Read no history, nothing but biography, for that is life without theory." So Disraeli once said, but it is not a maxim that can be applied to Napoleon III. His life contained so many adventures, conspiracies and love affairs, his court was so well provided with gossip and intrigue, his career reached such depths and such heights of fortune, that it is no wonder that his biographers have not had time to stop to ask what he achieved as a statesman. They would have been surprised to know that he was, in the opinion of Lamar-

[1] ALAN B. SPITZER, The Good Napoleon III, *French Historical Studies*, II (1962), p. 329.

tine, the greatest politician France had had since Talleyrand, and possibly even greater than he.

It is not from any personal animosity that they refuse to treat him seriously. On the contrary, for it can be said of few, as it can be said of him, that no one who ever knew him detested him or even found him disagreeable. His gift for making friends was quite extraordinary, and even his bitterest enemies concede that he was an amiable man. That, in fact, is how they damn him. He was a pleasant man, they say, with good intentions, no doubt, but with no political gifts and with none of the ability necessary to carry out his grandiose schemes. He was a rake, an adventurer, a dreamer, a charlatan, but nothing like his uncle, of course.

He ended as he began, in exile, and his critics have enjoyed showing that his failure was inevitable. He gradually divested himself of much of his power; and they have assumed that he did so because he was compelled to yield before the growing strength of the opposition, and decided to give up his control of the state in order to retain his throne. His Liberal Empire collapsed after little more than a hundred days; and they have assumed that it was a mere epilogue to his reign and not the consummation of his work. His government did not include the old parliamentary leaders; and they have asserted, therefore, that his supporters were mere nonentities and henchmen. They enjoy quoting the pretty phrase attributed to him: "The empress is legitimist, my cousin is republican, Morny is Orleanist, I am a socialist: the only Bonapartist is Persigny and he is mad"; and from this they conclude that the Second Empire represented nothing but a jumble of second-hand ideas. Some claim that it was established almost accidentally, under the influence of force and excitement, that it had no real roots in the country, and that its motto should have been not "Liberty, Equality and Fraternity" but that given to it by Marx, "Cavalry, Infantry and Artillery."

It is extraordinary how reputations are made and unmade in history. The great achievements of Castlereagh, for example, were condemned to a hundred years of oblivion very largely by the superior wit of his rival Canning and by the famous phrase of Byron; and likewise, under the influence of his royalist successors, Oliver Cromwell was spurned as a bigot and a tyrant for twice that time, until his letters and speeches were published to show what he was really like. In the other direction, it is well known how Napoleon

I looked after his own reputation and how he created the legend
about himself which made his name into a positive political force.
After Waterloo, he became the martyr of St. Helena, whence he
preached the gospel of his own glory, proclaiming the excellence of
his intentions and encouraging posterity to forget everything in his
reign that was not to his credit. His political enemies were in
power for a bare fifteen years. Louis-Philippe erected monuments
to his glory and brought his ashes back to France as those of a
national hero. Napoleon III gave him another twenty years of
official worship, published his correspondence in fifty volumes and
so made it impossible for anyone ever to deny his greatness. His
reputation never had to contend seriously with popular hostility
or ignorance.

Exactly the opposite happened to Napoleon III. His martyrdom
in the fortress of Ham took place before his reign; and though it
helped him to gain his throne, it came too early to influence historical opinion. In 1873 he planned to repeat the return from
Elba, but died before he could do so. The literary world was
largely hostile to him and vilified him as *Napoléon le petit*. The
two best histories of his reign are by a republican and a royalist,
and the French school textbooks have long reflected the views of
his political enemies, who obtained the professorships after his fall.
He has, indeed, never been allowed to speak for himself: his published correspondence barely fills a few volumes and most of it
dates from his early days of exile. There is nothing resembling the
huge series on his uncle to show what he was really like as a ruler.

There has thus grown up a myth about Napoleon III as a sort
of counterpart to the legend about Napoleon I. It began with the
story that he had been elected president because the royalist politicians thought he would be a tool in their hands, a story that they
invented to flatter their own importance. There is, in fact, incon-
trovertible evidence that they supported him because they saw that
he was bound to win; and Thiers, who never erred on the side of
modesty, would have stood himself had he thought he had any
chance at all. The story that he was allowed to take his seat in
parliament in June 1848 because he was considered harmless and
an imbecile is also an invention from the same source. Rumors were
spread that he could not speak French, that his hobby was rearing
eagles in cages, that so conscious was he of his own incompetence
that he had opened negotiations of his own accord to secure the

return of the legitimist pretender. The politicians who met him, however, quickly saw how wide all this propaganda was of the truth. Montalembert, the leader of the liberal Catholics, was much impressed when he first went to see him in October 1848. "I cannot conceive," he noted in his diary, "where his reputation for incompetence comes from."

It is time, therefore, that the abuse of his enemies should be appreciated in its true light and not accepted as impartial history merely because they happened to be distinguished men. What has been said about him should be put aside and an attempt should be made to study the facts and the primary sources. The man, however, cannot be assessed unless his work is also assessed, and that is why biography without history is not enough for him.

His standing as a statesman must depend to a very considerable extent on the way in which the Liberal Empire is interpreted. Napoleon I claimed in exile that his object had always been to establish liberty, and that the Hundred Days were destined to inaugurate a new era of peace and constitutional monarchy. No one has believed him, and quite rightly, for his character and his career made it impossible for him to accomplish such a metamorphosis. Is it right, however, to dismiss the similar claims of Napoleon III? Was he a liberal only in opposition and a despot as soon as he got the reins of power into his own hands?

In truth, he was probably a determined believer in the merits of neither liberalism nor despotism, but an opportunist above all else. He had thought a great deal about the art of success, and he was determined not to repeat the mistakes that had made others, and especially his uncle, fail before him. Politics was for him "the application of history." The task of the statesman was to study history and to discover which of the driving forces in the world had passed forever and which would triumph. Success would come to him who judged correctly which way the wind was blowing and trimmed his sails accordingly; to him who always made sure to lead events and not to be dragged by them. He must represent the aspirations of his epoch; and that is why his flattering courtiers pleased him by saying, "Sire, you are the century."

"In the end," he once declared, "it is always public opinion that wins the last victory." He concluded from his study of history, and in particular from his study of the history of England, the most successful of monarchies, that "It is not chance that determines the destinies of nations; it is not an unforeseen accident that over-throws or maintains thrones. There is a general cause that deter-mines events and makes them follow logically from each other. A government can often violate law and even liberty with impunity, but if it does not put itself openly at the head of the great interests of civilization, it can have only an ephemeral existence." He would always seek to give the French what they wanted.

In 1848 he was, to an extraordinary extent, "the man of the century"; and he did not owe his success simply to the attraction of his name. He represented better than anyone else the French peas-antry, whose hearts were on the left but whose pockets were on the right, who were fond of being "advanced" in theory but who, in the practical conduct of life, sought only the traditional rewards for their labor—property and social advancement for their chil-dren. Similarly, Napoleon was at once conservative and radical, a lover of peace but also a lover of glory, an unbeliever married to a religious wife—a bundle of contradictions, but of the very con-tradictions that were innate in the great majority of his subjects.

He was the only politician of the time who could be conservative without being retrograde. The proclamation of universal suffrage had cast terror into the old parliamentary leaders, who hastened to modify and limit it as soon as they returned to power. Napoleon alone knew how to place himself at the head of such an electorate, to lead it in the direction he chose and so to prove that it could be a perfectly harmless and conservative force. When he fell in 1870, no one could seriously think of abolishing universal suffrage; and this is not the least of his contributions to the development of the institutions of his country.

He consolidated universal suffrage rather in the way that Sir Robert Walpole and the Pelhams had consolidated parliamentary monarchy in England. They had made the king's government work by giving the House of Commons and the gentry what they wanted, by providing pasture enough for all the hungry beasts in politics and by following a policy that was popular with the nation. So likewise Napoleon made his government work by offering the electorate what it wanted, in return for support on matters to which it was indifferent. The centralization of Louis XIV and Napoleon I placed immense power in the hands of the government, and without the approval or initiative of its head very little could be done. Napoleon III argued that the details of politics mattered little to the peasants, and that they did not care whether there were one or two parliaments in Paris or none at all. He thought that what really interested them was how to finance improvements in their daily existence, how to build roads to their farms and railways to their markets, how to bring water to their villages and how to establish local schools for their children, and how, on top of all this, to find the money to maintain their hospitals and their almshouses, to repair their churches and to embellish their village halls. The centralization of the country required the peasants to pay taxes for these very purposes, but they had to send their money to Paris and then to beg it back from the government. The government was willing to help those who helped it. It redistributed the taxes in the form of subsidies to the villages that voted favorably in the elections. It offered part as a bait, just before the elections, and the rest as a reward if the results were satisfactory. It seemed a good bargain to many who cared nothing for politics and hence the unanimous votes which the opposition attributed to force.

A good deal of force and intimidation was, of course, used but not on the great majority of ordinary men. The system was more subtle than that. Napoleon had by far the best organized party in the country, for he had at his disposal the civil service, which now reached the zenith of its prestige and its power. The prefects, enjoying their heyday and reproducing in the provinces the glitter of the imperial court, were not simply administrators but the veritable political leaders of their departments. They gave much time to the task of making converts to Bonapartism, wooing the aristocracy with dinner parties and balls, wooing the bourgeoisie with jobs and favors, wooing above all the masses with the gift and the promise of material benefits. They took the credit for the prosperity that the country enjoyed; and it is largely thanks to them that the Second Empire was afterwards remembered as the good old days when men used to play games with golden coins.

They could speak to almost every peasant in the country through the mayors of the villages, appointed by the government and so invested with all the authority that comes from being an official of a centralized state like France. These mayors presided over the elections in the villages; and they made sure that the people understood the "social contract" of the Second Empire. They did not compel any man to vote for Napoleon or his official candidates, and they did not falsify the returns of unanimous results: they just made it unwise to cast a contrary vote. The system of voting was different from that now used in England. The voter was not presented with a list of candidates and asked to place a cross against one of them. Instead, he was required to put in the box a ballot paper which he had to produce himself, bearing the name of his favorite. These ballot papers were generally supplied by the candidates; but the government had the advantage that it sent the ballot paper of the candidate it supported with the card that entitled an elector to vote. The ignorant, therefore, frequently came to vote with their electoral cards and their government ballot papers, which they put in the box as though they were the only ones that could be used. When some poor peasant came to the village hall with a ballot paper that an opposition agent had given him, the mayor presiding over the box would at once spot it.

"Ah!" he would say. "Haven't you got any other ballot paper apart from that one?"

"Why, yes, Monsieur le Maire."

"Show me."

The elector shows several. The mayor takes the official candidate's and says, "Here, my good man, this is the *good one;* put the others down." Then the mayor puts it into the box. Or he would say, "Put the ballot paper you've got into your pocket and take this one: this is the *good one.*"

Such proceedings took place when the mayor was a paternal figure and the elector a submissive peasant. But sometimes a more arrogant man would march into the voting hall and demand a ballot paper. He is given the official candidate's. He asks for "another one." The mayor says there are no others. The man insists. The mayor gets angry. A row would start and in the end the man would probably be thrown out. Of course, the mayor would receive great sympathy; for was not this desire to vote against his advice a challenge to his authority, a doubt cast upon his knowledge of how administrative business should be transacted? It was for personal reasons, as much as because of their political preferences, that the mayors lost their tempers with organizers of opposition. They looked upon dissent as a personal insult. One mayor, no more pompous than most, thus writes to his prefect: "Yesterday three men traveled over my commune, putting up red posters everywhere in favor of M. Casimir Perier. When I and a gendarme asked them by what right they were putting up notices on the wall of

the town hall without my authorization, they replied in an *impertinent* manner, that they had no need of my authorization."
This was a slur on his dignity and his rage can be imagined.

The mayors had valuable allies in the schoolmasters, who were likewise agents of the state. Here is a report from one of them to show how they acted: "As secretary of the town hall, entrusted in this capacity with the preparation of all the election documents, I was able to exercise far greater influence on the elections. In conjunction with the village constable, I distributed the ballot papers I received from Monsieur le Préfet to the electors. I strongly supported the candidature of M. Arnaud, the government's candidate. I tried to make the electors understand that we must all without exception consolidate the plans of our august emperor by a unanimous vote. Despite this, I was compelled to redouble my zeal and energy owing to the fact that some agitators had led astray a large number of electors and particularly twenty electors at a village not far away, who had been earnestly solicited to vote for M. Dupont Delporte and were completely disposed to vote for the latter and in consequence to reject the government's candidate. Having heard this vexatious news, I went to make them see the error into which they had fallen. To prove to them that the government is good, I gave them knowledge of a letter which Monsieur le Maire of the commune had received from Monsieur le Préfet, in which it is said that a new subsidy of 220,000 francs had just been given to the department to be divided between the communes that had suffered in the floods of 1856. In the presence of this testimony of the solicitude of the government, will you be so ungrateful, I told them, as to refuse it your cooperation: and at once they all threw down the ballot papers that had been given to them and came at once to the town hall to vote for M. Arnaud."

In the course of the reign this system gradually disintegrated, and by 1869 it had pretty well collapsed. Napoleon himself hastened its collapse by his own measures. He found it unsatisfactory despite, and even because of, the almost absolute power that it gave him. One day, talking with the duc de Plaisance of his days as president of the republic, he said regretfully, "Ah! Those were the days!" Plaisance said things did not seem to have worsened for him. "You are quite wrong, my dear duke," replied Napoleon. "At that time it was all life and movement around me; today it is silence. I am isolated, I no longer hear anything." He was expected to do everything himself, but inevitably, in practice, he could not. He had to bear all the responsibility, nevertheless, while his ministers wielded their immense power without adequate control from parliament or from each other. Both he and they soon perceived that such checks were desirable, quite apart from any ideological reasons, simply in the interests of more efficient government. He saw, too, that he could hardly go on preaching liberty to the rulers of Europe when he did not practice it himself. He was getting old, moreover; and yet as things stood, all the achievements of the reign hung on the life of one sick man. He must provide for the future and found institutions that would render his work permanent.

Many of his earliest supporters had no wish to continue with the old system either. They may have been docile enough when he emerged clothed in all the prestige that his immense victories at the plebiscites gave him; but now they thought it was time they should share his power. They could no longer win their elections in their constituencies simply by declaring their loyalty to him, by saying, as did an old veteran of Waterloo, "If you re-elect me, I shall, as before, support the empire and we will repeat together, 'Long Live The Emperor'." They now had to meet the powerful challenge of an opposition which promised all the utopian joys the age could imagine. They could no longer defeat them by the old system; so they had to outdo them at their own game and promise even more, with liberty to crown it. In this way did they become supporters of a Liberal Empire, which was thus created not by the opponents of Napoleon but by his old supporters, converted like him. They had the good fortune to find in Émile Ollivier a leader who had one of the rarest and most elevated minds of his day, and who was able to organize them and to bring their vague ambitions to success.

The Liberal Empire was an attempt to break the vicious circle of revolution and reaction in which France had been caught since Louis XVI. It sought to effect progress without revolution, in the belief that reforms could be obtained only gradually, whereas revolutions, being essentially violent, would never achieve their ends because they inevitably created new problems and brought divisions, emigrations and reaction in their train. It held that France could not turn at once from despotism to parliamentary government; and it established a representative form of government as a first step. It was not muddled thinking that led it to maintain that if France wished to imitate nineteenth-century England, she should first start by copying her neighbor's preliminary institutions of the seventeenth and eighteenth centuries.

It is possible to argue therefore that since Napoleon III tackled, and for a time successfully solved, the most fundamental problem in French politics, he can claim a place among the great statesmen of the century. When the prejudice against him has died down, it will very likely be recognized that he came near to achieving as much in politics as his uncle achieved in administration and in war.

9.

How Success Spoiled the Risorgimento

Raymond Grew

❖❖❖

EDITORIAL NOTE: *The unification of Italy is the textbook example of the victory of European Liberal nationalism. It is ostensibly the exception to Namier's rule about the defeat of liberalism by nationalism in central Europe. In Italy, so the argument runs, liberalism and nationalism proved complementary. The Risorgimento was modest in aim and not excessively bellicose; the resulting Italian state proved socially and institutionally restrained—a worthy stepchild of French and English liberalism. The parliamentarian Cavour succeeded where the rigid doctrinaire Mazzini had failed. What a contrast to the brutal, cynical,* Blut mit Eisen *Bismarck who sought unification by force and mocked representative institutions. These views, like most historical clichés, contain an element of truth; but they are caricatures long since disregarded by serious historians. But the general outlines of the clichés persist principally because the revisions have tended to be limited to personal assessments, not the basic facts in the case. Cavour's image has tarnished but his achievement has not. The publication of his correspondence revealed a cynical diplomat of the Bismarckian stripe baiting the woolly Napoleon III and neatly entrapping the muddleheaded Austrians. More recently Denis Mack Smith has painted a far less tolerant or idealistic Cavour confronting the radical idealist, Garibaldi.*

Raymond Grew, in this highly sophisticated essay, argues that the endless debates between champions of Mazzini or Garibaldi and Cavour tend to confuse, not illuminate, the most important issue. This is a point easily lost in the pageantry of Risorgimento heroics. The leaders of the Risorgimento unwittingly and unconsciously established the future character of unified Italy. The victory of Cavour's Liberal nationalism was too complete. Men of moderate stamp retained control. Radicals and democrats were carefully shunted aside, used where necessary but kept from positions of power. Mass participation in politics was restricted, not

enlarged, by the victory of liberalism. But this all happened in the
warm glow of success. Garibaldi surrendered his idealistic Sicilian
peasants to Cavour's cynical Baron Ricasoli without ever realizing
that he had betrayed them. He thought of Italy while Cavour
thought of the need for moderation.

I

The making of a united Italy is one of the magnificent stories of
the nineteenth century, and hundreds of historians have been
tempted to test their prose in the telling of it. For all of them the
events of 1859 and 1860 are the climax. Here the ideas of at least
half a century, painted in broad, bold strokes, reach fulfillment in
a series of particular events, best depicted in neat and colorful
miniatures. The ideas developed during the Napoleonic experience
lead to the vague yearnings of the Carbonari, the mysticism of
Mazzini, and the practical program of Cavour; they are then expressed in the clash of armies, the clamor in the *piazzas* of a score
of cities, Garibaldi leading his redshirts, and Cavour excitedly
rubbing his hands. Perhaps it is because the story is so good that
the relationship between those ideas and the particular climactic
events of 1859 has been so little explored. A close analysis of their
connection suggests something of crucial significance for all of modern Italian history: no one intended Italy to achieve her unification
in the way she did; no one consciously wanted the political system
of united Italy to be what it became. In those very months of triumph, from April to December 1859, the Risorgimento itself came
to be conceived in new and narrower limits.

It is too easy to see the events of 1859 marching in perfect order
to the rhythmic needs of a narrative. The volunteers streaming
across the Ticino show the growing enthusiasm for unification and
provoke Austria into rash hostility. After an agonizing moment of
uncertainty, war is declared; and the French prove true to their
word. Revolutions then sweep across the Duchies and into the
Romagna, extending the war and displaying a unanimity of popular sentiment that is itself the climax of years of propaganda and
daring. In contrast to those of 1848, however, these revolutions
are bloodless, and they succeed. The provisional governments which
replace the departed dukes then do the work of destiny by sub-
ordinating themselves to the agents of Cavour. Suddenly, hopes are

dashed as the Truce of Villafranca ends the war, providing merely
for the addition of Lombardy to the Piedmontese domains, but
Italy's nationalists remain steadfast. The provisional regimes in
Tuscany, the Duchies, and the Romagna maintain order and
earnestly adopt Piedmontese coinage and tariffs. They hold assemblies where, with happy unanimity, the demand is made for their
annexation by Piedmont. In effect, Europe is presented with a
fait accompli, the accomplishment of rare restraint. The dark
hour of Cavour's resignation has proved to be a new dawn. Northern Italy, save Venice, becomes one country. Cavour's policy has
triumphed after all.

Seen in this light, the political events in Italy from the outbreak
of the war to the end of 1859 are a mere supplement to the drama
of the war itself and a logical extension of Cavour's general policy.
Such a view is not wrong, although it tends inevitably to a somewhat unhistorical tone, but it is inadequate. It treats the Risorgimento as the contagion of a common sentiment rather than as a
multiform political movement concerned with real and important
issues. It misses the point that while skillfully conducting this
campaign Italy's leaders were, without meaning to and certainly
without facing the fact, doing much to determine what the politics
of united Italy would be like. It was during this period of fulfillment that the Risorgimento became a movement which largely
eliminated the masses from participation in politics. So conceived,
it discouraged the discussion of those political questions which
had been its substance. It restricted to a minimum those political
and social changes which had been its promise. Administrative
fiat and dictatorship became the means for making decisions.

The narrowing of popular participation in the movement to
unify Italy began before the war. The volunteers who made their
way to Piedmont that spring provided the greatest demonstration
of Italian political consciousness in ten years. Nearly twenty
thousand had arrived by March;[1] yet the leaders of Piedmont
were never comfortable with this exciting sign of the success of
their policies. They had suggested that those men being con-
scripted into Austrian or local Italian armies come to serve in

[1] The best figure for the number of volunteers from January 15 to March
25 is 19,656 (Comando del Corpo di Stato Maggiore, Ufficio Storico,
La guerra del 1859 per la indipendenza d'Italia, vol. I, *Narrazione.*
Rome, 1910, p. 117).

Piedmont instead, thinking, with somewhat exaggerated realism, that these would be the only ones likely to come. There was, however, a graver reason for that suggestion: those avoiding conscription would be soldiers first and political demonstrators second. Volunteers, in contrast, were notoriously susceptible to infectious ideologies and were likely to be more loyal to Garibaldi than to formal military discipline. Thus the government remained ambivalent in its attitude toward these men, mostly students and not such a motley crew after all,[2] who in increasing numbers slipped across the borders to prove, through the risks they took, their personal courage and their confidence in Piedmont. These and the other reasons, domestic and diplomatic, for the government's hesitance are easily understood. This was a movement that created an atmosphere of chaos. It was one that might easily get out of hand and begin to define its own political goals. It might even produce an unfortunate revolt across the Ticino or in the Duchies.[3] The hesitance those reasons produced meant that the leading state in Italy could not support the demonstration of widespread belief in its leadership, that the opportunity to make a more popular movement of its policy had to be missed, that the war of Italian liberation would be a battle of professional armies, that neither the popularity of Garibaldi nor the political and military potentialities of the thousands ready to rally to him could be effectively used.

[2] Garibaldi, who could at times be quite discerning, was always bothered that there were few peasants and predominantly men of the middle class among his volunteers. See RAFFAELE COLAPIETRA, Intorno al pensiero politico di Garibaldi. *Nuovo rivista storica*, XLIII (1959), 28–29.

[3] For the reasons for favoring conscripts and the general attitude toward them see the letters of La Farina, in effect the government agent in these matters, to Giuseppe Clementi, December 21, 1858 and January 8, 1859 in AUSUNIO FRANCHI, ed., *Epistolario di Giuseppe La Farina*. Milan, 1869 (hereafter cited as "*Epistolario*"), vol. II, pp. 96, 110; La Farina to Mazzi, January 29, 1859 (manuscript in the Instituto per la Storia del Risorgimento, Rome, busta 110, n. 22), the relevant passages of which are omitted by Franchi. La Farina's letters to Leonzio Armelonghi, January 3; to Bolognini, January 13 and 30; and to Ermano Barigozzi, January 18 (*Epistolario*, vol. II, pp. 107, 114, 125, 117) also deal with these matters. The *Piccolo corriere* had taken a formal stand on the question of volunteers in the issues of January 3 and 17, 1859. The danger of undisciplined troops had been argued, and led to many protests, in the July 28, 1858 issue. For the fear of this activity leading to revolution, see especially La Farina's letters to Giacomo Medici, January 1, 1859, and to Bolognini, January 30, *Epistolario*, vol. II, pp. 109, 125.

The same sort of fear prevented the moderates from advocating local insurrections in the spring of 1859. The war plans of the previous year had included local revolts both as the war's justification and as a device for extending it outside Lombardy. Yet these plans, so precise in 1858, became increasingly vague as the time came to use them. The National Society, which still thought of itself as the agent of revolution, shared all of Cavour's concern that revolt might break out too soon, either fail or spread too far, endanger the diplomatic security of Piedmont or allow more radical forces to triumph locally and then use their position to modify Piedmont's. When at last the National Society issued the call to revolt, it was muffled and faint. The moderates had turned from revolution; they preferred to have Italy's fortunes decided with the more limited risks of battle.[4]

No real revolution occurred in Italy in 1859, no popular participation in government as in 1848. The revolt in Milan was a calm transference of powers, directed in part by an agent of Cavour immediately after the departure of the Austrians.[5] A revolution might have taken place in Tuscany if the grand duke had not left before anything more serious than a demonstration was necessary. Again an ambassador of Cavour, Carlo Boncompagni, and the Tuscan moderates kept things well in hand so that the complications of unneeded enthusiasm were avoided. In Modena and the Romagna, too, the nationalists rose only as

[4] For a sample of the National Society's attempts to explain its lack of instructions and its own inaction, see *Epistolario*, vol. II, pp. 117–26, 137, 143. Vincenzo Salvagnoli was typical when he had argued that if Europe left Italy to solve her problems alone, reliance would be placed on revolution, which, he warned, might become general (VINCENZO SALVAGNOLI, *Della indipendenza d'Italia*. Florence, 1859, pp. 56–58). Or see the letter of Marco Minghetti to Giovanni Malvezzi, April 29, 1859 (ALDOBRANDINO MALVEZZI, *Intorno alla origine della lega dell'Italia Centrale nel 1859*. *Rassegna storica del Risorgimento* [RSR], XLV, fasc. 3 [July–September 1958], 380). Alfredo Oriani (*La lotta political in Italia*. Vol. II, Bologna, 1943, p. 345) notes that the enthusiasm for Piedmont had come to cover the abdication of enthusiasm for revolution. Even Viscount Arthur de La Guerronière had distinguished between subversive and national revolutions in his *Napoleon III et l'Italie*. Paris, 1859. The plans for a revolution in Venetia seem not to have been abandoned until after Villafranca, however (Luigi Carlo Farini to La Farina, July 15, 1859, *Epistolario*, vol. II, p. 189).

[5] DOMENICO DEMARCO, *Le "Assemblee Nazionali" e l'idea di costituente alla dimane del 1859*. Florence, 1947, pp. 34–35. Cesare Giulini was the agent. He arrived June 4; the "revolt" was June 5.

the Austrians left. Marco Minghetti, who was one of those closest to Cavour, had seen such cautious waiting as a means whereby the Romagna could avoid the "political question," a strange goal for a revolution. These were rather coups d'état, and, in contrast to the National Society's premature attempt in Parma, they relied on the proximity of Piedmontese troops. Minghetti was relieved that his country's future would now be "the necessary consequence of great happenings" and "no longer the work of any party." [6] Politics as the public discussion of the form and methods of government was to be avoided.

In each town a faint legality was maintained, as the existing city council appointed a provisional government of moderate nationalists.[7] The provisional governments tended to see their function as an extension of diplomacy. They were to do what Piedmont alone dared not: replace the previous government and then hand their authority to Victor Emmanuel. Thus any opposition, diplomatic or domestic, was faced with that surest of political weapons, the accomplished fact. Wherever possible the treaties of 1848 were re-invoked,[8] and with little concern for the legality of their mandate the provisional governments then handed the full powers they claimed to a commissioner of Piedmont. Usually within a week an agent of Cavour exercised the full political power of the province.[9] And Cavour's followers, in or out of office, tended to

[6] Minghetti to Malvezzi, May 6, 1859, in GIOVANNI MALVEZZI, Origine della Lega. *RSR*, XLV, 38–81. The local committee in Parma took over from the regency which Maria Luisa had established on the day the committee was formed, May 1. When, on May 3, her army declared its loyalty to the duchess, the regency returned to power. She left again on June 9, and a new committee was appointed. At no time was there any serious disturbance.

[7] Milan, June 5, DEMARCO, p. 40; *Le assemblee del Risorgimento.* Rome, 1911, vol. I, p. 46. Florence, April 27, *ibid.,* vol. III, p. 622. Modena, June 13, *ibid.,* vol. I, p. 513. In Modena the *municipio* actually ruled, having taken over from the regency. Massa and Carrara, April 27–28, had something of a bloodless revolution with fewer of the legal formalities preserved. Parma and Piacenza, June 10, *ibid.,* pp. 647–49. Bologna, June 12, where the councils had some wider popular support, *ibid.,* p. 351.

[8] In Lombardy and Parma; in Modena too, although the movement there tended quickly to go beyond the precedents of 1848.

[9] The *congregazione* of Milan simply declared itself "l'interprete naturale de suoi concittadini nelle circostanze straordinarie" (proclamation of June 5, *Le assemblee,* vol. I, p. 263). Count Belgioioso replaced the former *podesta* and Giulini was added to the *congregazione;* Victor Emmanuel accepted protection of the province on June 8, three days after the

accept in the name of freedom the gravest restrictions on its practice. They could, like a group about to found a newspaper in Tuscany, volunteer for censorship believing that there would come "a time of free discussions";[10] and they expected a similar "sacrifice" from their more radical opponents. It is not surprising that under the new dispensation radicals and Mazzinians found they had no more rights in theory and perhaps fewer in practice, partly because the efficient men of the new government knew so well who the Mazzinians were.[11]

But when the talk of the political and social changes which the Risorgimento must bring about had lessened, so did the pressure for reform. After their patriotic addresses to Victor Emmanuel and their somewhat fawning ones to Napoleon III, the provisional governments had made it a point to make few changes. The exigencies of war supported their own political desire to avoid

"revolt" (ibid., pp. 263–65). In Modena Luigi Zini, as "commissario straordinario" with the Piedmontese troops was added to the municipal government on June 15, on its second day of power. He called in the Piedmontese troops. Farini, named by Cavour the same day, took over power on the 19th (ibid., pp. 514–17). In Parma Pallieri took over the reins of power on June 17, exactly one week after Maria Luisa's departure (ibid., pp. 646–52). In Tuscany and the Romagna the process took longer. Victor Emmanuel accepted the protection of Tuscany on April 30, three days after the revolt; but Boncompagni did not really begin his duties until May 11 (ibid., vol. III, pp. 632–35). In the interim, however, even the consulta went surprisingly unused (DEMARCO, p. 56). D'Azeglio did not arrive in Bologna until July 11, a month after the change of governments there; he was granted full powers three days later (Le assemblee, vol. I, pp. 291–92).

[10] When Leopoldo Cempini, Carlo Fenzi, and Piero Puccioni wrote Ricasoli, July 5, 1859, asking permission to found La Nazione, they made this comment after promising not to embarrass the government and offering "di sottoporci a quelle misure di previdenza che il Governo crederà opportuno di stabilire" (MARCO NOBILE and SERGIO CAMERANI, eds., Carteggi di Bettino Ricasoli. vol. VIII, Florence, 1952, p. 292). La Farina even believed that the National Society had been banned in Tuscany (La Farina to Ricasoli, January 1, 1860, in MARCO TABARRINI and AURELIO GOTTI, eds., Lettere e documenti del Barone Bettino Ricasoli. vol. IV, Florence, 1888, p. 133).

[11] The complaints of arrests in ANGELO BROFFERIO, I miei tempi. Turin, 1860, vol. XIII, pp. 285–307, vol. XIV, pp. 1–129, are famous. Primo Uccellini (Memorie di un vecchio carbonaro ravegnano. Rome, 1898, p. 112) tells of the uniting of the Mazzinians and the National Society in Ravenna and how, after he had refused to join his fellow Mazzinians in this, "Vittorio Emanuele Re d'Italia" was written on his house, the provisional government pursued him, and the new police chief, a former Mazzinian and friend, made things difficult for him.

controversy, and the provisional government of Tuscany spoke for them all when it declared that any reordering of institutions should be postponed until the "great enterprise is completed." Such postponement ran the risk, of course, of becoming permanent; but to men determined to avoid the errors of 1848 it appeared a "sacred duty" to avoid "untimely innovations." [12] The provisional government in Milan had shown its doctrinal liberalism by abolishing the death penalty, declaring the civil equality of Jews, and allowing political exiles to return.[13] The *giunta* in Bologna did these things, too, and even reduced tariffs and adopted the Napoleonic Code while demonstrating its reliable hardheadedness by prohibiting all newspapers and political writings from its first day in power. Yet the old bureaucracy was maintained, and the police little altered. Indeed, it had to be explained to the public by proclamation that these institutions of former repression had, with few changes even in personnel, now become trustworthy.[14] Except for such brief flurries of activity, the Piedmontese commissioners found themselves presented with full powers essentially unlimited by the preceding acts of the provisional governments; and Cavour's men, Boncompagni, Luigi Carlo Farini, Diodato Pallieri, and Massimo d'Azeglio, made appointments to major administrative posts and picked their own advisers with surprisingly little regard for those who had so happily handed the reins to them. When the provisional governments dissolved, the moderates of daring quickly gave way to still milder moderates of greater respectability.

[12] Proclamation of April 28, 1859, *Le assemblee,* vol. III, p. 623. This had been a moderate principle. See SALVAGNOLI, p. 80.

[13] DEMARCO, p. 40.

[14] *Le assemblee,* vol. I, pp. 373–74. The ban on newspapers (and the establishment of the official *Monitore di Bologna* to "illuminate citizens") was announced on June 13. The magistrates and all employees were confirmed in their offices the same day. The *gendarmeria* was dissolved but the *veliti* announced on June 14 was made up of the same men after they had taken an oath to the new government. The reassurances about them were published June 14 and 28. The busy government did not get around to freeing political prisoners until June 21, although it did declare a modest dole to families deprived of their support by absent soldiers (of 30 baiocchi or about ⅓ lire per family) (Collection of proclamations, edicts, and documents concerning Italy with special emphasis on Bologna, 130 vols., in the library of the Harvard Law School. Only some of these are reprinted in *Raccolta degli atti governativi pubblicati nelle provincie delle romagne e del Emilia dal 12 giugno 1859 al marzo 1860.* Bologna, 1860). Tuscany also emphasized modestly increased programs of public works (proclamation of Ricasoli, n.d., in *Le assemblee,* vol. III, p. 642).

The changes they tended to institute were not those evoked by visions of a better society but those which resulted from administrative need. The extensive authority given the commissioners had a precedent in the granting of dictatorship to Victor Emmanuel, a step which had on all sides been regarded as essential, so much so that to suggest constitutional guarantees in the interim seemed an affront to the *Re Galantuomo*.[15] This authority came to be wielded by others who, in his name and with doubtful constitutionality, limited the freedom of the press, applied the penal code, prorogued parliament, levied tariffs and taxes.[16] It is a tribute to the probity of these provincial dictators that this power was not more seriously misused. But the constitutional precedents were dangerous, and the procedures used were often unfortunate. Piedmontese laws were extended by fiat without either theoretical concern for their merits or careful study of local conditions. It was in Lombardy that the processes of bureaucracy first began to deal (as they would later in the rest of Italy) with some of the crucial issues no assembly had discussed. The Piedmontese court system was extended there by decree; the new penal code, with its dangerously complex clauses on religious liberty, was announced, and the limited local government to be allowed in Lombardy was defined.[17] Even these laws were often violated in practice, and the new Italian state experienced from the first some of the censorship and arbitrary imprisonment that had been familiar under other regimes. But the pattern for Italy's administration was set. It

[15] The National Society had long agreed on and propagandized for the necessity of Victor Emmanuel's dictatorship without limitations. Garibaldi felt much the same way (CARLO TIVARONI, Garibaldi e la dottrina della dittatura. *Rivista del Risorgimento italiano,* vol. II [1897], pp. 668–71).
[16] TEODOSIO MARCHI, *Le Luogotenenze Generali, 1848–1915, nel diritto costituzionale italiano.* Rome, 1918, pp. 39–42, 67–68. Marchi notes the significant fact that such procedures were never questioned in parliament (*ibid.,* p. 69).
[17] This took place, of course, while the Piedmontese parliament was prorogued. The court system was modified in decrees of July to October. The measures of local government, announced on October 23, providing for taxpayer suffrage for councils but an appointed *podestà,* caused some resentment in Lombardy. The penal code, whose provisions limiting the right of imprisonment were nevertheless violated, prohibited the clergy from "turbamenti" of public conscience and the peace of the family (GAETANO ARANGIO RUIZ, *Storia costituzionale del Regno d'Italia, 1848–1898.* Florence, 1898, pp. 115–18; ALBERTO AQUARONE, *L'unificazione, legislativa e i codici del 1865.* Milan, 1960, pp. 3–4, 9–19).

would be highly centralized and ruled by Piedmontese codes which protected liberty with few fundamental guarantees.

After the truce at Villafranca, these regimes were no longer directly supported by the power of Piedmont, and the commissioners turned their authority over to the local leaders with whom they had been working.[18] These provincial governments then had to secure a popular sanction, and soon each of them followed Farini's lead from Modena in calling for elections to provincial "national assemblies." The suffrage, which varied in the different provinces, was announced by decree. With some pride it was usually added that the elections would in fact be free, although Baron Bettino Ricasoli included the warning that those who dared disturb the concord of Tuscans would be punished. Prefects were instructed to take a "beneficent initiative" in the naming of candidates in order that the election would not be "pre-empted by parties," and to encourage the political dominance of reliable citizens. Still, the prefects were expected to act at least with decorum; and the voting appears not to have been outrageously rigged.[19]

When they met, the provincial assemblies showed the implications of politics which narrowed the popular participation in Italy's

---

[18] Farini resigned on July 27 but accepted the dictatorship again the next day from the *municipio* of Modena (*Le assemblee,* vol. I, pp. 518–20). D'Azeglio resigned on July 29, and the *giunta* named Leonetto Cipriani to replace him on August 1 (*ibid.,* pp. 293–95). Boncompagni resigned August 1, leaving the government under Ricasoli as president of the council, a post to which Boncompagni had named him (*ibid.,* vol. III, pp. 652–53). Pallieri resigned August 8, turning power over to Giuseppe Manfredi (*ibid.,* vol. I, pp. 653–54).

[19] Istruzione intorno alle prossime elezioni, Aug. 8, 1859, by Giuseppe Montanari (*ibid.,* p. 362). There could not be, he argued, any divisions by class or party where the *generalità* wanted a free and national government. Still, he expected his intendants to direct the organization of electoral committees and to cooperate with reliable citizens in preparing for the elections, but he carefully said that the government did not mean that men of "partiti estremi" should be excluded. Ricasoli boasted of the freedom that would be allowed in Tuscany in the proclamation of August 4 (*ibid.,* vol. III, pp. 655–56); but Demarco (p. 53), says it was made clear that supporters of the house of Lorraine should not run. Essentially, universal suffrage was allowed everywhere but in Tuscany, where the laws of 1848 were applied, although according to Demarco there was an effort to restrict the right to vote to those who would have been able to vote according to the tax rates of 1848, but this was not consistently carried out (pp. 53, 63).

unification, eschewed (and often prevented) political discussion, ignored the aspirations for reform, and depended so heavily on administrative fiat. The records of those assemblies, which provide an insight into the attitudes of the men so earnestly pursuing Cavourian policies, have been largely neglected by historians. They reveal that those conventions were deliberative bodies only in form.

Despite the hint of democratic aspirations in their titles, these national assemblies were notable for their abnegation. Each of them declared the downfall of the old regime after minimal discussion and by a unanimous vote. But they treated those regimes as if they had abdicated rather than as if they had been overthrown and pictured themselves as preventing anarchy rather than making a revolution. The somewhat miscellaneous lists of their former rulers' failings which were drawn up in the assemblies avoided any theoretical justification for the most important and permanent political change in modern Italian history. The assemblies chose Victor Emmanuel to be their king and maintained the interim regimes; but impressed, as astute men were bound to be, with the role of foreign affairs in determining Italy's fate, they conducted themselves like diplomats rather than legislators (thus the excessive encomiums of Louis Napoleon). They were carrying out a demonstration rather than fulfilling a natural right. They therefore expected unanimous votes. And nearly every vote, whether secret or open, was unanimous; indeed, the favorite argument for voting secretly was that this would make a better demonstration, while without such secrecy a negative vote might be recorded by mistake. Only in Tuscany and Parma was there ever anything approaching debate.[20] Yet in Tuscany, where regional pride was strong, so

---

[20] Not many, however, went so far as Manfredi in praise of Louis Napoleon; he saw that the Risorgimento in accepting Victor Emmanuel was catching up with France, which had shown the post-republican stage of politics in turning to the emperor (manifesto of August 8, *Le assemblee,* vol. I, p. 654). A typical demand for unanimity is Gioacchino Rasponi's statement as *relatore* in the Romagna assembly for the bill declaring Victor Emmanuel their king on September 7 (*ibid.,* p. 393). The arguments for secrecy were most fully developed in Parma and Piacenza (*ibid.,* pp. 716–17). An exception was Tuscany, where the vote for union with Piedmont was 164 to 1. In the second session of these assemblies, called to vote for the regency of the Prince of Carignano, the vote on proroguing the assemblies got some opposition, 60 to 7 in Parma, 11 to 5 in the Romagna. Parma actually voted down one proposal from the floor but for essentially technical reasons; there were everywhere some mild procedural disagreements. The Romagna resolutions came close

important a question as whether the new Italian state should be a federation was dismissed as "too vast, too complex, and . . . too academic, to be unfolded before this Assembly." In Parma the Piedmontese *Statuto* was adopted with no discussion of its merits.[21]

This is what the emphasis on "concord" was coming to mean; Farini made it clear in his address to the assemblies in Modena and Parma. "Concord," he said, "has been until now our greatest strength, but this concord is composed of elements which, united in their ultimate and highest end, are nevertheless diverse by their nature." It was, he implied, only the pressure of European politics which had kept such diversity from flying apart (he was becoming grateful for the limitations of circumstance). With disarming clarity he added that the great difficulty had been for so long a time to hold their movement within the "limits traced by cold reason of state." [22] It was the importance of maintaining just those limits that D'Azeglio had in mind when he declared, on taking charge in Bologna: "If you know how to obey, you will know how to fight and win." He added that discipline and order had no roots where discords flamed. And when he departed, he warned the Romagnols: "One single danger menaces you: discord and disorder." [23] In all the assemblies, the deputies frequently asserted that they were not revolutionaries. They said that not merely to put the British and French at ease; they were reassuring themselves. They sensed that they wanted little change; they knew that by limiting discussion they would be safer from the dangers both

---

to implying natural rights (see especially the proclamation of July 22, *ibid.*, p. 357, and the *relazioni, ibid.*, pp. 355–93). In Modena a biblical precedent was cited for the right to decide, popularly, the form of government (see *relazione* of Lucchi, *ibid.*, p. 542). There was usually some general talk of the evils of despotism, Italy's destiny as a nation, and the obligations to Piedmont (*ibid.*, pp. 641, 644-45, 693-703). Following the French system, proposals were first discussed in the half-dozen *uffici* to which the representatives were assigned by lot. There may have been some fairly free (and unrecorded) discussion here although it is likely that the dominance of the prominent men who were also the friends of those in power was at least as great in the smaller groups.
[21] Giovanni Battista Giorgini, as *relatore* in the Tuscan assembly of the bill for accepting Victor Emmanuel, August 20 (*ibid.*, vol. III, p. 694). Significantly, this is the only assembly in which the question was raised. Tuscany, however, adopted the *Statuto* with an ambiguous reservation protecting her peculiar institutions (*ibid.*, p. 747).
[22] Farini's address of November 7. The same one was given to the Modena and the Parma assemblies (*ibid.*, vol. I, pp. 567, 760).
[23] Proclamations of D'Azeglio of July 11 and 28 (*ibid.*, pp. 355, 359).

of change and of dissension. Faced with nearly all the major issues
of nineteenth-century politics at once, they hoped to postpone the
controversial ones.

II

The manner and tone of the politics of a united Italy were being
determined, but the followers of Cavour who dominated those
politics in 1859 took pride in being pragmatists. If in a sequence
of crises their practices whittled away at their own liberal vision
of the Risorgimento, they were scarcely aware of it. The inter-
action of ideas and events is always subtle, but the effect of that
subtlety in this case is easily overlooked because the methods employed by Cavour's followers and the political system they created
are, when seen with hindsight, so easily explained by calling these
men "moderates." In this period the term was usually reserved
for those like Cavour, Minghetti, Farina, Ricasoli, or perhaps
D'Azeglio, who by the 1850's had come to dominate Italian politics
—for those who were politically influential, decently nationalist,
and loyally monarchist.

Often members of the aristocracy or at least men who could
move with ease in such circles, these followers of Cavour had
become reformers in the Enlightenment tradition of scientific
societies and agricultural associations. They had discovered, like
Cavour, that successful pig farming required political reform.[24]
Often they had, like Minghetti with Pius IX, tried to work within
the old regimes. Finding themselves stifled there, and touched by
the Mazzinian dream, they came to think in more than provincial
terms. Yet they felt a deep distaste for revolution, and it was easy
for them to lead Italians in learning from the failures of 1848.
They found a pattern for reform without revolution in the contemporary history of England and France, models made natural
for them by their own international connections. Thus the moderates tended to advocate representative institutions while remaining
suspicious of politics and contemptuous of parties, for they had
learned from Antonio Rosmini that parties are "worms which de-
vour the fabric of society." [25] They adopted liberal economic theory

[24] Cited in KENT ROBERTS GREENFIELD, The man who made Italy, in *Studi
in onore di Gino Luzzatto*. Milan, 1950, vol. III, p. 185.
[25] Even in 1858 the National Society had begun to extend its attacks on
"sects" to parties. The moderates' suspicions of political parties had deep
roots. See LUIGI SALVATORELLI, *Il Pensiero politico italiano*. Turin, 1949,

and believed in the importance and inevitability of economic growth. Here they most directly appealed to Italy's small middle class of merchants and lawyers. Combining a respect for the traditional institutions of power (such as the monarchy and the military) with demands for change, they easily adopted the tone of realism and naturally shared the fears of a Lord Malmesbury.[26]

Finally, they were compromisers who were keenly aware of the weakness of their position; for compromise, as a principle, makes the dullest of political programs. Mazzini could fail and maintain a following. The moderates were certain they must succeed in winning much of what the nationalists wanted whenever they had the chance or lose their dominance. That conviction both stimulated their courage and increased their caution. It explains Cavour's panic that the war might not begin in April and his famous loss of temper on learning the news of Villafranca. These displays of emotion were not, as often interpreted, merely signs of an uncharacteristic flaw or uncontrolled patriotism. For the moment Cavour's policy had failed, and out of Mazzini's steady flow of prognostications, dire and utopian, the warnings against an alliance with France stood out as apparently proved. Yet the Cavourian policy did not collapse, and the Risorgimento contains no greater testimonial to the sagacity of the moderates than their conduct of Italian affairs in the months following Villafranca.

The moderates thought of themselves as liberal as well as nationalist, but the methods they employed in 1859 had done much to make a liberal state less likely. Like their ideological cousins elsewhere in Europe, Italian moderates had run too far from the

---

pp. 304, 114, 234, 333–34, on the distaste for parties in the thought of Cesare Balbo, Vincenzo Gioberti, Rosmini, and Cavour. For Cavour's own parliamentary practices prior to this period see D. MACK SMITH, Cavour and Parliament. *Cambridge Historical Journal*, XIII (1957), 37–57. Minghetti, who cites Rosmini in his wise book, *I partiti politici e la ingerenza loro nella giustizia e nell' amministrazione*. Bologna, 1881, pp. 188–89, takes 200 pages to find the justification for parties only in the inevitable differences on utility in politics. He did not allow for disagreement on anything more fundamental and hoped even then that the "progress of science and civilization would restrict the circle of parties and attenuate dissension" (*ibid.*, p. 216).

[28] Malmesbury wrote Sir James Hudson, January 13, 1859: "In a war so begun the republicans of every possible hue, the dreamers of every impractical theory, the exiled pretenders to thrones, and all, in short, who seek revenge, gain or power, will expect to find their account" (Earl of Malmesbury, *Official Correspondence on the Italian Question*. London, 1859, p. 15).

failures of 1848. Determined to avoid fatal political divisions, they had sought unanimity less through agreement than by postponing all "lesser" issues, all questions but unification.[27] Postponement in practice proved to be decision without discussion. Determined this time to succeed, they had stressed the military virtues of discipline and order. The very concepts of unification and liberty had been vigorously and deliberately separated as distinct issues unnecessarily cumbersome when taken together.[28]

Only a program which took advantage of the ambitions of Piedmont, the aims of the lower middle class, and the discontents of the lower middle and artisan classes could have won widespread support. Only one with which Louis Napoleon could associate himself and which Great Britain could accept was likely to succeed. The moderates, with only occasional slips, provided that program. To do so, however, they expressed ideas which were the critique of the policies they pursued. They sounded like Gladstone but performed like Guizot. Confident there was a law of progress, the moderates believed they had opened Italy to its beneficial effects. They could rely on time to correct their omissions.

The moderates' policies in these exciting months of 1859 are important to historical understanding, then, for a number of reasons. Those policies succeeded, and they established the kind of political system under which united Italy operated: a highly centralized state dominated by the bureaucracy with effective power limited to a small group of men with similar backgrounds and interests. Those policies are important, too, precisely because what the moderates did was not what they had advocated. To

[27] The necessity for the postponement of issues other than unification was a cardinal point in the doctrine of the Italian National Society, but it was a theme of Mazzini, too. Even in 1861 he said he would look to the founding of a sort of legal aid society "to defend individual liberty" if it were not for the absence of Venice and Rome from the Italian union (Mazzini to Andrea Gianelli, *Scritti di Mazzini*, vol. LXXI, Imola, 1935, p. 19).

[28] The National Society consistently insisted on this separation. Salvagnoli wrote (*Indipendenza d'Italia,* p. 21) : "Non si confonda la questione della indipendenza con quella della cultura e della libertà." Garibaldi agreed that unification was more important (*Edizione nazionale degli scritti di Giuseppe Garibaldi,* III, *I Mille.* Bologna, 1933, p. 222). The dangers of such a separation are especially clear in the futurist and fascist, F. T. Marinetti, who declared: ". . . oggi più che mai la parola 'Italia' deve dominare sulla parola 'Libertà'" (proclamation to Italian students, November 29, 1914, republished in his *Futurismo e fascismo.* Foligno, 1924, p. 97).

begin with, a great deal about the kind of Risorgimento they would direct had not been determined by the spring of 1859. The moderates themselves did not know whether the war would extend to the Papal States, Sicily, or even to Tuscany; there was little deliberation about the role revolutions might play. Even the old hope for something like a constituent assembly to follow a successful war had not been clearly rejected. As enemies of Mazzini, the moderates had denounced his tactics and condemned his means; but they had not, even in their own thinking, altogether divorced themselves from his vision of the future. In August Farini could still insist that a united Italy would not be centralized *alla francese,*[29] and Minghetti years later would not understand the impossibility of fulfilling that promise.

More important, the moderates were both deeply nationalist and devoted to the concept of parliamentarism. The very assemblies which so avoided debate had medals struck for the men who had volunteered and monuments built to commemorate the actions of the populace.[30] Perhaps it was the implications of social unity within nationalism which the moderates understood best, but they did not shun the suggestion of domestic freedom which was part of the meaning of independence. The moderates were fond of the word "liberty," and they had freely promised it as the fruit of their labors. For them a national parliament was the very symbol of unification; justice through law was the highest achievement of the state. In the chamber of deputies or in the various assemblies they expected their representative institutions to be treated with respect, and they took delight in parliamentary procedures.[31] They

[29] *Il Piccolo corriere d'Italia,* August 26, 1859.

[30] In Modena and Reggio they were formally declared "benemeriti" of the *patria,* August 23, 1859 (*Le assemblee,* vol. I, p. 557). In Parma and Piacenza a medal was struck in their honor while it was carefully insisted that they had gone spontaneously and not at the prodding of local committees. See the comments of Guido Della Rosa, *relatore* of the bill, September 12, 1859 (*ibid.,* pp. 709–11). The provisional *giunta* of Bologna, in its June 28 address to Napoleon III, boasted of the "spontaneity of sacrifice" shown by the volunteers (*ibid.,* p. 353). The *consiglio* of Milan argued, in its proclamation of June 8, that the vote for annexation had already been made by thousands of volunteers (*ibid.,* p. 264). The Tuscan praise of their volunteers took place in the session of November 7 (*ibid.,* vol. III, pp. 728–29).

[31] ALBERTO CARACCIOLO, *Il parlamento nella formazione del Regno d'Italia.* Milan, 1960, pp. 9, 20, 40–41, 52–53; DOMENICO ZANICHELLI, *Studi di storia costituzionale e politica del Risorgimento italiano.* Bologna, 1900, p. 27. An excellent example of the moderates' attitude on these questions is the

espoused liberal economic theories which implied social changes
that, in the Italy of the 1850's, were in fact revolutionary. Their
deviations from such programs they saw only as the result of
practical necessity. But their very practicality made it difficult for
them to see how far they had strayed from such abstract standards
and made it impossible for them to understand the charge that
they had moved always in the direction of their immediate class
interests.

This is why to their opponents the moderates seemed cynical,
and why the charge of bad faith added such anguish to Italian
political disputes. When Garibaldi resigned from the army in the
autumn of 1859, the conflicts in political views so long suppressed
or ignored began to appear. Enforced inactivity had proved too
much for him, and, with public bitterness, he destroyed the illusion
that Italian nationalists were happily cooperating. Yet Garibaldi
had been too much influenced by the cry for "concord" to assume
a clear political position. He expressed, rather, his frustrated
activism and the dangerous contempt for politics which often
marked his views, allowing himself to be used by a political opposition with clearer goals.[32] The moderates, on the other hand (especially with Cavour out of office), did not realize how secure their

---

ponderous work by PIETRO CASTIGLIONI, *Della monarchia parlamentare e
dei diritti e doveri del cittadino secondo lo statuto e le leggi del Piemonte*.
2 vols., Milan, 1859. A loyal Cavourian, Castiglioni accepts all the restrictions on liberty of recent practice and Piedmontese law; yet he insists on
arguing for the necessity of such limits in the categories of the purest
liberalism.

[32] Thus COLAPIETRA, Pensiero politico di Garibaldi. *Nuova rivista storica*,
XLIII (1959), 30, says he was "imborghesito" in the Piedmontese army
and notes (*ibid.*, p. 9) his "peasant" distrust of parliament. Always an
advocate of dictatorship in times of crisis, he felt that deputies, at the
mercy of their electors, lacked courage and merely reflected the corruption
of society (see his letter to Marcel l'Allemand, December 3, 1869, cited in
TIVARONI, Garibaldi e la dittatura. *Rivista storica italiana*, II, 671). Like
the moderates, he distrusted parties (*Le memorie di Garibaldi*. Bologna,
1932, pp. 402–03). Significantly, the specific issue which led to Garibaldi's
public break with the moderates was the use of the largely volunteer army
in the Romagna (see GIUSEPPE MAZZATINTI, Contributo alla storia del
1859. *Achivio storico del Risorgimento umbro*, I [1905], 74–77; and
ALESSANDRO ALESSANDRINI, *I fatti politici delle Marche*. Macerata, 1910,
vol. II, pp. 26–27). He had learned, at last, that the government, even
of Rattazzi (and despite his friendship with Victor Emmanuel) would
not allow action independent of it regardless of the loyalty of the actors.
He had forgotten the lesson by the time of Aspromonte and his Roman
ventures.

position was. Having for long tended to see parties as a manifestation of the selfishness of their opponents, they reacted with anger instead of the generous tolerance their position justified. The split between the National Society and the *Liberi Comizii* and between Cavour and Garibaldi became bitter, deep, and open.

As eminently practical men, the moderates reflected with some sensitivity the political pressures of their time. Their policy was formed by the nature of the domestic as well as the diplomatic scene. And this makes an understanding of what the moderates did of further importance to the historian. They did not distort the truth when they acted as if the middle class was weak and assumed that there was no clear popular pressure for any specific program opposed to theirs. Indeed, they were probably right in viewing themselves as the only ones capable of unifying Italy. Even their convinced opponents found it difficult to make a clear and politically effective critique of their policy. With all their skill Angelo Brofferio and Agostino Bertani could not. They sensed that Cavourian policies were stranding the nationalists of the left with no alternative but to acquiesce in the moderates' triumph or withdraw from politics. By the autumn of 1859, they were indignant but frustrated. They tended to share the moderates' impatience with "detail" which prevented a careful formulation of alternative policies, and they made their criticism in terms of moral categories which could too easily be made to seem unconnected with political reality. Most enfeebling of all, these opponents of Cavour were themselves impressed by success. Despite their sincerity, they betrayed the poverty of their position as they returned again and again to an ill-defined mystique of revolution.[33]

[33] Bertani maintained a similar viewpoint in his insistence that all might be different if only Sicily had remained independent a bit longer (*Della opposizione parlamentare*. Milan, 1865, p. 19). Even Mazzini did no better in his hope first that the provisional governments would stay independent of Piedmont and then that they would prepare for revolution (as if Piedmont had refused their requests for annexation) (GIUSEPPE MAZZINI, Il moto italiano. *Scritti editi ed inediti di Giuseppe Mazzini*, vol. LXIV, Imola, 1932, pp. 114, 117–18). His promise that they could thus save Italy, or at least their own honor, was poor politics (*ibid.,* p. 119). For a picture of even the doctrinaire Mazzini disarmed by Cavour's success from making any but a faint tactical and moral complaint, see his, I due programme. *ibid.,* vol. LXVI, Imola, 1933, pp. 74–80. In his Delenda Carthago, published January 1, 1860, he says that the provinces should unite with Piedmont only on condition that the latter pursue the national cause, which had been Daniele Manin's position in 1856.

Finally, taken all together, these policies the moderates so practically pursued during the triumphant months of 1859 played their part in much of subsequent Italian history. The way in which Italy was united left a dull, persistent ache in the Italian body politic. The exclusion from politics of most Italians was part of that legacy. Garibaldi came to represent the participation through direct action of those who had been left out. It was this which made him seem a threat to Cavour in 1860 and caused the prime minister to view the general with such harsh fear. The tendency to substitute men proved in Piedmont for local leaders (including even those who had been active in the National Society), the split with Garibaldi, the intolerance toward the parliamentary left (and the habit of seeing in it all the dangers of the Parisian proletariat) led to the narrowing of the political base of the new Italy. This was a moment, however, at which the urban lower middle class and some leading artisans were gaining a new political self-consciousness. When years later they were admitted to effective political life, they tended first to fight the battle of their past deprivation. Italy's political base was not broad enough to support a system of two parties, while the exclusion of democrats and Catholics left an increasingly isolated ruling caste. And the beleaguered, earnest moderates could not forget the moments of unanimity they had claimed in 1859; for them, disagreement would always smack of a selfish partisanship, a decline from the greatness of Cavour's age.

"Unconditional unitarianism" one of the moderates' opponents labeled this attitude, in arguing that inherently it led to the sacrifice of liberty.[34] But that tendency was the more dangerous because united Italy suffered from the lack of traditions of legality and precedents of restraint. These shortcomings, too, were part of the legacy of moderate policy. One could not effectively cite the authority of constitution and laws when they were the product neither of some dominant ideology nor of a publicly welded compromise. They had been expedients, so tightly tied to the needs of the moment that they lost dignity as circumstances changed. They had been weakened from the first by the reliance on dictatorship in Piedmont and in the provinces. It would remain a temptation, as in the plebiscites of 1860, to use the instruments of rep-

[34] BERTANI, p. 15.

resentative government primarily for safe demonstrations which left a slight sense of sham. Urbano Rattazzi was only the first of a long line of lesser successors to be tempted by Cavour's gaudier successes. Well before Aspromonte or the days of Agostino Depretis, he had done his part in 1859 to make corridor intrigue and the extra-constitutional support of the king an important part of Italian politics. Too often diplomatic triumphs would seem, as they had in 1859 but with more reason, the only way of over-coming domestic division. And in the decade after 1860 parliament was plagued, in addition to its regular burdens, by the need to serve as the constituent assembly which had not been held. It is no wonder that the new legal codes were exceedingly cautious and inappropriately close to their French models. They, too, became a source of disappointment and dissatisfaction.[35]

Disappointment was deepened by the fact that, in the process of achieving national union, nationalism itself had been somewhat tainted. Caution and realism had led, in 1859, to that regional self-interest which made Tuscany hesitant to join with the Duchies and both of them reluctant to associate their claims to the diplo-matically dangerous ones of the Romagna.[36] The Perugian patriots had been abandoned; and if, in a few bloody days, they had dis-played the weakness of revolution, they had established, too, the unheroic limits of Piedmontese realism.[37] The cession of Nice was another of those bitter blows to the sanguine nationalist, a list of which could easily be extended to 1866. Many of these disappoint-ments are a measure of how weak the forces were which worked for Italy's union. Indeed, an assessment of the difficulties the moderates faced suggests that unification was neither so inevitable nor so imminent as most contemporaries thought. In this sense, the moderates accomplished more than they could claim. But the dis-covery of what unification did not achieve led to the recognition

---

[35] AQUARONE, pp. 3–4, 9, 17–21, 37, 79–80; CARACCIOLO, pp. 15–18; GIUSEPPE TALAMO, *La Scuola dalla legge Casati alla inchiesta del 1864.* Milan, 1960, pp. 22–48; DEMARCO, pp. 164–65.

[36] MALVEZZI, Origine della Lega. *RSR,* XLV, 384–99. Ricasoli showed his sensitivity on this score as he insisted that his stand was "prudent and provident" but not "egoistic" (Ricasoli to Farini, August 6, *ibid.,* p. 391).

[37] For the Perugian petition see BEATRICE RASCHI, *Movement politico della città di Perugia del 1846 al 1860.* Foligno, 1904, p. 75. The vote September 7 in the Romagna assembly, on the suggestion of Minghetti, to do all they could for the Marches and Umbria, shows an awareness of the unattrac-tiveness of their position (*Le assemblee,* vol. I, p. 398).

of what narrow aims moderates had. When coupled with the assumption that Italian unification was a nineteenth-century necessity, it led to the feeling that the moderates had been guilty of some subtle treachery, of having stolen something.[38]

But by far the most important legacy of the moderate policy was the disappointment in the Risorgimento, in Italy itself, which grew to haunt Italian politics. The discontent with Piedmontese laws, the sense of having been cheated out of the old dream of a constituent assembly arose even before the new state was established and spread as a criticism of the foundation of the regime. Inevitably the left lamented the fall from its ideals, but even the conservative Alfonso La Marmora confessed a decade later that the means by which Italy had been made embarrassed those who later governed.[39] Much of the caution of 1859 had been meant to reassure Europe, but even this could be self-defeating. With self-righteous perceptiveness the *Westminster Review* complained at the time that the Italians had shown "more sagacity than energy," that their freedom had been won "by a fortunate deficiency of vehemence and excitement." [40] Italy's dependence on other countries had been made too clear; and these things, like the limited role granted the provisional governments, deprived the successful Risorgimento of 1859 of the heroic tradition of its predecessor. The famous post-unification political apathy was more than a letdown once the one great goal was achieved. It expressed a sense of disappointment with the past as well as the present. The feeling of the revolution *manquée* was born with the successes of 1859,

---

[38] The moderates were by temperament as well as program ill-equipped to excite the popular imagination. The perceptive young Henry Adams predicted at the time that Italy would "adore Garibaldi's memory, and only respect Cavour's" (letter to his brother, Charles Francis, June 9, 1860. Henry Adams and Garibaldi. *American Historical Review*, XXV [1919–20], 248).

[39] La Marmora was thinking especially of the extra-legal cooperation with men such as Garibaldi (cited in FEDERICO CHABOD, *Storia della politica estera italiana dal 1870 al 1896*, vol. I, *Le premesse*. Bari, 1951, p. 324). The yearning for the constituent assembly (and the feeble hope that it might take place even after the winning of Rome) is noted by DEMARCO, pp. 168–70, 174–84. See also LEONE CARPI, *Del riordinamento amministrativo del regno*. Bologna, 1860. These articles first appeared in the official and friendly *Monitore di Bologna*. Bertani's lamentations are often eloquent, *Opposizione parlamentare, passim*.

[40] *Westminster Review*, N. S., XXVII (1861), 187.

and Boncompagni confessed more than he meant when, in 1871, he noticed that Italy was "more fortunate than great." [41]

While the attention of all concerned was concentrated on the skill and luck with which political unification was at last being achieved in Italy, the meaning of that unification was being determined with far less attention. The moderates were almost pathetically eager to establish that Italians could behave with the popular restraint and political responsibility of Englishmen and Frenchmen. And that rather limited aim they attained. But in doing so they bore the burden not only of Italy's history but of their neighbors' as well. They could have been more generous to the classes beneath them if they had not confused them with the more demanding masses of the industrialized countries. They could have won a wider following if their opponents had not had ready at hand all the arguments against Whiggish limitations developed in the different context of Britain and France. What was done in 1859 is explicable in terms of the needs then felt and understandable in terms of the values the moderates held; and by so assessing it, one can escape the traditional polemics. The crucial months of 1859 stand, then, as something of a turning point; but their historical importance lies more deeply in the opportunity they afford for studying the ideals and realities of the Risorgimento. What was then done, when every act was a political decision, teaches something about the balance of forces in Italy as well as the weaknesses of that practical liberalism so common to the nineteenth century. As for the deeds themselves, one need only ponder them to recognize within the exciting story the importance of the precedents then set and of the pride Italian patriots could not feel in a country so compromisingly formed.

[41] Boncompagni is cited in CHABOD, p. 13. For the sense of letdown, see *ibid.,* pp. 3–79. Chabod himself, however, tends to see this reaction as a necessary consequence of unification (*ibid.,* pp. 509–12). Pietro Gobetti in his famous *Coscienza liberale e classe operaia.* Turin, 1951, p. 35, notes the absence of "grandi miti."

10.

The Bismarck Problem

Franz Schnabel

❧❧

EDITORIAL NOTE: *Bismarck, A. J. P. Taylor once argued, is the German barometer, the real measure of German self-esteem. Since Bismarck always stands more than life size, he easily rises above German doubts about themselves. While given to occasional hysteria or temper tantrums, he rarely lost his nerve, never his self-confidence. Franz Schnabel, the distinguished historian of nineteenth-century Germany, wrote this essay in 1949, when German self-esteem ran very low, after participating in an international congress of historians on Europe and Nationalism. The subject and the time gave rise to many second thoughts. Schnabel also wrote in the shadow (and consciously so) of the distinguished three-volume critical biography of Bismarck by the Liberal Eric Eyck. Schnabel, a professor at the University of Munich, thought and wrote in a non-Prussian, Catholic tradition. He saw Bismarck as a latter-day Metternich, the last brilliant practitioner of the old school of diplomacy. But there was a difference. Bismarck marred the practice by bringing the brutal temper of an east Prussian Junker to a refined gentleman's game.*

    Bismarck improvised. He was a political pragmatist determined to save the Prussian social order, traditional values, and his job (not necessarily in that order). He believed that each would be lost should liberal, democratic, or radical nationalist views prevail. To thwart these forces he worked or considered working with every important political faction and each principal social element. He employed dictatorial authority, then democracy, to beat down Liberalism. Then he used the emotion of nationalism at least in part to deflect radical enthusiasm. He played upon the social peril and anti-Catholicism to capture the Liberals. He undercut, traduced, or seduced opposition groups. But he could never have succeeded had German Liberals not discovered what Henry James called "the bitch goddess Success." Having, as Namier so tartly puts it, sacrificed "Freiheit" from "Einheit, Freiheit, Macht," they prepared to recapture it by taking it away from others.

Schnabel's essay is a tour de force, a brilliant, sweeping review of the cardinal factors of nineteenth-century German history, and a reassessment of the interplay of ideas and institutions. Schnabel delivers a penetrating sketch of what Bismarck was rather than who he was. "Das Problem Bismarck" is in some ways complementary to Namier's essay, but it deals with specific problems in the course of German liberalism and nationalism after 1848. Schnabel is not concerned with Bismarck the imperial chancellor, whom he regards as a failure, nor with Bismarck the manipulator of an alliance system. Schnabel addresses himself, in the tradition of German federalist historiography, to ethical and philosophic matters quite as much as political and pragmatic problems.

The empire which Bismarck founded lasted half a century. When it fell, historians centered their interest upon the personality and life work of this man who, more than any other, put his own stamp upon the second half of the nineteenth century. What was written before 1918 on this great problem must now be considered for the most part obsolete. After the collapse of the German Empire and the monarchies in the middle and small German states, the archives were opened and a profusion of important, unknown documents brought to light. The events which took place in Germany between 1918 and 1945 were such, moreover, as to make men question what Bismarck did and said, what he was and what he wanted. Or, they made men change what he brought about. One after another, all Bismarck's opponents have risen again; once more they have borne testimony against him. The multitude of those who in his lifetime heaped praise upon him, citing the success of his endeavors, were too hasty in their conclusions. Men had to learn from experience, like those before them, that only a much later age can pass final judgment on success in history—the empire which began so brilliantly stood but for fifty years. There were times, to be sure, when Bismarck himself spoke with profound pessimism of the durability of his achievement. After his dismissal, domestic and foreign difficulties in fact continued to multiply. But dominant public opinion brushed aside any suggestion that the course along which Bismarck had directed German and European history was responsible for this state of affairs. The more painfully obvious were the shortcomings of his successors and the emperor under whom they served, the easier it seemed to bring forward the founder of the Reich in edifying contrast to them.

After the first catastrophe in 1918, however, the spiritual descendants of the earlier German liberalism and democrats took the field. They established Bismarck's responsibility for the predominance of the policy of "Blood and Iron." They voiced regret that ever since Bismarck the people and the parties had always played the role of followers or opposition, but not of participants in responsibility in the "authoritarian state" which bore the impress of the Prussian system. Bismarck was also criticized for having over-estimated the vitality of the Austro-Hungarian monarchy and neglected therefore to bring about *Anschluss*. Thereafter, as cupidity increasingly took the place of concern for the state and political life as such, as the masses ceased to think of the interests of the state, which guaranteed law and order, and should have provided their rational guide to action, as nationalism and neoromanticism, literary scribblings (*Literatentum*) and theories of the "folk" (*Volk*) gained the upper hand, Bismarck's reputation began to decline correspondingly. Though once, in an exchange of opinions with Gottfried Kinkel,[1] he drew a distinction between his soul, the "soul of a diplomat," and the heart of the patriotic leader, the heart of a poet, men at that time began to draw closer again to the patriots of the period when unification was being prepared. They were extolled because they wished to unite all "folk comrades" (*Volksgenossen*) and "bring home" the *"disjecta membra"* into the empire for which they strove, and because they wished therefore to reorganize Europe upon the basis of folk membership (*Volkstum*) and tongue. In this way, men knew, the old princely policy of territorial incorporations could be continued by a new, folkish policy of incorporations; but they did not gladly have their attention drawn to the fact that it was the doctrines of German romanticism which first really brought the nationalities of eastern Europe into movement. But, in the twentieth century, the national state conception reached a complete *reductio ad absurdum;* it brought incalculable disaster upon millions who were driven from their homes because of the language they spoke and the people to which they belonged. Not surprisingly, therefore, men found reason

[1] Gottfried Kinkel (1815–82), German revolutionary poet, professor at Bonn; aided to escape (1850) from prison by Carl Schurz.

to re-examine critically the entire national state movement since 1815, which had resulted in endless disorder, two world wars, and catastrophe; nor was it surprising either that they called up again those opponents of Bismarck who combated his power-permeated concept of the state, his alliance with the German national state idea, and who condemned the division of Europe into national states and demanded a European federal structure.

Thus the age of Bismarck lies today concealed in profound obscurity. We do have the documents at hand, but interpreting them is difficult because, living in devastated lands, we find it hard to attain that lofty and far-off vantage point where the historian must take his stand. In earlier ages, when historical awareness had not yet been formed, men came quickly to their own aid in explaining things. Among us, too, resentment will bring about simplification. States and empires, it is said, decline for the same reasons by which they rise. Thus an effort has been made to find a single trace that goes from Bismarck to Hitler, from the "Iron Chancellor," the man in cavalry boots, to the National-Socialist policy of violence. But this means forgetting the popular and revolutionary forces which had been at work ever since 1815. To remember where we must seek in German history for the spiritual ancestors of modern demagogy, of explosive ideologies, of the extolling of violence, we need merely read the sentences written in 1833 by Heinrich Heine in which he drew the outlines of the future German revolution. At that time Lorenz Oken,[2] the philosopher of nature who has been lauded as the "great revolutionary," tried to start a movement of revolutionary enthusiasm among the youth in Germany and was expelled from the University of Jena, on Goethe's decision, as a "Catilinarian." As always, things were expected to take place faster than they actually occurred. But, under the immediate impact of the Hambach Festival of 1832 which J. G. A. Wirth[3] organized, Heine felt so bold as to prophesy:

Kantians unwilling to hear of any piety in the phenomenal world either, ruthlessly upsetting the foundations of our European life, will make their appearance. Armed Fichteans unwilling to be

[2] Lorenz Oken (1779–1851), German scientist and philosopher, leading philosopher of nature of the romantic period.
[3] Johann Georg August Wirth (1798–1848), German democratic leader; organizer of the Hambach Festival of revolutionary youth, May 27, 1832.

hampered by aught in their fanatic willfulness will take the stage. But most terrible of all will be the philosophers of nature, unleashing the daemonic forces of the German pantheism of yore and thus awakening that battle passion which fights not to win, but merely to fight. . . . To some extent, Christianity has mitigated that Germanic battle passion. But once the Cross is broken, then the clangor of that wildness of which the Nordic poets sing and speak so much will be heard again. . . . But when you hear such a crashing and clanging as was never before heard in the history of the world, then a drama will be played out in Germany, alongside which the French Revolution will seem but a harmless idyll. To be sure, things are still quiet among us; we do not as yet know whether the Crown Prince of Prussia or Dr. Wirth will come to power in Germany. But do not believe that one day to come these will appear upon the scene as the real actors. They are only the curs running about in the empty arena and snarling at each other, before the hour comes when the troop of gladiators enters who will fight for life and death. And that hour will come! The peoples will gather round Germany, as if seated upon the banks of an amphitheater, to see the great battle-play.[4]

It must be admitted that in the procession of such antecedents there is no place for Bismarck. It is still our task to define his position in the history of Europe, and to determine what were the opportunities that were then open to him and to other, positive forces in German history, as well. These were opportunities which he hampered or destroyed. During the last war a valuable start in this task was made by Erich Eyck. His three-volume biography of Bismarck was written and published outside of Germany. It is a work of high scholarly standing. Based upon knowledge of all the German and European sources, it is well written and to the point. It is, in fact, the first large, rounded biography of Bismarck. None the less, its description of Bismarck cannot be accepted as definitive. The discussion already under way over this important work must be continued; it can become fruitful and contribute to solving the problems which we still find in understanding Bismarck, the man, and his life work. We must frankly say that Eyck was able to write an imposing and easily understood work because he examined the play of opposing forces from a fixed position. But unfortunately, in taking this position, Eyck did not rise above the times. He stayed down amidst the embattled political

[4] TEMPEL HEINE, ed., *Werke*. Leipzig, n.d., vol. VII, pp. 424–26 (modified).

parties. True, the author, thanks to his great skill as a writer, was able to leave the polemics of those strife-filled decades far behind him. Only a few presently current turns of phrase hinder the flow of the narrative here and there. The personal greatness of Bismarck is recognized, and the author, when he comes up against the weaknesses of Bismarck's foes, does not keep silence about them. But Eyck is convinced that the national-liberal movement of the sixties was on the right track, that it could really have established the German national state in conformity with its own ideals. Eyck belongs among those opponents of Bismarck who may be called "German Whigs." They included persons in the highest reaches of society, including the royal family and the liberal princely courts. For the new Bismarck biographer, Gladstone is the lofty ideal of a statesman. Eyck, who lives in England, has written a fine monographic study on Gladstone. Bismarck, the great hater, held no other statesman of his time in such scorn as "the Grand Old Man" who let his policy be guided by humanitarian and even pacifist ideals, opposed the advance of imperialism, approached the Irish nationalist movement in an accommodating spirit, and extended the suffrage for the British parliament. According to Eyck, Bismarck's interference with the development of conditions for the rise of a statesman like Gladstone in Prussia and Germany was the source of all the evil to come for Germany and for Europe.

By now the reader will have realized that Eyck accepts without further ado the position that the isolated national state with centralized institutions was the only correct and possible solution of the "German question," the only one corresponding to the strivings of the German people for unity. He directs his criticism just at the methods which Bismarck employed. In Eyck's opinion, if Bismarck had given more consideration to the ideals of his liberal allies, the internal structure of the new Reich would have met the needs of that day better and would have been more durable as well. Moreover, it would have been possible to found the Reich without using the violent methods which Bismarck did. Eyck voices most profound regret that the new state was born with the flaw of lawbreaking and violence, and that German liberalism developed from a party of law and order into a service group of success worshippers.

Certainly, this is not a new train of thought. There were always at least a few liberal and democratic writers in Germany, during and after Bismarck's imperial chancellorship, who held firm to ideals of freedom and humanity, deplored their loss in Germany when it came under Prussian control, and therefore remained at all times critics of Bismarck. But they produced no major historical work. They were not able to distinguish and correctly to evaluate, upon the basis of detailed research, the various streams within the liberal and democratic movement. They had no importance compared with the specialists, from Sybel down to Erich Marcks, who did the valuable scholarly service of refuting the claims which the reigning monarch [William II] made on behalf of his grandfather [William I, "the Great"]; but these erstwhile leading historians took part in the movement of liberalism into Bismarck's camp, they defended it and found it to be in conformity with the needs of modern times. Eyck is the first person who has managed to put forward the position of the liberal opponents of Bismarck in a large, well-supported analysis. Since Eyck's work is becoming known in Germany at a time when, after a lapse of almost half a century, the spiritual and political ideas of western European liberalism are again acceptable, there is a danger that the old myth, which justified and praised Bismarck as the *"Realpolitiker"* will now be replaced by a new historical myth. All the more must our thanks go to Eyck for his analysis, which affords us a reason for examining in a fundamental way the problems of Bismarck's achievements and establishing the facts in the matter.

Hans Rothfels, now of the University of Chicago, has set down in a far-reaching critique, "Problems of a Bismarck Biography," the principal points which must be made against Eyck's approach. Not only did he carry the analysis forward, he also greatly simplified it. The assumption that the goal which Bismarck and the liberals shared—the little-German (*kleindeutsch*) national state under Prussian leadership—could have been achieved without the methods employed by Bismarck, and that Bismarck brought the *kleindeutsch* empire into ill repute by his methods, is one which cannot be proved. All the evidence we have supports the position that the powers accepted only unwillingly the formation of a new national state in the heart of Europe. Either, like Napoleon III, they wished for "compensations," or they were surprised by Bismarck's procedure and did not have time to prepare themselves spiritually and materially to counter it. All the virtuosity of

Bismarck's manipulation of the rival powers, his skill in the handling of men and his daring as well, were required to achieve the goal. It was not alone the extension of Prussian power which the other states disliked. They did see with misgivings that the traditions of Frederick the Great had been taken up again, that the old policy of rounding-off the borders of Prussia and conquering new territories which at an earlier time had been directed against Saxony, now led to the annexation of Schleswig-Holstein and the kingdom of Hanover. But the program of establishing a national state, which at the outset had nothing to do with the Prussian drive for expansion and a Frederician policy, gave the powers no less reason for anxiety and interference. Whether or not German nationalism became an ally of Bismarck, the liberals would have come into conflict with Europe. As early as the Hambach Festival of 1832, when most of the participants were wholly under the influence of the French revolutionary spirit and of Franco-German fraternization, the speakers could not refrain from rejecting France's claim to the left bank of the Rhine, and J. G. A. Wirth dared openly to express the view that the desired unification of Germany "very probably" would also have as a result the return of Alsace-Lorraine to the ancient homeland. The executive committee of the festival then eliminated this phrase from the official minutes, "in deference to the friendly French people," and there were many who took amiss the speaker's "slip." But the *"furor teutonicus"*—as the favorite catchword of the Bismarckian period ran—burned brightly precisely after 1859, and without Bismarck's intervention. The *kleindeutsch* patriots were scarcely ready to grant compensations to Napoleon III and to renounce the left bank of the Rhine. The German variety of nationalists in St. Paul's church [where the national assembly met in Frankfurt in 1848] had thrashed it all out! How many times had the verse *"So weit die deutsche Zunge klingt!"* [5] ("Where'er is heard the German tongue!") been reiterated within its walls, as the basis for far-reaching claims! Amid great applause a speaker in the national assembly at Frankfurt declared that one could not draw the sword for the Germans in Schleswig and at the same time abandon South Tyrol. It became evident at St. Paul's church that there were irredenta in many parts of Europe; the courts and governments of

[5] A famous patriotic poem, *The German's Fatherland,* by Ernst Moritz Arndt.

the powers agreed that to treat status as a people (*Volkstum*), nation and national state, as mutually equivalent expressions, was a "Germanism." They saw it as a great error which, as Ernest Renan expressed it in 1882, "if it came to dominate, would hurl Europe into immense wars and destroy its civilization." As a matter of fact, the governments feared the ideology of the German liberals and democrats more than the ambitions of the Prussian statesman. True, the *kleindeutsch* program was limited to strict boundaries, but once released and given wing by its first success, the movement would necessarily develop its latent tendencies and would then be able to make use of Bismarck's power methods. We need merely to recall the great interest which was given to the question of the "Germans in the outside world" at the festivals of gymnastic, rifle, singing and Schiller societies since 1840. After 1859 this element of national ambition kept emphatically to the front; even the *Kleindeutschen* could not remain free of it. It was expected in the European courts after 1871 that a period of pan-Germanic expansion would begin, and there was astonishment and a return to calm feelings when it was seen that such plans were far indeed from Bismarck's mind.

But the movement of folk groupings was the very force which, as soon as it could attain freedom for development, had to bring disorder and war upon Europe. Among the peoples of Europe, ambitious to make their own states, the belief in humanity and the solidarity of free nations, each developing along its own lines, did not prevent an embittered struggle from breaking out at once over the frontiers of provinces and folk groupings. Though still in vain, Robert Blum,[6] together with the leaders of the nationalities of eastern Europe, had already sought to bring about the dismemberment of the Hapsburg Empire, in order to split away the Germans of Austria from all the other nationalities, bringing the Germans into a centralized unified republic. This goal was not abandoned. Yet its achievement would have brought European chaos, as Metternich and Grillparzer in Vienna, the mid-point of many nations, had predicted. In our own day, we have experienced its terrible results. The beginnings of a secular nationalist "revivalist movement" were already quite strong in 1848. Blum, it is

[6] Robert Blum (1807–48), German political leader; head of left at Frankfurt assembly; executed (November 1848) by Austrians for part in Vienna uprising.

true, did not become the "leader and arouser of the people," and no one in Germany was called upon to play the role which was enacted in Hungary by Louis Kossuth; to a remarkable degree the German movement on behalf of a national state ran an anonymous course. Then Bismarck, having brought the liberals both into alliance and into subordination, took the rudder; thereafter there was no place for a patriotic leader like Gottfried Kinkel. Bismarck held fast to the traditions of the old statecraft, and thereby placed the German movement under the command of the state-centered conception. He maintained it in the form of a constitutional monarchy, in correspondence with the relationship of forces which existed within Germany after almost all German states had received such constitutions. The wars which he waged were in their own way wars for unification. They were not organized as people's wars, but were conducted in the strict forms laid down in the armies of the kings, and with strict, wholly political aims. We must always recall to our memories the sentence which proved such breadth of vision and which has received such frightening confirmation: "What ought to be placed in that part of Europe which is at present occupied by the Austro-Hungarian monarchy? New creations in this soil could only be of a revolutionary character."

This—and just this—was the decisive course of events. Bismarck thwarted not only the beginnings of a liberal and democratic movement, but he restrained the development of [central] European nationalism in general, which for specific, historically verifiable reasons had arisen in close relationship with the liberal and constitutionalist conception, but, where it could develop, ended in dictatorship, the centralized unitary republic, and unlimited expansion. How Louis Kossuth, Mazzini and Daniele Manin were extolled in the democratic journals of bourgeois democracy, *Didaskalia* and *Gartenlaube,* although they were certainly not liberal and constitutionalist politicians; one wished to extend Hungary to the crest of the Carpathians, the other Italy to the Brenner frontier! Even Ferdinand Lassalle had entered upon a similar path, though he started from a different point of departure; he was a fervent patriot, and he would have favored, in fact, a *grossdeutsch* socialist centralized republic. The extent to which the liberal upper bourgeoisie could construct a barrier from its own resources is very questionable. They could not bring forth, and could not desire, an arouser of the people. Into the gap stepped the statesman who had nothing in common with the dictators of the nationalist period, but had his origin in classic diplomacy and statecraft.

For historical science it is a question of assigning to Bismarck his correct place in the historical sequence, not of justifying him or "vindicating his honor." He had naught to do with the doctrines of folk and living space (*Lebensraum*), with the old imperial idea, or with what Eichendorff [7] so ironically called "modern patrioteering" (*moderne Vaterländerei*); the patriots and national heroes, as they arose everywhere in the wake of nationalism, were of different stamp. In his old age he permitted himself to take pleasure in popularity and noisy hero-worship, which were foreign to aristocratic times. But he did not owe his successes, certainly, to the "Third Estate" or to the masses, but rather to the mastery with which he controlled the rules of the older diplomacy. Actions and transactions involving the courts and states had been developed to a high level of science and art in the chancelleries of the Italian Renaissance and the absolute monarchy of the French type. European unity was smashed to bits upon this mosaic pattern of politics, and Machiavellianism came into practice. After the kings and their counsellors had brought this to pass, nationalism pushed them aside, took over and further developed their methods and works, and adapted them to the needs of the masses who were coming into prominence. The history of the rise and decline of classic diplomacy has still to be written, however rich the sources available for it; we have only fragments from the hands of experienced diplomatists. Bismarck is the last great representative in the line of classic diplomats, which begins with the famed Venetian ambassadors and the papal nuncios of the sixteenth century. He did not in any way create a new type, but rather acted out to the full an old and strong departmental tradition. Even in his time diplomacy was in the process of becoming a bureaucratized profession with a strict course of training and a caste-stratified pattern of promotion. When Junker Bismarck, then only the squire of Schönhausen, still on the lowest rungs of his career as officer and jurist, entered their caste as an outsider, those who had served according to the rules were discontented. While he had deserved well of the crown in his service as a deputy, he

[7] Joseph, Freiherr von Eichendorff (1788–1857), German romantic poet.

had made his way into diplomacy by the detour of parliament. But he soon acquired the gentlemanly training of the international high society of Europe, to which stratum he belonged by origin and effort; his first assignment to Frankfurt as Prussian envoy to the federal Diet gave him an opportunity to acquire experience and develop his abilities. His memoirs still give us today a direct impression of the way in which, in the style of the old diplomacy, he evaluated the forces at work in every situation which confronted him, and tested, and to some extent calculated through, all possible combinations one after another. Thus he was a "member of the guild" with Choiseul, Kaunitz, Talleyrand and Metternich, all of whom left us their memoirs; however different were the states and interests which they represented, politics was for each of them an exact science concerned with calculable magnitudes. We may let the question rest whether there is a difference of spiritual rank between Bismarck and his great predecessors, and it has been observed of his manner of negotiating that he had been in the habit of peddling his wool on the market square in Stettin. Talleyrand and Metternich, the bishop of the Gallican church and the Rhenish nobleman, had still absorbed the lofty intellectual culture of the ancien régime. But, in the last analysis, the East Elbian Junker had belonged to the exclusive student *Korps* at the University of Göttingen, educated himself in the world of society, and always maintained a French recess in his mind.

To be sure, Bismarck, as minister of a constitutional monarch, had to count no longer only with potentates, courtiers and favorites. He had to play not only in the "concert of Europe," but also on the instrument of parliament as well. And here then was to be seen the limits beyond which the old classic diplomacy did not reach. The great transformation which was taking place in that period of the awakening of nationalism and its democratic concomitant, consisted precisely in the fact that it was no longer the governments which led the peoples, but the peoples which decided for the governments. Thereby an element was introduced into politics which escaped all calculation. So long as Bismarck had dealings only with the czar and Gorchakov, with the empress and the ladies of the court, that is, with the great ones whom someone who knew people well could see through to some extent, his diplomatic art could hew to the old methods which earlier had been formed under the world dominance of mathematics and mechanics. But, with the rise of pan-slavism, all calculations became uncertain. Bismarck took German nationalism into custody and utilized it, subordinated it to the state conception and made it available for diplomatic craft. It was a very unequal alliance which was concluded then—a true *societas leonina,* for the Prussian state received the lion's part; the nationalist movement had to permit limits to be drawn to its activity, with regard to domestic freedom as well as to "pan-German" tendencies. For the time being, Bismarck was the master; and the world in which he felt at home and moved with complete security was the grand world of the courts and aristocratic society. There he sought for the decisions, exactly as had been done in bygone times in the manner depicted in the historical writings of Ranke. Bismarck and Ranke, the contemporaries, belong together most intimately from this point of view as well, and everything, furthermore, which was common to them—the objective comprehension of reality, the conviction of the primacy of foreign policy, the doctrines of the power-state and the legitimacy of political action—came out of the school of the old diplomacy. Following the same pattern, Bismarck and Ranke both fundamentally looked upon the state from the top downwards, while the patriots saw it as their task in politics and science to judge public affairs from below, upon the basis of the rights and requirements of the people. This celebrated formulation, which fixes the difference between the enlightened-absolutist and the democratic conceptions of public life, was first coined by Arndt; Treitschke took it over from him and misunderstood it. Even in his later life Bismarck limited the labors of the statesman and the diplomat to governments and courts; he was always foreign to the newly developing diplomacy which had to devote its energies to the fatiguing tasks of directing large staffs and studying the peoples and the economic and social phenomena of distant lands. Bismarck was not equal to working in the new world of the popular forces which had come into movement—consider the fiasco of his domestic policy after 1871! In just the same way the historian Ranke did not judge correctly those parties in the past in which, alongside the diplomats and court theologians, primal forces from below forced their way. Bismarck never did learn, as Napoleon did, to flatter the crowd. He was gripped by narrow class prejudices as was another leading statesman of his time. Hence he inaugurated his social policy principally for considerations of power politics and preferred such solutions as were, in his view, adapted to strengthening the state. Even when he desired, he was unable to negotiate with deputies and party leaders as skillfully as with ambassadors and ministers of other powers. He always looked upon Windthorst[8] as just the former minister of a defeated royal house who only sought revenge in gathering the Catholics around himself; he never even made the effort to achieve an understanding of the endeavor of the Catholic portion of the population to help shape the inner structure of the new Reich. And he made just as little effort to develop in August Bebel [9] and his party a willingness to cooperate upon the basis of even the slightest concession. There is no doubt that his narrow and unchanging horizon served to strengthen his national-liberal and conservative allies in their lack of understanding for the Christian and Social-Democratic labor movement.

Thus Bismarck is to be understood as a historical phenomenon only upon the basis of the old statecraft, with its lofty intellectuality and self-sufficiency, in which the people played no part. He created the German national state within the framework of the old state system and with the old methods; after him, it went into decline. One has to look at Hindenburg and Ludendorff and compare them to the earlier leaders of German destinies in order to realize that Germany used to live more decently. The charge has often been made, and is emphatically repeated by Eyck, that Bismarck took no care to provide for the new generation, and tolerated no independent persons of quality around him. His collaborator in St. Petersburg, Leopold von Schlözer, always called him "the Pasha." But yet it was rare for him to encounter in the government departments such fine and upstanding personalities as Schlözer himself; when he did meet them, he did not withhold his respect. Furthermore, not only in the chancelleries and governments, but in the other domains of life in the era of rising nationalism, with the entry of the masses into history, noble personalities were forced into the background behind robust and servile characters.

In the old classic diplomacy to which Bismarck belonged, it

[8] Ludwig Windthorst (1812–91), German political leader; minister of justice in Hanover (1851–53, 1862–65), leader of Center Party in the German Reichstag after 1870.
[9] August Bebel (1840–1913), German political leader; founder and leader of German Social-Democratic Party.

was true that the principles and methods which are included under the name of Machiavellianism had been in long use; it remains to be seen whether, in this respect, Bismarck acted without restraint to an unusual degree. Where it is required by reason of state, Machiavelli considers anything to be permissible. He recommends lying, breaking treaties, deceit, violence; one must be a lion and a fox at the same time, and success justifies the most outrageous villainy. But, on the other hand, as the sagacious and honorable Johann Jakob Moser[10] taught in the eighteenth century, the small state cannot build upon force; therefore it must build upon law and justice. But it is obvious that the "minor powers," when they became involved in the affairs of the world, have been the most perfidious, while the great powers maintained their strong positions and no longer had to pursue a shifty course. The Prussian state was the most recent and smallest of the powers. This is the explanation of many of the acts of treacherous behavior which are to be found so frequently in the history of Prussian policy. But Talleyrand, too, who certainly had a great power behind him, was never squeamish, and in Bismarck's time Prussia was so great a military power that it did not need small expedients. But Bismarck always applied the methods of deceit or violence which seemed useful to him, without meditating upon them. A statesman who saw his state as incomplete, he was moved by ambition to make it larger; moreover, the increase of power by all means was a personal necessity for him. He brought about three wars with complete deliberateness, as he frankly admitted afterwards. He dragged the king of Hanover into war in order to drive him from his throne, confiscated his property in violation of an agreement, and then had parliament forbid him to make restitution. He concluded the Reinsurance Treaty with Russia against Austria and carefully concealed this fact from his ally. It is not possible and not necessary to enumerate here all the misdeeds or improprieties of his foreign and domestic policy. Even at the time they were brought to light of day by those affected, and were vigorously discussed by contemporary public opinion; but when he was successful, his power became so great that all who were dependent by function or character, bowed their heads and worshipped his genius. It was an ill harbinger of things to come that these were the leading intellectuals; previously humanitarian or liberal in

[10] Johann Jakob Moser (1701–85), German juridical scholar and teacher.

attitude, they wished to remain on top as time passed, whatever came to pass. Eyck has carefully brought out in the course of his narrative every instance of violation of law and justice, of violence, of unfair conduct of affairs on the part of Bismarck; we now know much more of what he did than contemporary polemists knew at the time. We possess for no other statesman, not even for Talleyrand, so elaborate a register of his sins. Bismarck had the additional misfortune of finding a historian who pursued the old sinner through every twist and turn of his career.

But, what is more, the picture of Bismarck was drawn even more unflatteringly because of his personal idiosyncrasies. Words exist to conceal ideas, went the celebrated paradox coined by Talleyrand. Such behavior was not to Bismarck's taste. Though he was able to watch his step, he did not find it easy. He carried over into political controversy the coarse language he had used as a member of a student *Korps* at the university and as a reserve officer in the army. He never acquired the self-control which one learns in the chancellery of state or *salon* society. For him at least, parliament was not the best school at which to prepare for diplomacy. Furthermore, he tended to make his criticism too slashing. He took delight in witty conversation, which he spiced with the kind of merry tale and unexpected jest his adversaries would then turn against him. He did not scruple to speak his mind. He said openly that he would not be balked by trifles. Other cynical turns of phrase from his lips soon became public knowledge. Such cynicism, also, set his successors a bad example. His imitators mimicked his cynicism, but not his honorable traits. The time was not far off when the reigning monarch, in his overbearing arrogance, hardly cut the figure of a prince or nobleman. In a world of rapidly growing wealth and splendor, William II was more the *parvenu* than the aristocrat.

No one will deny, therefore, that Bismarck and William II introduced into politics the habit of acting harshly toward ostensible weakness, and the use of strong words, so that ever-larger sections of the German people were summarily stigmatized as enemies of the Reich. Such conduct was foreign to the despots in previous times, because they sat, lonely and silent, upon the thrones in their Escorials. To be sure, many a cynical, blunt remark ("a crime, but not a mistake") has come down to us from Napoleon, who was dependent upon the crowd. However, he too adapted very easily to the new opinions taking form among the people; what is more, he too failed. Like Hegel, the "Prussian" in philosophy, Bismarck inculcated in the German Empire the belief that one "shouldn't be squeamish" [*"Nicht viel Umstände zu machen"*]. The role which the Junkers from east of the Elbe were now called upon to perform was, perhaps, particularly appropriate to them. Every reformer, from Freiherr vom Stein down to the liberals of the pre-Bismarck period, was indeed convinced, of course, that Prussia would have to renew herself upon the basis of the forces and institutions of Rhenish and Westphalian Germany. As a matter of fact, despite Bismarck, the center of gravity of the German national movement in the nineteenth century did lie in the west, where the Rhenish economic leaders were at home and democracy had roots in the life of the people. In northern Germany the liberal movement won influence only in the cities. In that area, the authentic Prussia of old, which was Bismarck's homeland, his methods were quickly adopted and imitated. Freiherr vom Stein and his collaborators had not worked wholly without success in Prussia; Berlin in the time of Schinkel,[11] and Königsberg in the time of Theodor von Schön, the Kantian and Prussian reformer,[12] gladly put a long distance between themselves and Frederick's Prussian system. But now, by Bismarck's example, anyone who had any power whatever to use found himself encouraged to act more abruptly. Only where constitutional courts were able to exercise effective control was there any safeguard against utter disregard of law and justice. This flouting of right under law was frankly proclaimed at the time in the form of the right of necessity, as was done in 1914 in the invasion of Belgium.

We may be surprised, therefore, that the leaders of the Prussian-German state adopted such methods when they had ceased to be customary among legitimate monarchies after Napoleon's fall. We must ascribe to Bismarck a large individual share in promoting this development. In Prussia itself professional diplomats looked amiss at these methods. Bismarck was, after all, not only an outsider, but a man out of the ordinary, from whom one could look

[11] Karl Friedrich Schinkel (1781–1841), German architect and painter, particularly active in Berlin.
[12] Theodor von Schön (1772–1856), Prussian statesman; took liberal role in east Prussia in war against Napoleon.

for a coup d'état; he was, therefore, of the same ilk as the men of 18 Brumaire and 2 December. We forget too easily how deep an impression was made by the reappearance of Bonapartism at a time when the nineteenth century was becoming more and more bourgeois, in an age of liberalism and belief in progress. It was a stupendous phenomenon which aroused misgivings lest the means and resources of liberal democracy prove inadequate in the difficult and hard time just beginning. If anything encouraged Bismarck to enter upon the path of violence, it was certainly the conduct of Prince Louis Napoleon. There is reason, furthermore, to investigate more deeply the extent to which he also felt encouraged by Cavour's example; the Piedmontese was a great "realist" who also drove many princes from their thrones and yet did not become dependent upon extremism. But, beyond doubt, many aspects of Bismarck's life work trace back to the French Second Empire. That is all just history now. It would be difficult to find threads which extended from that time into the twentieth century. The general character of Caesarism or dictatorship as such, exemplified in the Renaissance and once again brought into being by Napoleon I, was such a thread. The twentieth century, on the contrary, did not find its exemplars in the great realists and proponents of reason of state, but rather in the theory and practice of violence as created by the nationalists of eastern Europe and Italy. Kossuth, Mazzini and Garibaldi mobilized the youth of their nations and led them in hosts, again and again, to destruction. They aroused men's instinctual passions. In general, they were demoniac in character for they adopted chimerical goals, used the most extreme methods, and remained relatively indifferent to success, which neither they nor their imitators met. Bismarck had no part in all their doings, not even when, in 1866, he entertained a plan to rouse up the Czechs and Magyars. Though he may have learned from Napoleon III, still we do not find in him any trace of admiration for the demoniac figure of Napoleon I. In his youth, he went through his "romantic" period; but, once the storms of youth were past, *déborder* became foreign to his nature. The traditional rules of conduct provided that in cases of extreme necessity one need not think twice about using any weapon at hand. If we wish to probe for the ultimate cause of all the processes which gave rise to Napoleon, to Bismarck and to the leaders of the nationalities, as well as to their methods and goals, we will become aware that, in general, these processes are rooted in modern humanity. It clearly was not at all the same thing when the old sovereign states used their machinery of power to define their interests, and when national sovereignty came into play. The sovereign nation, once it was swung into action, did not readily accept any limitation of its scope.

We cannot condemn these methods and accept their goals. Bismarck could attain his purposes only by such methods. How else could he have bound together the eastern and western halves of the Prussian monarchy, closing the gaps that lay between them? The king of Hanover acted cautiously and beyond criticism. He took his stand squarely on law and avoided taking any part in the conflict between the two big powers! In order to respect the rights of Hanover, Bismarck would have had to give up any hope of making the Prussian state a single territorial unit. But he wished the Prussian body politic to have one compact territory, which would enable it to prevail completely in the North German Confederation. When this was won, he turned at once to his next goal and established the German Empire. Prussia could have existed in it even if she did not have Hanover and Hesse. In any case, in spite of the federal organization of the state, which was inevitable at the time, the decisive fact remains that Bismarck did not free himself from the old political conception of the isolated, territorially-compact, state body. In this old classic policy, Machiavellianism, because it arose in fact out of the struggle of sovereign powers, was not something put in afterwards, but the principle of its very life. Though national sovereignty merely took the place of the princely sovereigns, it vastly intensified, as we know, the drive of Machiavellianism, extended it widely and made it all-inclusive.

We may correctly speak of Bismarck's being "misunderstood" nowadays in the sense that his work and activity have been viewed apart from their connection with the previous system of states and its political conceptions. Bismarck's conduct was dictated by a line which traced back to Frederick the Great, Richelieu, Gustavus Adolphus and Maurice de Saxe. They all contributed to the destruction of Western unity, to the establishment of sovereign states, and to their mighty expansion by conquest, treaty-breaking and violence against the weak. For a long time, Bismarck merely put modern nationalism to his own uses. He was, first and fore-

most, the managing director of a state which played the role of
a great power in the European state system of five great powers
and many smaller powers; as yet, Prussia was not "saturated"
within this state system. Once he said that Prussia wore too heavy
armor for her small body. It is an image which corresponds to
the old political thinking. Bismarck did not learn the new meta-
phors of nationalism. He was concerned with the interests of the
state, with the state as a rational system of analysis and action.
Hence he remained strange to the voluntarisms of the period of
national states and democracy. The program and slogans of nationalism—natural living space, historical borders, assimilation and
national will—which derived in part from the French Revolution
and for the rest from German romanticism, were widespread
among the liberals in the sixties and seventies, and were already
being fully acted upon among the eastern European peoples. Bismarck did not heed any of these slogans; he disregarded this program. Even when he annexed Alsace and Lorraine, military considerations were paramount in his mind. He belonged to the system
of states as it had been, when states looked out for themselves and
wished to please only themselves, when the interests of the state
were all that was at stake and the interests of the people were
only of secondary concern. He brought two new great powers,
Prussia-Germany and Sardinia-Italy into the old European state
system. As a result, he transformed the "European concert." The
forces which later put an ax to the entire historical state structure
had been in being for a long time, and Bismarck had to reckon
with them. But he still hoped to be able to bring them under
control.

The methods used by Bismarck therefore derived from the old
policy of European governments. It saw in power the proper purpose of the state. It had extricated the states from the medieval
bonds of universalism, and involved them in the struggle for
hegemony or balance of power. Modern nationalism was a new
form of this spirit of separatism. Therefore, Bismarck had been
able to make it his ally; with it he brought new elements of power
into the battle array. He saw that, as a result, Europe would have
to make rapid progress toward ruin. But he thought that the
traditional state system, in whose categories he thought and acted,
was strong. It would survive the profound contradiction which
he brought about when he created a Prussian-German national

state in central Europe and at the same time tried to protect and preserve the pure dynastic states against the nationalities in eastern Europe. For historical judgment this question is therefore clearly crucial: was there, in fact, any chance in Bismarck's time of giving up the free competition of interests? It would have made superfluous the old methods by which affairs had been conducted until then. Could there have been established as a consequence, cooperative life of men and peoples upon Christian principles, or at least a system corresponding to these principles more closely than the previous system? It cannot be maintained that Bismarck did not dare to set himself against his time. He thrust himself very energetically athwart the liberal and democratic movement, which certainly belonged to the advancing forces of the time, and hindered their development. On the other hand, the Frederician tradition in which he grew up was no longer a vital force at that instant; it regained its power during Bismarck's lifetime and mainly by his exertions. The choice was up to him. Would he remain under the spell of the old diplomacy and adopt in consequence its theory that the compact national state was the necessary form in which the nations could achieve their fulfillment? In that case, to be consistent, he would have had to "write off" the Hapsburg monarchy. But he did not. Or would he feel himself called upon to seek new paths in order to satisfy the nations of central and eastern European territories into a jumble of lands like the Balkans?

A statesman who did not accept the compact national state certainly had no lack of allies and forces at his disposal. Everywhere the majority of peoples still adhered to their hereditary princes. Of course, a small ducal state with a serene highness at its head no longer furnished an adequate area in which to function. But numerous connections had by then been set up between countries. Extension of the Prussian customs union (*Zollverein*) was possible; it was wholly justified by economic conditions, and only the school of the old diplomacy thwarted its achievement. Above all, however, the German Confederation could have been further developed. After the events of 1848 and 1849, the governments, including that of Prussia before Bismarck came upon the scene, were ready. Moreover, the question whether the vital rights of the nation could not be satisfied in this way as well, still remained completely open. The Danubian monarchy of the Hapsburgs was not to be saved. It could break apart into national states. There would be frightful struggles especially in territories of mixed national composition. Or the Hapsburg realms could be transformed into a central European federation of nations, each living its own life again under new constitutional arrangements. In Vienna, as in Berlin, the decision had not yet been taken. Despite 1848–49, the awakening of the nationalities in eastern Europe had only begun. They took what they could use and were as yet not out of control. Only in the eighties did radicalism finally break through to them as a consequence of the system of 1866. There had been a time when national hatred between Englishmen and Scotsmen was elemental and fierce, yet it had been buried. To be sure, with the Irish this did not come successfully to pass. The examples of the United States and France were beyond contradiction. The nationalities were also set in motion by the doctrines of German romanticism. But after 1849 there was everywhere very great fear of Russia, and Pan-Slavism was still just something happening within literary romanticism. There was a profound basis in the course of modern history for the endeavor of all the peoples of Europe to develop, each in its own way, toward the goal of forming its own state. They were still in the habit of calling in a king from old dynasties, from foreign lands. Personal union was found to be a satisfactory solution, and there were many other such solutions. The demand for a compact national organism came only from a few parties, and was chiefly a product of the scholars. Furthermore, if a statesman knew world conditions, he could not help but see the problems of the Continent more profoundly than could Bismarck, whose policy was limited to the Continent. He could not escape the deep contradiction which cleaved apart the entire age: when nationalism had free course, it led to a dismemberment of Europe; at the same time, the technology of communications, which in the shape of the locomotive had already outrun the small states and was a pacemaker for the nation and for democracy, was advancing. It was overcoming distance ever more quickly and thereby compelling a changeover to world communications and a world economy.

There was, therefore, a good basis in the actual conditions for federal union of the central and eastern European peoples. The new arrangement could be developed upon an existing foundation with existing forces and energies. Any other goal signified an extension of the revolutionary policy which had already shaken Europe for so long a period of time. The revolutionary forces at various times had brought to the forefront one or another artificial power-state. These forces now included as well the active portion of the urban bourgeoisie which, as Ranke said at the time, dreamed that they could "construct out of their wits" their fatherland. Some constructed a *kleindeutsch* monarchy, others a *grossdeutsch* centralized republic. But the time when Bismarck was preparing and carrying through his work was also filled with plans tied to existing reality. Constantin Frantz was only the most active and the intellectually most important of those who told Bismarck that the security which the German people so urgently required when future world decisions would be made, could not be guaranteed by means of the isolated national state, and by the combination of alliances which Bismarck with great skill formed anew time and again. It should not be said, therefore, that the conceptions of a federative Europe were mere literature. The very *kleindeutsch* doctrine which came so conveniently to Bismarck's hand, had been elaborated in scholars' studies. And it is not correct either to say that the conception of a central European federation of national states was premature, that it would only be justified when the nations would come to fear their own likeness unto God and saw themselves placed between two rising world powers. The moment quickly passed during which, as fate would have it, serious discussion of such a federation of Europe was possible. No one talked any more of union of the nations of central and eastern Europe, or of a Europe existing upon the basis of its own strength. Only in Bismarck's time could this idea have been carried out and the self-laceration of the nations prevented. It was already obvious that the appearance of Russia in central Europe, which anyone could see by 1849, was a world event of incalculable consequences. It necessarily opened up a new world epoch, with new methods in diplomacy and a new European attitude.

Here one may well object that no serious opponent of Bismarck, able to carry through such a policy, came forward. Controversial historiography, though it has its rights like any other, should never lose from view the fact that Germany at that time had lived for many centuries in political decrepitude. The German Confederation did indeed constitute a new beginning, but it was not yet a living political organism. Metternich, on whom rests responsibility for the three decades of German history from 1815 to 1848, permitted political life in the individual states to go farther. It was certainly of great value that the German people got the habit of acting in accordance with free political forms in the legislatures of south and central German states. But 1848 was the penalty paid because only those who supported the national state solutions had set programs. Austria's leadership in fact signified stagnation and reaction. Bismarck was the only statesman who took energetic action; he opened the valve to release the accumulated energies. An immense conflict in German life now broke out again, to be decided once and for all—on the one side the House of Hapsburg, which for centuries had found its profit in maintaining things as they were; and on the other Frederician policy brought back to life! The liberals joined Bismarck's camp when he began to prove successful. The more they had previously placed their hopes upon Prussia and the Prussian monarchy, while rejecting Prussian methods, the longer was their resistance. The power of the personal factor in history was displayed with particular vigor in this regard. Yet the fact remains that the organization of Germany permitted of no delay, and that, in any event, whenever Austria would prove hesitant, Prussia would act.

Although Bismarck was therefore able to drive German history along the road to disaster, clearly he did not shoulder sole responsibility. It was borne equally by those other German forces still in existence at the time which did not set up a rival leader of equal stature. He was far superior to his liberal adversaries, like Roggenbach[13] and Benningsen,[14] who wished to give a different constitution to the national state. One looks in vain in Prussia for a statesman of rank who would have been able to carry on the policy of peaceful dualism. In the middle-sized states there were no German princes as active on the *grossdeutsch,* federalist side as the grand duke of Baden was in the *kleindeutsch,* liberal camp; none was so popular as Duke Ernst of Gotha, the "sharpshooter duke." Even Windthorst did not have his king's support; he was only an administrative minister and, when the hour of decision drew near,

[13] Franz, Freiherr von Roggenbach (1825–1907), German statesman, active in the government of Baden; favored a liberal, *kleindeutsch* Reich.
[14] Rudolf von Benningsen (1824–1902), German political leader; leader of the National-Liberal Party.

had once more been dropped from the ministry of state. In any case, we must look into the actual capacity of Count Beust[15] as a statesman who, in the years of the foundation of the Reich, was Bismarck's leading opponent. Did he lose out to Bismarck because the Prussian statesman took a course of action which did not look far into the future, and so was much simpler and easier to follow? Because Bismarck opened the way for his policy, and followed it with no scruples of conscience, brushing aside violently considerations of law and justice? But it is still very doubtful whether the governing caste of the old Austrian monarchy would have permitted any statesman to carry through fundamental reorganization. It is true, of course, that Count Julius Andrássy,[16] who was certainly a statesman of scope, received a free hand for a foreign policy which differed very greatly from that previously in effect. The nationalities brought forth personalities like Deák,[17] who wished to guide nationalism along orderly channels. But, while Bismarck gave the example and brought on the decision, it was the Magyars who none the less were the essential driving force. The Czechs, on the contrary, hesitated for a while. At that time, there were important intellectuals among them. For a long time they endeavored to achieve peaceful reorganization of the monarchy, they kept in sight the danger threatening them from the East. But, for much too long, the answer which was given in Vienna, and in Berlin as well, was that things would not be changed under any circumstances. Archduke Franz Ferdinand [18] came much too late. But it is often true in history that when the political turn of affairs is propitious, it brings forth the statesman who is needed. Who will deny that there were still many chances of development which even the Austrian court could not reject in the long run? It was Bismarck who destroyed these prospects. It may reasonably be doubted that, in the long run, such a federal

[15] Friedrich Ferdinand, Count von Beust (1790–1886), Saxon and Austrian statesman; led opposition to Bismarck as premier of Saxony (1858–66), and Austrian foreign minister (1866–71).

[16] Julius, Count Andrássy (1823–1900), Hungarian statesman, as foreign minister of Austria-Hungary concluded alliance with Bismarck (1879).

[17] Ferencz Deák (1803–76), Hungarian leader of moderate liberals; established *Ausgleich* of 1867 with Austria.

[18] Archduke Franz Ferdinand of Hapsburg (1863–1914), heir to Austrian throne, whose slaying at Sarajevo precipitated World War I; advocated collaboration of Germans, Magyars and Slavs within Hapsburg monarchy.

state would have been able to provide security against the over-whelming growth of Russia. But the fact remains that there were forces in central Europe which could have been spared and com-bined, which the rivalries and competition of the national state system used up at an enormous rate. Because of his origin and character, Bismarck was never able to take this path; in fact, as a result, he gave an intensely personal direction to the history of Germany and Europe. The situation which he faced at the start of his career was that the peoples of Europe were attacking the work of the Congress of Vienna; they wished once more to destroy it. But the decision was his that this would come about only by way of annexations and militarism, and that the nations had to adopt the capitalist system in self-preservation. Thus, very much against his will, he did most to bring about the dissolution of cen-tral and eastern Europe into purely independent national states.

We now know the steps by which this disaster, as we must call it today, was brought about. From the very first day of his official activity, Bismarck with fiery zeal loosened the ties with Austria, forced it out of Germany, abandoned it to the struggle of nationali-ties within it and created the Prussian-German state which could maintain itself only by alternating alliances with other power-states in the fashion of the old political system. The enormity of the enduring alliance with Russia against Austria was in itself a demonstration of the extent to which the new empire was totally incorporated into the great power system, entirely abandoned to the uncertain play of forces between the powers, and remaining wholly dependent upon one man's virtuosity. The many eulogists of Bismarck among German historians have praised to the highest his ostensible moderation in making the armistice with Austria at Nikolsburg in 1866; because it prevented the collapse of Austria at that moment, the later national radicalism of all nationalities found cause to regret it. In truth there is nothing in it either to be praised or blamed. The whole system of 1866, this last and much extolled "masterpiece" of the old style, resulted at once in the decline of the Hapsburg Empire. Thus it was the cause of the isolation and downfall of the Bismarckian Empire as well. The nationalities were in fact encouraged by the success of the German movement. They took advantage of the weaknesses of the mon-archy which had been defeated on the battlefield. As soon as the nationalities lay free and unprotected along the Russian border, central Europe in turn could no longer maintain its own position. The old statecraft was utterly confounded.

In the latest biography of Bismarck there is little or no mention of all these historical points which illuminate and call into question not so much Bismarck's means and methods as his goals. A biographer of Bismarck whose critical views are taken over from the arguments of the liberal movement in favor of the national state, remains a prisoner of the time; he can only draw a false picture. We achieve a different result when we look at things in the broader relationships, including the entire course of development until the present day. The leading statesman of Prussia did not recognize, or, because of personal idiosyncrasy, could not recognize, that the old diplomacy led only to the old struggle for hegemony in Germany and in Europe, and that, with the entrance of newly awakened elemental forces, this struggle would necessarily result in dismemberment of Europe. That this was already visible was publicly demonstrated by Bismarck himself in numerous expressions of anxious foreboding, but he did not break through to a new decision. Thus success was possible only in the old way, by violation of law and justice, and in the end by a final rupture with all historic relationships. All too easily the German people became habituated to going farther in this direction, far beyond what Bismarck wished, wanted or expected. To be sure, alongside the "legitimacy of princes" there was a new "legitimacy of peoples." For a long time, the former had been repeatedly violated by the princes themselves, and the latter led to an enduring rule of violence. Though everything was beginning to slip into motion, the Prussian statesman believed that he could expand the power of his king and his state in the manner of the old princely revolutions and at the same time maintain the old structure of society. It is not true that the German people lost their traditions only because of Bismarck. Since the downfall of the old empire, how much had been cut short, how many old legal safeguards had been abandoned since then, even as the result of liberal legislation—the individual became personally free, but lost his corporative protection at the same time. In our history books there is absent a great and tragic chapter on the "death struggles of the nineteenth century." We call it tragic because it developed with a certain necessity and led to chaos. Despite the French Revolution, it was not the French but the German people who were shattered to their very depths by this destiny. Because they lacked a genuine tradition, romanticism contrived tradition for them. Ludwig Jahn,[19] and the applause which he gained, were by that time warning signs of the unhistorical and destructive results this new tradition would have. It is true that historical and individualistic thought is a product of German romanticism. It is true that historical research now encompasses all times and peoples and is conducted with greater diligence than ever before, so that every historic form is imitated in every area of cultural life. Yet it is also probably true for just these reasons that the ruling spirit of the nineteenth century became and remained most profoundly unhistorical. Bismarck gave a powerful impetus to this development. His activity demonstrates the old adage that men often want the causes, but not their results. The concentration of forces, tremendous for the time, which he brought about, again and again compelled the amputation of old and still vigorous relationships, even when they have become part of the new constitutional life. Freedom could not be granted. Although the greatness and richness of German life until then had consisted in the multiplicity of its regions (*Stämme*) and states, the activities of the spirit began to become uniform under Bismarck. He vigorously accelerated this development, which was rooted in the modern world. Because their program became inapplicable, the liberal parties of all shades had to remain powerless. The conception of law and justice could not be applied in practice because there was always cause to use hastily, methods not beyond reproach.

It is a fact that a state finds it difficult to re-establish itself when its moral foundations have been shattered, when law and justice, which are the foundation of states, are held in scorn, when its leaders, citing expediency, exempt themselves in their policies from those very principles without which no state and in general no human society can be maintained. Even the acceptance of Christianity in the declining Roman Empire could no longer prevent its collapse. The centuries during which European civilization ripened into world civilization were also centuries filled with endless struggle, wars without number, lawbreaking and acts of violence with an incessant struggle for power, for hegemony or balance of power.

---

[19] Friedrich Ludwig Jahn (1778–1852), German teacher of gymnastics, organized nationalist movement of gymnastic groups (*Turnverein*).

It developed out of the spiritual and moral forces of the Romanic and Germanic nations, from antiquity, Christianity and Germanic life, and it could thrive because the competition of states and peoples was still an emanation of the will to remain multifarious, not to become uniform. By this will the elements of resistance to any unbounded extension of power over the conception of law and justice were strengthened again and again. Bismarck, too, was fully aware that freedom from law had to lead to slavery for all. It is therefore a most fundamental question to know how Bismarck tried to bring into consonance his Christianity and his oft-times slight respect for law. There is hardly reason any more to doubt seriously that he did not embrace modern religious indifferentism, but achieved and practiced a devout Christianity. This is shown by numerous documents from his hand, not intended to prove such a point; there can be no deceit in them. But the universality of the Christian world view hardly ever came alive in him. We should not attribute it too much to the fact that he learned to know Christianity only in the pietist conventicles of the East Elbian landed estates, and was hence less concerned to overcome distress in a Christian spirit than to have an opportunity to live out his personal faith. The man whom he replaced in leadership of European affairs, Prince Metternich, was certainly farther from living Christianity, but carried within himself more of the spirit of universality. This resulted from the period of time in which Metternich worked and from the tasks of the Hapsburgs. It is difficult to maintain a fundamental difference between them; both held their position in the modern state world. But Bismarck intervened in it and brought it to its downfall; he could no longer provide it with a new foundation.

By destiny and tendency Bismarck's profession became the modern political system of reason of state and embattled interests. He found joy in this activity. He considered that territorial compactness and the independence of modern great states, which recognize legal order among themselves only in the shape of alternating alliances, constituted not merely a valuable, but in fact a final achievement of civilization. In order to safeguard and to extend this system of state power, he promoted the welfare of the people, though wholly in the spirit of the old statecraft, and was convinced that only a power-state could guarantee happiness and prosperity. Since the situation in which he found himself demanded his active intervention, he was not squeamish in the choice of his means and did not seek farther afield after new, better ways. He took for granted the state world in which he lived, and believed that Prussia was called upon to achieve something valuable in this system. He considered a compact state organism in the heart of Europe to be a higher form of life than a federation of states carried to another stage of development. There were many esteemed thinkers who, though they had their doubts, still sought to justify the statesman and to encourage him in this course. Powerful intellectual currents of the time assisted in this change. They led farther and farther away from the conception of law and from Christianity. But the statesman did not wholly realize what an alliance he was accepting. The life work which he built was certainly not profoundly thought out, but one would do injustice to its master if one were to forget that the spiritual life of his time had in general lost all direction, that numerous and contradictory standpoints were represented with scholarship of equal breadth and with equal impressiveness, and that it was extremely difficult for the statesman to reach a position of fixity and validity. The creator of the Second German Empire remained entirely gripped by the contradictions of his age. He made shift with the old means and the old purposes. This had never before led to enduring order; now the passions were all aroused as well. Bismarck took part in this release from control. He believed that he could utilize the new impulsion to be found in the crowd for the power of his state, and at the same time limit it by a rational system called reason of state. He did not come to a realization that in a world of such confusions there are tasks which go far beyond the state, and that it was becoming extremely necessary to bring the state back to its original purpose, to help establish the good, the right, the higher order. His position remained that the statesman's task consisted in nothing more than development of the state. Were there statesmen who saw farther than he? We cannot be sure. But he did become the first man of his time. Upon him depended essentially the further course of events. In history, however, only those forces are preserved which devote themselves to world historic goals. And the only standard by which peoples and civilizations can be measured and differentiated is whether a belief in a higher world order lives on in them.

11.

The Imperialism of Free Trade

John Gallagher & *Ronald Robinson*

❖❖

EDITORIAL NOTE: *English liberalism was essentially pacific. So runs one of history's more durable myths. Richard Cobden believed that permanent international peace must follow the general adoption of free trade. Setting aside the awkward fact of Liberal enthusiasm for the Crimean War (for which a special explanation can be made), one must still explain the stern repression of the Sepoy Rebellion in India and the brutal Opium Wars in China. But every historian of the mid-nineteenth century knows that this period was, in Britain at least, also the zenith of anti-imperialism. The virtues of free trade, peace, and prosperity made overseas holdings a nuisance and an expense. The Durham Report (1839), that brainchild of imperial reformers, developed the principle of self-government which was applied through mid-century to the white colonies of settlement.*

John Gallagher and Ronald Robinson hold that this traditional view of imperialism and liberal pacifism is wrong. Studies of the empire produce the wrong answers, they argue, because they apply the wrong questions to the wrong problem. The error lies in a mistaken assessment of the imperial situation and the definition of empire. There are, claim Gallagher and Robinson, degrees of political control even as there are levels of economic involvement. There is, in fact, an "informal empire," consisting of areas over which the imperial power has degrees of de facto, not de jure, control. This argument suggests an important historiographic problem. Ironically both the historians who hold the Hobson-Lenin view of imperial economic determinism and those who dissent, preferring to chart political activity within the formal empire and discuss imperialism as an aspect of world politics, disagree in their assessment of the situation but are in accord on the facts. They agree that there was a period of mid-century indifference to the empire, ascribable to Liberal laissez-faire, followed by an imperial revival in the late nineteenth century. Some historians attribute this to a failure of Liberalism, to a growing reaction to the shoddy, dull, materialistic culture of the liberal-industrial era at home. Restraint and tolerance were a bore. Imperialism provided excitement, direct or vicarious—a sort of global world series. Other historians argue that economic liberalism failed and they hold that imperialism was the pursuit of new areas for investment of surplus capital and the quest for new markets.

Gallagher and Robinson begin by arguing that the facts are incorrectly stated. The mid-Victorian period, the heyday of Liberal laissez-faire and allegedly the great era of anti-imperialism, was actually an age of large-scale expansion. They find nothing strikingly new in the jingoism of the late nineteenth century save that the most desirable areas of expansion had been exploited long before the African landgrabs of the 1880's and 1890's. By implication they raise an interesting problem: German Liberals look vulgar and crude bargaining with power and exploiting other peoples; yet British Liberals may have been just as crude, but masked their acquisitive self-interest with sanctimonious avowals of principles of freedom. The point may be unfair, but the question remains to be answered.

I

It ought to be a commonplace that Great Britain during the nineteenth century expanded overseas by means of "informal empire" [1] as much as by acquiring dominion in the strict constitutional sense. For purposes of economic analysis it would clearly be unreal to define imperial history exclusively as the history of those colonies colored red on the map. Nevertheless, almost all imperial history has been written on the assumption that the empire of formal dominion is historically comprehensible in itself and can be cut out of its context in British expansion and world politics. The conventional interpretation of the nineteenth-century empire continues to rest upon study of the formal empire alone, which is rather like judging the size and character of icebergs solely from the parts above the water-line.

The imperial historian, in fact, is very much at the mercy of his own particular concept of empire. By that, he decides what facts are of "imperial" significance; his data are limited in the same way

---

[1] The term has been given authority by Dr C. R. Fay. See *Cambridge History of the British Empire*. Cambridge University Press, 1940, vol. II, p. 399.

as his concept, and his final interpretation itself depends largely upon the scope of his hypothesis. Different hypotheses have led to conflicting conclusions. Since imperial historians are writing about different empires and since they are generalizing from eccentric or isolated aspects of them, it is hardly surprising that these historians sometimes contradict each other.

The orthodox view of nineteenth-century imperial history remains that laid down from the standpoint of the racial and legalistic concept which inspired the Imperial Federation movement. Historians such as Seeley and Egerton looked on events in the formal empire as the only test of imperial activity; and they regarded the empire of kinship and constitutional dependence as an organism with its own laws of growth. In this way the nineteenth century was divided into periods of imperialism and anti-imperialism, according to the extension or contraction of the formal empire and the degree of belief in the value of British rule overseas.

Ironically enough, the alternative interpretation of "imperialism," which began as part of the radical polemic against the Federationists, has in effect only confirmed their analysis. Those who have seen imperialism as the high stage of capitalism and the inevitable result of foreign investment agree that it applied historically only to the period after 1880. As a result they have been led into a similar preoccupation with formal manifestations of imperialism because the late-Victorian age was one of spectacular extension of British rule. Consequently, Hobson and Lenin, Professor Moon and Mr. Woolf [2] have confirmed from the opposite point of view their opponents' contention that late-Victorian imperialism was a qualitative change in the nature of British expansion and a sharp deviation from the innocent and static liberalism of the middle of the century. This alleged change, welcomed by one school, condemned by the other, was accepted by both.

For all their disagreement these two doctrines pointed to one interpretation; that mid-Victorian "indifference" and late-Victorian "enthusiasm" for empire were directly related to the rise and decline in free-trade beliefs. Thus Lenin wrote: "When free competition in Great Britain was at its height, i.e. between 1840 and

[2] J. A. HOBSON, *Imperialism* (1902); V. I. LENIN, *Imperialism, the Highest Stage of Capitalism.* Selected Works (n.d.) vol. V; P. T. MOON, *Imperialism and World Politics.* New York, 1926; L. WOOLF, *Empire and Commerce in Africa* (n.d.).

1860, the leading British bourgeois politicians were . . . of the opinion that the liberation of the colonies and their complete separation from Great Britain was inevitable and desirable." [3] Professor Schuyler extends this to the decade from 1861 to 1870: ". . . for it was during those years that tendencies toward the disruption of the empire reached their climax. The doctrines of the Manchester school were at the height of their influence." [4]

In the last quarter of the century, Professor Langer finds that "there was an obvious danger that the British [export] market would be steadily restricted. Hence the emergence and sudden flowering of the movement for expansion. . . . Manchester doctrine had been belied by the facts. It was an outworn theory to be thrown into the discard." [5] Their argument may be summarized in this way: the mid-Victorian formal empire did not expand, indeed it seemed to be disintegrating, therefore the period was anti-imperialist; the later-Victorian formal empire expanded rapidly, therefore this was an era of imperialism; the change was caused by the obsolescence of free trade.

The trouble with this argument is that it leaves out too many of the facts which it claims to explain. Consider the results of a decade of "indifference" to empire. Between 1841 and 1851 Great Britain occupied or annexed New Zealand, the Gold Coast, Labuan, Natal, the Punjab, Sind and Hong Kong. In the next twenty years British control was asserted over Berar, Oudh, Lower Burma and Kowloon, over Lagos and the neighborhood of Sierra Leone, over Basutoland, Griqualand and the Transvaal; and new colonies were established in Queensland and British Columbia. Unless this expansion can be explained by "fits of absence of mind," we are faced with the paradox that it occurred despite the determination of the imperial authorities to avoid extending their rule.

This contradiction arises even if we confine our attention to the formal empire, as the orthodox viewpoint would force us to do. But if we look beyond into the regions of informal empire, then the difficulties become overwhelming. The normal account of South

[3] LENIN, *op. cit.,* vol. V, p. 71.
[4] R. L. SCHUYLER, *The Fall of the Old Colonial System.* New York, 1945, p. 45.
[5] W. L. LANGER, *The Diplomacy of Imperialism, 1890–1902.* New York, 1935, vol. I, pp. 75–76.

African policy in the middle of the century is that Britain abandoned any idea of controlling the interior. But in fact what looked like withdrawal from the Orange River sovereignty and the Transvaal was based not on any a priori theories about the inconveniences of colonies but upon hard facts of strategy and commerce in a wider field. Great Britain was in South Africa primarily to safeguard the routes to the East, by preventing foreign powers from acquiring bases on the flank of those routes. In one way or another this imperial interest demanded some kind of hold upon Africa south of the Limpopo River, and although between 1852 and 1877 the Boer republics were not controlled formally for this purpose by Britain, they were effectually dominated by informal paramountcy and by their dependence on British ports. If we refuse to narrow our view to that of formal empire, we can see how steadily and successfully the main imperial interest was pursued by maintaining supremacy over the whole region, and that it was pursued as steadily throughout the so-called anti-imperialist era as in the late-Victorian period. But it was done by shutting in the Boer republics from the Indian Ocean: by the annexation of Natal in 1843, by keeping the Boers out of Delagoa Bay in 1860 and 1868, out of St. Lucia Bay in 1861 and 1866, and by British intervention to block the union of the two republics under Pretorius in 1860.[6] Strangely enough it was the first Gladstone government which Schuyler regards as the climax of anti-imperialism, which annexed Basutoland in 1868 and Griqualand West in 1871 in order to ensure "the safety of our South African Possessions." [7] By informal means if possible, or by formal annexations when necessary, British paramountcy was steadily upheld.

Are these the actions of ministers anxious to preside over the liquidation of the British Empire? Do they look like "indifference" to an empire rendered superfluous by free trade? On the contrary, here is a continuity of policy which the conventional interpretation misses because it takes account only of formal methods of control. It also misses the continuous grasp of the West African coast and of the South Pacific which British seapower was able to maintain. Refusals to annex are no proof of reluctance to control. As Lord

---

[6] C. J. UYS, *In the Era of Shepstone.* Lovedale, Cape Province, 1933; and C. W. DE KIEWIET, *British Colonial Policy and the South African Republics* (1929), *passim.*

[7] DE KIEWIET, *op. cit.,* p. 224.

Aberdeen put it in 1845: ". . . it is unnecessary to add that Her Majesty's Government will not view with indifference the assumption by another power of a protectorate which they, with due regard for the true interests of those [Pacific] islands, have refused." [8]

Nor can the obvious continuity of imperial constitutional policy throughout the mid- and late-Victorian years be explained on the orthodox hypothesis. If the granting of responsible government to colonies was due to the mid-Victorian "indifference" to empire and even a desire to be rid of it, then why was this policy continued in the late-Victorian period when Britain was interested above all in preserving imperial unity? The common assumption that British governments in the free-trade era considered empire superfluous arises from over-estimating the significance of changes in legalistic forms. In fact, throughout the Victorian period responsible government was withheld from colonies if it involved sacrificing or endangering British paramountcy or interests. Wherever there was fear of a foreign challenge to British supremacy in the continent or subcontinent concerned, wherever the colony could not provide financially for its own internal security, the imperial authorities retained full responsibility, or, if they had already devolved it, intervened directly to secure their interests once more. In other words, responsible government, far from being a separatist device, was simply a change from direct to indirect methods of maintaining British interests. By slackening the formal political bond at the appropriate time, it was possible to rely on economic dependence and mutual good-feeling to keep the colonies bound to Britain while still using them as agents for further British expansion.

The inconsistency between fact and the orthodox interpretation arises in yet another way. For all the extensive anthologies of opinion supposedly hostile to colonies, how many colonies were actually abandoned? For instance, the West Africa Committee of 1865 made a strong and much quoted case for giving up all but one of the West African settlements, but even as they sat these settlements were being extended. The Indian empire, however, is the most glaring gap in the traditional explanation. Its history in the "period of indifference" is filled with wars and annexations.

Moreover, in this supposedly laissez-faire period India, far from

[8] Quoted in J. M. WARD, *British Policy in the South Pacific, 1786–1893*. Sydney, 1948, p. 138.

being evacuated, was subjected to intensive development as an economic colony along the best mercantilist lines. In India it was possible, throughout most of the period of the British Raj, to use the governing power to extort in the form of taxes and monopolies such valuable primary products as opium and salt. Furthermore, the characteristics of so-called imperialist expansion at the end of the nineteenth century developed in India long before the date (1880) when Lenin believed the age of economic imperialism opened. Direct governmental promotion of products required by British industry, government manipulation of tariffs to help British exports, railway construction at high and guaranteed rates of interest to open the continental interior—all of these techniques of direct political control were employed in ways which seem alien to the so-called age of laissez-faire. Moreover, they had little to do, particularly in railway finance, with the folk-lore of rugged individualism. "All the money came from the English capitalist" as a British official wrote, "and, so long as he was guaranteed five per cent on the revenues of India, it was immaterial to him whether the funds which he lent were thrown into the Hooghly or converted into bricks and mortar." [9]

To sum up: the conventional view of Victorian imperial history leaves us with a series of awkward questions. In the age of "anti-imperialism" why were all colonies retained? Why were so many more obtained? Why were so many new spheres of influence set up? Or again, in the age of "imperialism," as we shall see later, why was there such reluctance to annex further territory? Why did decentralization, begun under the impetus of anti-imperialism, continue? In the age of laissez-faire why was the Indian economy developed by the state?

These paradoxes are too radical to explain as merely exceptions which prove the rule or by concluding that imperial policy was largely irrational and inconsistent, the product of a series of accidents and chances. The contradictions, it may be suspected, arise not from the historical reality but from the historians' approach to it. A hypothesis which fits more of the facts might be that of a fundamental continuity in British expansion throughout the nineteenth century.

[9] Quoted in L. H. JENKS, *The Migration of British Capital to 1875* (1938), pp. 221–22.

II

The hypothesis which is needed must include informal as well as formal expansion, and must allow for the continuity of the process. The most striking fact about British history in the nineteenth century, as Seeley pointed out, is that it is the history of an expanding society. The exports of capital and manufactures, the migration of citizens, the dissemination of the English language, ideas and constitutional forms, were all of them radiations of the social energies of the British peoples. Between 1812 and 1914 over twenty million persons emigrated from the British Isles, and nearly 70 per cent of them went outside the empire.[10] Between 1815 and 1880, it is estimated, £1,187,000,000 in credit had accumulated abroad, but no more than one-sixth was placed in the formal empire. Even by 1913, something less than half of the £3,975,000,000 of foreign investment lay inside the empire.[11] Similarly, in no year of the century did the empire buy much more than one-third of Britain's exports. The basic fact is that British industrialization caused an ever-extending and intensifying development of overseas regions. Whether they were formally British or not, was a secondary consideration.

Imperialism, perhaps, may be defined as a sufficient political function of this process of integrating new regions into the expanding economy; its character is largely decided by the various and changing relationships between the political and economic elements of expansion in any particular region and time. Two qualifications must be made. First, imperialism may be only indirectly connected with economic integration in that it sometimes extends beyond areas of economic development, but acts for their strategic protection. Secondly, although imperialism is a function of economic expansion, it is not a necessary function. Whether imperialist phenomena show themselves or not, is determined not only by the factors of economic expansion, but equally by the political and social organization of the regions brought into the orbit of the expansive society, and also by the world situation in general.

It is only when the politics of these new regions fail to provide

[10] SIR W. K. HANCOCK, *Survey of British Commonwealth Affairs* (1940), vol. II, pt. 1, p. 28.
[11] A. H. IMLAH, British Balance of Payments and Export of Capital, 1816–1913. *Economic History Review,* 2nd ser., V (1952), 237, 239; HANCOCK, *op. cit.,* p. 27.

satisfactory conditions for commercial or strategic integration and when their relative weakness allows, that power is used imperialistically to adjust those conditions. Economic expansion, it is true, will tend to flow into the regions of maximum opportunity, but maximum opportunity depends as much upon political considerations of security as upon questions of profit. Consequently, in any particular region, if economic opportunity seems large but political security small, then full absorption into the extending economy tends to be frustrated until power is exerted upon the state in question. Conversely, in proportion as satisfactory political frameworks are brought into being in this way, the frequency of imperialist intervention lessens and imperialist control is correspondingly relaxed. It may be suggested that this willingness to limit the use of paramount power to establishing security for trade is the distinctive feature of the British imperialism of free trade in the nineteenth century, in contrast to the mercantilist use of power to obtain commercial supremacy and monopoly through political possession.

On this hypothesis the phasing of British expansion or imperialism is not likely to be chronological. Not all regions will reach the same level of economic integration at any one time; neither will all regions need the same type of political control at any one time. As the British industrial revolution grew, so new markets and sources of supply were linked to it at different times, and the degree of imperialist action accompanying that process varied accordingly. Thus mercantilist techniques of formal empire were being employed to develop India in the mid-Victorian age at the same time as informal techniques of free trade were being used in Latin America for the same purpose. It is for this reason that attempts to make phases of imperialism correspond directly to phases in the economic growth of the metropolitan economy are likely to prove in vain. The fundamental continuity of British expansion is only obscured by arguing that changes in the terms of trade or in the character of British exports necessitated a sharp change in the process.

From this vantage point the many-sided expansion of British industrial society can be viewed as a whole of which both the formal and informal empires are only parts. Both of them then appear as variable political functions of the extending pattern of overseas trade, investment, migration and culture. If this is accepted, it follows that formal and informal empire are essentially interconnected and to some extent interchangeable. Then not only is the old, legalistic, narrow idea of empire unsatisfactory, but so is the old idea of informal empire as a separate, non-political category of expansion. A concept of informal empire which fails to bring out the underlying unity between it and the formal empire is sterile. Only within the total framework of expansion is nineteenth-century empire intelligible. So we are faced with the task of refashioning the interpretations resulting from defective concepts of organic constitutional empire on the one hand and Hobsonian "imperialism" on the other.

The economic importance—even the preeminence—of informal empire in this period has been stressed often enough. What was overlooked was the interrelation of its economic and political arms; how political action aided the growth of commercial supremacy, and how this supremacy in turn strengthened political influence. In other words, it is the politics as well as the economics of the informal empire which we have to include in the account. Historically, the relationship between these two factors has been both subtle and complex. It has been by no means a simple case of the use of gunboats to demolish a recalcitrant state in the cause of British trade. The type of political lien between the expanding economy and its formal or informal dependencies, as might be expected, has been flexible. In practice it has tended to vary with the economic value of the territory, the strength of its political structure, the readiness of its rulers to collaborate with British commercial or strategic purposes, the ability of the native society to undergo economic change without external control, the extent to which domestic and foreign political situations permitted British intervention, and, finally, how far European rivals allowed British policy a free hand.

Accordingly, the political lien has ranged from a vague, informal paramountcy to outright political possession; and, consequently, some of these dependent territories have been formal colonies whereas others have not. The difference between formal and informal empire has not been one of fundamental nature but of degree. The ease with which a region has slipped from one status to the other helps to confirm this. Within the last two hundred years, for example, India has passed from informal to formal association with the United Kingdom and, since World War II, back to an informal connection. Similarly, British West Africa has passed through the first two stages and seems today likely to follow India into the third.

III

Let us now attempt, tentatively, to use the concept of the totality of British expansion described above to restate the main themes of the history of modern British expansion. We have seen that interpretations of this process fall into contradictions when based upon formal political criteria alone. If expansion both formal and informal is examined as a single process, will these contradictions disappear?

The growth of British industry made new demands upon British policy. It necessitated linking undeveloped areas with British foreign trade and, in so doing, moved the political arm to force an entry into markets closed by the power of foreign monopolies.

British policy, as Professor Harlow has shown,[12] was active in this way before the American colonies had been lost, but its greatest opportunities came during the Napoleonic Wars. The seizure of the French and Spanish West Indies, the filibustering expedition to Buenos Aires in 1806, the taking of Java in 1811, were all efforts to break into new regions and to tap new resources by means of political action. But the policy went further than simple housebreaking, for once the door was opened and British imports with their political implications were pouring in, they might stop the door from being shut again. Raffles, for example, temporarily broke the Dutch monopoly of the spice trade in Java and opened the island to free trade. Later, he began the informal British paramountcy over the Malacca trade routes and the Malay peninsula by founding Singapore. In South America, at the same time, British policy was aiming at indirect political hegemony over new regions for the purposes of trade. The British navy carried the Portuguese royal family to Brazil after the breach with Napoleon, and the British representative there extorted from his grateful clients the trade treaty of 1810 which left British imports paying a lower tariff than the goods of the mother country. The thoughtful stipulation was added "that the Present Treaty shall be unlimited in point of duration, and that the obligations and condi-

[12] v. T. HARLOW, *The Founding of the Second British Empire, 1763–1793* (1952), pp. 62–145.

tions expressed or implied in it shall be perpetual and immutable." [13]

From 1810 onwards this policy had even better chances in Latin America, and they were taken. British governments sought to exploit the colonial revolutions to shatter the Spanish trade monopoly, and to gain informal supremacy and the goodwill which would all favor British commercial penetration. As Canning put it in 1824, when he had clinched the policy of recognition: "Spanish America is free and if we do not mismanage our affairs sadly she is *English*." [14] Canning's underlying object was to clear the way for a prodigious British expansion by creating a new and informal empire, not only to redress the Old World balance of power but to restore British influence in the New. He wrote triumphantly: "The thing is done . . . the Yankees will shout in triumph: but it is they who lose most by our decision . . . the United States have gotten the start of us in vain; and we link once more America to Europe." [15] It would be hard to imagine a more spectacular example of a policy of commercial hegemony in the interests of high politics, or of the use of informal political supremacy in the interests of commercial enterprise. Characteristically, the British recognition of Buenos Aires, Mexico and Colombia took the form of signing commercial treaties with them.

In both the formal and informal dependencies in the mid-Victorian age there was much effort to open the continental interiors and to extend the British influence inland from the ports and to develop the hinterlands. The general strategy of this development was to convert these areas into complementary satellite economies, which would provide raw materials and food for Great Britain, and also provide widening markets for its manufactures. This was the period, the orthodox interpretation would have us believe, in which the political arm of expansion was dormant or even withered. In fact, that alleged inactivity is seen to be a delusion if we take into account the development in the informal aspect. Once entry had been forced into Latin America, China and the Balkans, the task was to encourage stable governments as good investment

[13] Quoted in A. K. MANCHESTER, *British Pre-eminence in Brazil*. Chapel Hill, 1933, p. 90.
[14] Quoted in W. W. KAUFMANN, *British Policy and the Independence of Latin America, 1804–1828*. New Haven, 1951, p. 178.
[15] Quoted in J. F. RIPPY, *Historical Evolution of Hispanic America*. Oxford, 1946, p. 374.

risks, just as in weaker or unsatisfactory states it was considered necessary to coerce them into more cooperative attitudes.

In Latin America, however, there were several false starts. The impact of British expansion in Argentina helped to wreck the constitution and throw the people into civil war, since British trade caused the seaboard to prosper while the back lands were exploited and lagged behind. The investment crash of 1827 and the successful revolt of the pampas people against Buenos Aires[16] blocked further British expansion, and the rise to power of General Rosas ruined the institutional framework which Canning's strategy had so brilliantly set up. The new regime was uncooperative and its designs on Montevideo caused chaos around the Rio de la Plata, which led to that great commercial artery being closed to enterprise. All this provoked a series of direct British interventions during the 1840's in efforts to get trade moving again on the river, but in fact it was the attractive force of British trade itself, more than the informal imperialist action of British governments, which in this case restored the situation by removing Rosas from power.

British policy in Brazil ran into peculiar troubles through its tactless attempt to browbeat the government of Rio de Janeiro into abolishing slavery. British political effectiveness was weakened, in spite of economic predominance, by the interference of humanitarian pressure groups in England. Yet the economic control over Brazil was strengthened after 1856 by the building of the railways; these—begun, financed and operated by British companies—were encouraged by generous concessions from the government of Brazil.

With the development of railways and steamships, the economies of the leading Latin American states were at last geared successfully to the world economy. Once their exports had begun to climb and foreign investment had been attracted, a rapid rate of economic growth was feasible. Even in the 1880's Argentina could double her exports and increase sevenfold her foreign indebtedness while the world price of meat and wheat was falling.[17] By 1913, in Latin America as a whole, informal imperialism had

[16] M. BURGIN, *Economic Aspects of Argentine Federalism*. Cambridge, Mass., 1946, pp. 55, 76–111.

[17] J. H. WILLIAMS, *Argentine International Trade under Inconvertible Paper Money, 1880–1900*. Cambridge, Mass., 1920, pp. 43, 103, 183. Cf. W. W. ROSTOW, *The Process of Economic Growth*. Oxford, 1953, p. 104.

become so important for the British economy that £999,000,000, over a quarter of the total investment abroad, was invested in that region.[18]

But this investment, as was natural, was concentrated in such countries as Argentina and Brazil whose governments (even after the Argentine default of 1891) had collaborated in the general task of British expansion. For this reason there was no need for brusque or peremptory interventions on behalf of British interests. For once their economies had become sufficiently dependent on foreign trade the classes whose prosperity was drawn from that trade normally worked themselves in local politics to preserve the local political conditions needed for it. British intervention, in any case, became more difficult once the United States could make other powers take the Monroe doctrine seriously. The slackening in active intervention in the affairs of the most reliable members of the commercial empire was matched by the abandonment of direct political control over those regions of formal empire which were successful enough to receive self-government. But in Latin America, British governments still intervened, when necessary, to protect British interests in the more backward states; there was intervention on behalf of the bondholders in Guatemala and Colombia in the seventies, as in Mexico and Honduras between 1910 and 1914.

The types of informal empire and the situations it attempted to exploit were as various as the success which it achieved. Although commercial and capital penetration tended to lead to political cooperation and hegemony, there are striking exceptions. In the United States, for example, British business turned the cotton South into a colonial economy, and the British investor hoped to do the same with the Mid-West. But the political strength of the country stood in his way. It was impossible to stop American industrialization, and the industrialized sections successfully campaigned for tariffs, despite the opposition of those sections which depended on the British trade connection. In the same way, American political strength thwarted British attempts to establish Texas, Mexico and Central America as informal dependencies.

Conversely, British expansion sometimes failed, if it gained

[18] J. F. RIPPY, British Investments in Latin America, end of 1913. *Inter-American Economic Affairs*, V (1951), 91.

political supremacy without effecting a successful commercial penetration. There were spectacular exertions of British policy in China, but they did little to produce new customers. Britain's political hold upon China failed to break down Chinese economic self-sufficiency. The Opium War of 1840, the renewal of war in 1857, widened the inlets for British trade but they did not get Chinese exports moving. Their main effect was an unfortunate one from the British point of view, for such foreign pressures put Chinese society under great strains as the Taiping Rebellion unmistakably showed.[19] It is important to note that this weakness was regarded in London as an embarrassment, and not as a lever for extracting further concessions. In fact, the British worked to prop up the tottering Pekin regime, for as Lord Clarendon put it in 1870, "British interests in China are strictly commercial, or at all events only so far political as they may be for the protection of commerce." [20] The value of this self-denial became clear in the following decades when the Pekin government, threatened with a scramble for China, leaned more and more on the diplomatic support of the honest British broker.

The simple recital of these cases of economic expansion, aided and abetted by political action in one form or another, is enough to expose the inadequacy of the conventional theory that free trade could dispense with empire. We have seen that it did not do so. Economic expansion in the mid-Victorian age was matched by a corresponding political expansion which has been overlooked because it could not be seen by that study of maps which, it has been said, drives sane men mad. It is absurd to deduce from the harmony between London and the colonies of white settlement in the mid-Victorian age any British reluctance to intervene in the fields of British interests. The warships at Canton are as much a part of the period as responsible government for Canada; the battlefields of the Punjab are as real as the abolition of suttee.

Far from being an era of "indifference," the mid-Victorian years were the decisive stage in the history of British expansion overseas, in that the combination of commercial penetration and political influence allowed the United Kingdom to command those

[19] J. CHESNAUX, La Révolution Taiping d'après quelques travaux récents. *Revue Historique,* CCIX (1953), 39–40.
[20] Quoted in N. A. PELCOVITS, *Old China Hands and the Foreign Office.* New York, 1948, p. 85.

economies which could be made to fit best into her own. A variety of techniques adapted to diverse conditions and beginning at different dates were employed to effect this domination. A paramountcy was set up in Malaya centered on Singapore; a suzerainty over much of West Africa reached out from the port of Lagos and was backed up by the African squadron. On the east coast of Africa British influence at Zanzibar, dominant thanks to the exertions of Consul Kirk, placed the heritage of Arab command on the mainland at British disposal.

But perhaps the most common political technique of British expansion was the treaty of free trade and friendship made with or imposed upon a weaker state. The treaties with Persia of 1836 and 1857, the Turkish treaties of 1838 and 1861, the Japanese treaty of 1858, the favors extracted from Zanzibar, Siam and Morocco, the hundreds of anti-slavery treaties signed with crosses by African chiefs—all these treaties enabled the British government to carry forward trade with these regions.

Even a valuable trade with one region might give place to a similar trade with another which could be more easily coerced politically. The Russian grain trade, for example, was extremely useful to Great Britain. But the Russians' refusal to hear of free trade, and the British inability to force them into it, caused efforts to develop the grain of the Ottoman Empire instead, since British pressure at Constantinople had been able to hustle the Turk into a liberal trade policy.[21] The dependence of the commercial thrust upon the political arm resulted in a general tendency for British trade to follow the invisible flag of informal empire.

Since the mid-Victorian age now appears as a time of large-scale expansion, it is necessary to revise our estimate of the so-called "imperialist" era as well. Those who accept the concept of "economic imperialism" would have us believe that the annexations at the end of the century represented a sharp break in policy, due to the decline of free trade, the need to protect foreign investment, and the conversion of statesmen to the need for unlimited land-grabbing. All these explanations are questionable. In the first place, the tariff policy of Great Britain did not change. Again, British foreign investment was no new thing and most of it was

[21] V. J. PURYEAR, *International Economics and Diplomacy in the Near East* (1935), pp. 216–17, 222–23.

still flowing into regions outside the formal empire. Finally the statesmens' conversion to the policy of extensive annexation was partial, to say the most of it. Until 1887, and only occasionally after that date, party leaders showed little more enthusiasm for extending British rule than the mid-Victorians. Salisbury was infuriated by the "superficial philanthropy" and "roguery" of the "fanatics" who advocated expansion.[22] When pressed to aid the missions in Nyasaland in 1888, he retorted: "It is not our duty to do it. We should be risking tremendous sacrifices for a very doubtful gain."[23] After 1888, Salisbury, Rosebery and Chamberlain accepted the scramble for Africa as a painful but unavoidable necessity which arose from a threat of foreign expansion and the irrepressible tendency of trade to overflow the bounds of empire, dragging the government into new and irksome commitments. But it was not until 1898 that they were sufficiently confident to undertake the reconquest of so vital a region as the Sudan.

Faced with the prospect of foreign acquisitions of tropical territory hitherto opened to British merchants, the men in London resorted to one expedient after another to evade the need of formal expansion and still uphold British paramountcy in those regions. British policy in the late, as in the mid-Victorian period preferred informal means of extending imperial supremacy rather than direct rule. Throughout the two alleged periods the extension of British rule was a last resort—and it is this preference which has given rise to the many "anti-expansionist" remarks made by Victorian ministers. What these much quoted expressions obscure, is that in practice mid-Victorian as well as late-Victorian policy makers did not refuse to extend the protection of formal rule over British interests when informal methods had failed to give security. The fact that informal techniques were more often sufficient for this purpose in the circumstances of the mid-century than in the later period when the foreign challenge to British supremacy intensified, should not be allowed to disguise the basic continuity of policy. Throughout, British governments worked to establish and maintain British paramountcy by whatever means best suited the circumstances of their diverse regions of interest. The aims of the mid-Victorians were no more "anti-imperialist" than their successors', though they were more often able to achieve them

[22] Quoted in CROMER, *Modern Egypt* (1908), vol. I, p. 388.
[23] *Hansard,* 3rd Series, CCCXXVIII, col. 550, July 6, 1888.

informally; and the late-Victorians were no more "imperialist" than their predecessors, even though they were driven to annex more often. British policy followed the principle of extending control informally if possible and formally if necessary. To label the one method "anti-imperialist" and the other "imperialist," is to ignore the fact that whatever the method British interests were steadily safeguarded and extended. The usual summing up of the policy of the free trade empire as "trade not rule" should read "trade with informal control if possible; trade with rule when necessary." This statement of the continuity of policy disposes of the over-simplified explanation of involuntary expansion inherent in the orthodox interpretation based on the discontinuity between the two periods.

Thus Salisbury as well as Gladstone, Knutsford as well as Derby and Ripon, in the so-called age of "imperialism," exhausted all informal expedients to secure regions of British trade in Africa before admitting that further annexations were unavoidable. One device was to obtain guarantees of free trade and access as a reward for recognizing foreign territorial claims, a device which had the advantage of saddling foreign governments with the liability of rule whilst allowing Britons the commercial advantage. This was done in the Anglo-Portuguese Treaty of 1884, the Congo Arrangement of 1885, and the Anglo-German Agreement over East Africa in 1886. Another device for evading the extension of rule was the exclusive sphere of influence or protectorate recognized by foreign powers. Although originally these imposed no liability for pacifying or administering such regions, with changes in international law they did so after 1885. The granting of charters to private companies between 1881 and 1889, authorizing them to administer and finance new regions under imperial licence, marked the transition from informal to formal methods of backing British commercial expansion. Despite these attempts at "imperialism on the cheap," the foreign challenge to British paramountcy in tropical Africa and the comparative absence there of large-scale, strong, indigenous political organizations which had served informal expansion so well elsewhere, eventually dictated the switch to formal rule.

One principle then emerges plainly: it is only when and where informal political means failed to provide the framework of security for British enterprise (whether commercial, or philanthropic or simply strategic) that the question of establishing formal empire arose. In satellite regions peopled by European stock, in Latin America or Canada, for instance, strong governmental structures grew up; in totally non-European areas, on the other hand, expansion unleashed such disruptive forces upon the indigenous structures that they tended to wear out and even collapse with use. This tendency in many cases accounts for the extension of informal British responsibility and eventually for the change from indirect to direct control.

It was in Africa that this process of transition manifested itself most strikingly during the period after 1880. Foreign loans and predatory bankers by the 1870's had wrecked Egyptian finances and were tearing holes in the Egyptian political fabric. The Anglo-French dual financial control, designed to safeguard the foreign bondholders and to restore Egypt as a good risk, provoked anti-European feeling. With the revolt of Arabi Pasha in 1881, the Khedive's government could serve no longer to secure either the all-important Canal or the foreign investors' pound of flesh.

The motives for the British occupation of 1882 were confused and varied: the desire, evident long before Disraeli's purchase of shares, to dominate the Canal; the interests of the bondholders; and the over-anxiety to forestall any foreign power, especially France, from taking advantage of the prevailing anarchy in Egypt to interpose its power across the British road to India. Nearly all Gladstone's cabinet admitted the necessity of British intervention, although for different reasons, and, in order to hold together his distracted ministry, the prime minister agreed.

The British expedition was intended to restore a stable Egyptian government under the ostensible rule of the Khedive and inside the orbit of informal British influence. When this was achieved, the army, it was intended, should be withdrawn. But the expedition had so crushed the structure of Egyptian rule that no power short of direct British force could make it a viable and trustworthy instrument of informal hegemony and development. Thus the Liberal government following its plan, which had been hastily evolved out of little more than ministerial disagreements, drifted into the prolonged occupation of Egypt it was intent on avoiding. In fact, the occupying power became directly responsible for the defense, the debts and development of the country. The perverse effect of British policy was gloomily summed up by Gladstone:

"We have done our Egyptian business and we are an Egyptian government." [24] Egypt, then, is a striking example of an informal strategy misfiring due to the undermining of the satellite state by investment and by pseudo-nationalist reaction against foreign influence.

The Egyptian question, in so far as it was closely bound with the routes to India and the defense of the Indian empire itself, was given the highest priority by British policy in the eighties and nineties. In order to defend the spinal cord of British trade and empire, tropical African and Pacific claims were repeatedly sacrificed as pawns in the higher game. In 1884, for example, the foreign office decided that British vulnerability in Egypt made it unwise to compete with foreign powers in the opening scramble for West Africa; and it was therefore proposed ". . . to confine ourselves to securing the utmost possible freedom of trade on that [west] coast, yielding to others the territorial responsibilities . . . and seeking compensation on the east coast . . . where the political future of the country is of real importance to Indian and imperial interests." [25] British policy was not one of indiscriminate land-grabbing. And, indeed, the British penetration into Uganda and their securing of the rest of the Nile Valley was a highly selective program, in so far as it surrendered some British West African claims to France and transferred part of East Africa to Germany.

IV

Thus the mid-Victorian period now appears as an era of large-scale expansion, and the late-Victorian age does not seem to introduce any significant novelty into that process of expansion. The annexations of vast undeveloped territories, which have been taken as proof that this period alone was the great age of expansion, now pale in significance, at least if our analysis is anywhere near the truth. That the area of direct imperial rule was extended is true, but is it the most important or characteristic development of expansion during this period? The simple historical fact that Africa was the last field of European penetration is not to say that it was the most important; this would be a truism were it

[24] Quoted in s. GWYNN and G. M. TUCKWELL, *Life of Sir Charles Wentworth Dilke* (1917), vol. II, p. 46.
[25] Foreign Office Confidential Print (East Africa), 5037.

not that the main case of the Hobson school is founded on African examples. On the other hand, it is our main contention that the process of expansion had reached its most valuable targets long before the exploitation of so peripheral and marginal a field as tropical Africa. Consequently arguments, founded on the technique adopted in scrambling for Africa, would seem to be of secondary importance.

Therefore, the historian who is seeking to find the deepest meaning of the expansion at the end of the nineteenth century should look not at the mere pegging out of claims in African jungles and bush, but at the successful exploitation of the empire, both formal and informal, which was then coming to fruition in India, in Latin America, in Canada and elsewhere. The main work of imperialism in the so-called expansionist era was in the more intensive development of areas already linked with the world economy, rather than in the extensive annexations of the remaining marginal regions of Africa. The best finds and prizes had already been made; in tropical Africa the imperialists were merely scraping the bottom of the barrel.

Sources and Acknowledgments

❋❋❋

R. MAX HARTWELL, The Rising Standard of Living in England, 1800–1850. *The Economic History Review,* Second Series, XIII (1961), 397–416. Copyrighted by the *Review*; reprinted by permission. Mr. Hartwell is a Fellow of Nuffield College, Oxford and co-editor of the *Review*. He has written extensively on social and economic history. His books include *Van Dienam's Land* and a forthcoming volume, *The Industrial Revolution.*

ASA BRIGGS, Cholera and Society in the Nineteenth Century. *Past & Present,* No. 19 (1961), 76–96. Copyrighted by *Past & Present*; reprinted by permission. Mr. Briggs is Vice Chancellor of Sussex University and the author of many studies in social and political history including *The Age of Improvement; Victorian People; Victorian Cities;* and the *History of the B.B.C.*

ROBERT A. KANN, Metternich: a Reappraisal of His Impact on International Relations. *The Journal of Modern History,* XXXII (1960), 333–39. Copyrighted by the University of Chicago Press; reprinted by permission. Mr. Kann is Professor of History at Rutgers University and has written extensively on problems of cultural, diplomatic, and institutional history. His works include *The Multinational Empire; The Hapsburg Empire, a Study in Integration and Disintegration;* and *A Study in Austrian Intellectual History.*

DOUGLAS JOHNSON, A Reconsideration of Guizot. *History,* New Series, XLVII (1962), 239–53. Copyrighted by the Historical Association; reprinted by permission. Mr. Johnson is Professor of History at the University of Birmingham. His studies of modern history include *Guizot* and *France and the Dreyfus Affair.*

IRENE COLLINS, Liberalism in Nineteenth-Century Europe. *From Metternich to Hitler: Aspects of British and Foreign History*

1814–1939. Historical Association Essays, edited by W. N. Medlicott. London: Routledge and Kegan Paul, 1963, pp. 25–44. Copyrighted by Routledge and Kegan Paul (U.K.) and Barnes and Noble (U.S.); reprinted by permission. Mrs. Collins is a member of the department of modern history at the University of Liverpool. Her studies of French and European history include *The Government and the Newspaper Press in France* and *The Age of Progress.*

LEWIS B. NAMIER, Nationality and Liberty. *Vanished Supremacies.* London: Hamish Hamilton, 1952, pp. 31–53. Copyrighted by Hamish Hamilton (U.K.) and Harper & Row (U.S.); reprinted by permission. The late Sir Lewis Namier was the author of many works in British and European history including *The Structure of Politics at the Accession of George III; England in the Age of the American Revolution; 1848: the Revolution of the Intellectuals; Diplomatic Prelude;* and *Europe in Decay.*

A. J. P. TAYLOR, Crimea: the War That Would Not Boil. *Rumours of Wars.* London: Hamish Hamilton, 1952. Copyrighted by Hamish Hamilton (U.K.) and Harper & Row (U.S.); reprinted by permission. Mr. Taylor is a Fellow of Magdalen College, Oxford and the author of many studies in European history including *The Origins of the Second World War; The Struggle for the Mastery in Europe, 1848–1918;* and *England, 1914–1945.*

THEODORE ZELDIN, The Myth of Napoleon III. *History Today,* VIII (1958), 103–09. Copyrighted by *History Today;* reprinted by permission of *History Today* and the author. Mr. Zeldin is a Fellow of St. Anthony's College, Oxford and the author of several studies of the political institutions and behavior of the Second Empire including *The Political System of Napoleon III.*

RAYMOND GREW, How Success Spoiled the Risorgimento. *The Journal of Modern History,* XXXIV (1962), 239–53. Copyrighted by the University of Chicago Press and reprinted by permission. Mr. Grew is Associate Professor of History at the University of Michigan. Currently working on problems of cultural and social history in nineteenth-century Europe, he is also the author of *A Sterner Plan for Italian Unity.*

FRANZ SCHNABEL, The Bismarck Problem. *Germany History: Some New German Views,* edited by Hans Kohn. Boston: Beacon Press, 1954. pp. 65–93. Copyrighted by George Allen & Unwin; reprinted by permission. Mr. Schnabel has held the chair of history at the University of Munich and is, among other things, the author of the multi-volume *Deutsche Geschichte im Neunzehnten Jahrhundert.*

JOHN GALLAGHER & RONALD ROBINSON, The Imperialism of Free Trade. *The Economic History Review,* Second Series, VI (1953), 1–15. Copyrighted by the *Review;* reprinted by permission. Mr. Gallagher is a Fellow of Trinity College, Cambridge, and Mr. Robinson is a Fellow of St. John's College, Cambridge. Together with Alice Denny, they are the co-authors of *Africa and the Victorians.*

EUGENE C. BLACK is Associate Professor of History at Brandeis University. Currently working on problems in Victorian and nineteenth-century European history, he is the author of *The Association* and *Posture of Europe.*

hARPER ♦ TORChBOOKS

American Studies: General

HENRY STEELE COMMAGER, Ed.: The Struggle for Racial Equality   TB/1300
CARL N. DEGLER, Ed.: Pivotal Interpretations of American History   TB/1240, TB/1241
A. S. EISENSTADT, Ed.: The Craft of American History: Recent Essays in American Historical Writing
Vol. I TB/1255; Vol. II TB/1256
CHARLOTTE P. GILMAN: Women and Economics ‡ TB/3073
MARCUS LEE HANSEN: The Immigrant in American History   TB/1120
JOHN HIGHAM, Ed.: The Reconstruction of American History △   TB/1068
ROBERT H. JACKSON: The Supreme Court in the American System of Government   TB/1106
LEONARD W. LEVY, Ed.: American Constitutional Law: Historical Essays   TB/1285
LEONARD W. LEVY, Ed.: Judicial Review and the Supreme Court   TB/1296
LEONARD W. LEVY: The Law of the Commonwealth and Chief Justice Shaw   TB/1309
RALPH BARTON PERRY: Puritanism and Democracy   TB/1138
ARNOLD ROSE: The Negro in America   TB/3048

American Studies: Colonial

BERNARD BAILYN, Ed.: The Apologia of Robert Keayne: Self-Portrait of a Puritan Merchant   TB/1201
BERNARD BAILYN: The New England Merchants in the Seventeenth Century   TB/1149
JOSEPH CHARLES: The Origins of the American Party System   TB/1049
CHARLES GIBSON: Spain in America †   TB/3077
LAWRENCE HENRY GIPSON: The Coming of the Revolution: 1763-1775. † Illus.   TB/3007
PERRY MILLER & T. H. JOHNSON, Eds.: The Puritans: A Sourcebook   Vol. I TB/1093; Vol. II TB/1094
EDMUND S. MORGAN, Ed.: The Diary of Michael Wigglesworth, 1653-1657   TB/1228
EDMUND S. MORGAN: The Puritan Family   TB/1227
RICHARD B. MORRIS: Government and Labor in Early America   TB/1244
WALLACE NOTESTEIN: The English People on the Eve of Colonization: 1603-1630. † Illus.   TB/3006
JOHN P. ROCHE: Origins of American Political Thought: Selected Readings   TB/1301
JOHN SMITH: Captain John Smith's America: Selections from His Writings. Ed. with Intro. by John Lankford   TB/3078

American Studies: From the Revolution to 1860

MAX BELOFF, Ed.: The Debate on the American Revolution, 1761-1783: A Sourcebook △   TB/1225

RAY A. BILLINGTON: The Far Western Frontier: 1830-1860. † Illus.   TB/3012
EDMUND BURKE: On the American Revolution. ‡ Edited by Elliott Robert Barkan   TB/3068
WHITNEY R. CROSS: The Burned-Over District   TB/1242
GEORGE DANGERFIELD: The Awakening of American Nationalism: 1815-1828. † Illus.   TB/3061
WILLIAM W. FREEHLING, Ed.: The Nullification Era: A Documentary Record ‡   TB/3079
FRANCIS GRIERSON: The Valley of Shadows: The Coming of the Civil War in Lincoln's Midwest TB/1246
JAMES MADISON: The Forging of American Federalism. Edited by Saul K. Padover   TB/1226
JOHN C. MILLER: Alexander Hamilton and the Growth of the New Nation   TB/3057
RICHARD B. MORRIS, Ed.: The Era of the American Revolution   TB/1180
FRANCIS S. PHILBRICK: The Rise of the West, 1754-1830. † Illus.   TB/3067

American Studies: Since the Civil War

W. R. BROCK: An American Crisis: Congress and Reconstruction, 1865-67 º △   TB/1283
W. A. DUNNING: Reconstruction, Political and Economic: 1865-1877   TB/1073
ROBERT GREEN MCCLOSKEY: American Conservatism in the Age of Enterprise: 1865-1910   TB/1137
VERNON LANE WHARTON: The Negro in Mississippi: 1865-1890   TB/1178
A. RUSSELL BUCHANAN: The United States and World War II. † Illus.   Vol. II TB/3044; Vol. II TB/3045
FOSTER RHEA DULLES: America's Rise to World Power: 1898-1954. † Illus.   TB/3021
ROBERT L. HEILBRONER: The Limits of American Capitalism   TB/1305
SIDNEY HOOK: Reason, Social Myths, and Democracy   TB/1237
WILLIAM E. LEUCHTENBURG: Franklin D. Roosevelt and the New Deal: 1932-1940. † Illus.   TB/3025
ARTHUR S. LINK: Woodrow Wilson and the Progressive Era: 1910-1917. † Illus.   TB/3023
GEORGE E. MOWRY: The Era of Theodore Roosevelt and the Birth of Modern America: 1900-1912. † TB/3022
RUSSEL B. NYE: Midwestern Progressive Politics: 1870-1958   TB/1202
WILLIAM PRESTON, JR.: Aliens and Dissenters: Federal Suppression of Radicals, 1903-1933   TB/1287
JACOB RIIS: The Making of an American. ‡ Edited by Roy Lubove   TB/3070
PHILIP SELZNICK: TVA and the Grass Roots: A Study in the Sociology of Formal Organization   TB/1230
IDA M. TARBELL: The History of the Standard Oil Company: Briefer Version.‡ Edited by David M. Chalmers   TB/3071
GEORGE B. TINDALL, Ed.: A Populist Reader ‡   TB/3069

† The New American Nation Series, edited by Henry Steele Commager and Richard B. Morris.
‡ American Perspectives series, edited by Bernard Wishy and William E. Leuchtenburg.
* The Rise of Modern Europe series, edited by William L. Langer.
** History of Europe series, edited by J. H. Plumb.
¶ Researches in the Social, Cultural, and Behavioral Sciences, edited by Benjamin Nelson.
§ The Library of Religion and Culture, edited by Benjamin Nelson.
Σ Harper Modern Science Series, edited by James R. Newman.
º Not for sale in Canada.
△ Not for sale in the U. K.